CW00832826

EVERY VOTE COUNTS

EVERY VOTE COUNTS

The Story of India's Elections

NAVIN CHAWLA

HarperCollins *Publishers* India

First published in India in 2019 by
HarperCollins *Publishers*
A-75, Sector 57, Noida, Uttar Pradesh 201301, India
www.harpercollins.co.in

2 4 6 8 10 9 7 5 3 1

P-ISBN: 978-93-5302-600-4
E-ISBN: 978-93-5302-601-1

Typeset in 11/15 Sabon LT Std
Manipal Digital Systems, Manipal

Printed and bound at
Thomson Press (India) Ltd.

This book is produced from independently certified FSC® paper to ensure responsible forest management.

To the true heroes of the Indian election story: the thousands of dedicated polling officials, including teachers and revenue staff as well as police officials, all of whom walk the extra mile to enable the country to vote

Contents

Preface

DURING my years in the Election Commission of India, I enjoyed my frequent interactions with students. I tried not to refuse invitations to campuses and addressed almost fifty across the country. I looked forward to the lively question-and-answer sessions that followed my lectures. Among the frequently asked questions was why the Commission did not do something to prevent criminals from being elected to parliament. The audience would be disappointed when I replied that the jurisdiction to amend the law lay with parliament and not with the Commission. How could lawbreakers be lawmakers, asked the students almost in one voice. While I extolled the many strengths of the Commission, the students in turn asked what we were doing about money power.

It was once again students who raised the issue of transgenders and asked why they had not been recognized as a separate entity, which we then proceeded to do. When questions such as these were raised, they were met with huge applause. At the end of the sessions, students would cluster around me to ask more questions. Often enough they wanted to know whether I was writing a book on elections. My reply was invariably that I would think about it.

When I finally set about the task of writing this book, I realized how vast the subject was. I needed to condense into a single volume the nuts and bolts of election management, a history of current practices and challenges we confronted and those that lay ahead. I took a cue from my lectures to make the narrative personal with anecdotes from my own experience.

When I began my research, I found there was very little information available on how India's early elections had been conducted in the first four decades after Independence. None of the early chief election commissioners had written any books on their electoral experiences, nor, to the best of my knowledge, kept diaries or notes that were accessible to a researcher. It was with some difficulty that I was able to get a little information on our first chief election commissioner Sukumar Sen from his daughters, one living in Kolkata and the other in London. My inquiries regarding K.V.K. Sundaram drew a blank. It was therefore welcome that T.N. Seshan, J.M. Lyngdoh, T.S. Krishnamurthy and S.Y. Quraishi had contributed to the still fledging literature on the subject.[1]

To the question why I chose to write eight years after leaving the Commission, I am reminded of the time that I decided to write a biography of Mother Teresa (now St Teresa of Kolkata). Fifteen years into my association with her, I first discussed the idea of a biography with the legendary literary agent Gillon Aitken in London. He was sufficiently enthused to pursue me with reminders. After a few such exchanges, I wrote back to say that I was not unduly concerned if other books on the subject were published before I was ready with mine. Others had their stories to tell while I had mine. When the biography that I worked on for five years was finally published in the winter of 1992 in the United Kingdom, it immediately found its own

---

1 T.N. Seshan, *A Heart Full of Burden*, New Delhi: UBS Publisher's Distributors, 1995; J.M. Lyngdoh, *Chronicle of an Impossible Election*, New Delhi: Penguin India, 2004; T.S. Krishnamurthy, *The Miracle of Democracy*, Noida: HarperCollins, 2008.; and S.Y. Quraishi, *An Undocumented Wonder: The Great Indian Election*, Delhi: Rupa Publications, 2014.

niche in an already crowded field. Hopefully, this offering on India's elections would contribute towards the history and functioning of a widely admired institution.

During the four years when I was an election commissioner, I gained experience that came with conducting twenty-eight assembly elections for the states and Union territories. There is no doubt that this readied me for the Big One—the general election of 2009. There could be no substitute for the hands-on learning that I gained while travelling throughout our vast country on official work, encountering different traditions and cultures. Each part of the country revealed its own difficulties for which there were often no tailor-made solutions. Wherever possible, I consciously travelled through some districts by road instead of flying from point to point. This enabled me to get acquainted with local officials and their problems over a cup of chai. I gained insights that would often not trickle up at formal reviews.

A credible electoral system is the very core of democracy. A glimpse into our history since gaining independence in 1947 illustrates the importance accorded to free and fair elections. The framers of the Constitution had the prescience to dedicate a separate section to deal with elections, providing unqualified powers to the Commission for their superintendence, direction and control. With remarkable foresight they envisaged the Election Commission to be a fiercely independent body. They were also careful to leave it with sufficient residuary powers to deal with unforeseen situations that might emerge.

Into these unchartered waters came universal adult franchise which, as is well known, had a difficult passage in the West. Meanwhile, India with barely 16 per cent literacy in 1947 and with the added problems caused by the uneven integration of princely states and a traumatic Partition, had taken a major leap of faith. Many observers predicted doom from the start. However, the vision of the early architects of the freedom movement was translated into successful reality by the tenacity of a handful of civil servants and the early election commissioners. This I seek to bring out in the chapter on India's first general election of 1951–52.

The early chapters include a kaleidoscopic account of the efficacy of the electoral machine—the subject of study in management schools globally. The chapter titled 'Notes from the 2009 General Election' amplifies this. Yet not everything about the election scenario is praiseworthy. I have examined some of the unwelcome trends across three chapters on money and muscle power, 'paid news' and 'post-truth'.

I would have liked to examine at least half a dozen important assembly elections held during my tenure, including Bihar (October–November 2005), West Bengal (April–May 2006), Uttar Pradesh (April–May 2007) and Karnataka (May 2008). I chose instead to examine the 2008 assembly election in Jammu and Kashmir in some depth, for this election was of importance beyond the state's own boundaries. The multilayered processes that the Commission followed to ensure fairness and transparency in the face of almost insurmountable odds has merited a chapter.

Much has been written about Maoist extremism but, as far as I know, no one has written about the problems of conducting elections in Maoist-affected areas. I have deliberately not strayed into the complex reasons for the origin or persistence of this conflict. This was arguably the foremost challenge I faced in the 2009 general election. Hopefully, this confrontation with Maoist forces will recede.

I have devoted a full chapter on Electronic Voting Machines (EVMs). This has become especially relevant because in the last few years this machine, which was once described as 'a national pride' by the Karnataka High Court, has come in for intense criticism. It has stoked controversy where to my mind none exists. I have traced the history of the EVM and the introduction of the Voter Verifiable Paper Audit Trail (VVPAT)—the printer recently created to corroborate the EVM results.

During the course of writing this book, some seminal election-related concerns were raised. These included the feasibility of conducting simultaneous elections to parliament and state legislative assemblies once every five years. The introduction of compulsory voting was another such proposal. Since these had come up during my years in the Commission, I decided to explore both in a chapter on emerging trends. Finally, without dwelling on the unjust personal attack launched by N. Gopalaswami against me, I have highlighted what I consider to be an issue of vital importance: the role of the CEC vis-à-vis the election commissioners. Is he truly the 'first amongst equals'? Or was that but the pious hope of the Supreme Court?[2] I believe this is a question that is crying out for constitutional reform.

In the Appendix, I have looked beyond elections in India to Bhutan in our neighborhood. A decade ago, Bhutan's fourth king Jigme Singye Wangchuk chose to make a dramatic change towards representative democracy, bucking the trend of many nations, which have instead lurched towards dictatorship. I had been invited to observe all the three general elections in Bhutan and am therefore uniquely placed to report on its transition into a democracy.

We are often hailed as the world's largest democracy but we were that even at Independence. What is more remarkable is that Indian elections have always been held on time, and with considerable competence—no easy task given the size of our electorate. The result of each election held so far has been accepted by winners and losers alike. This has proved the success of one of the boldest democratic enterprises ever undertaken where people from diverse backgrounds and cultures coalesced to form a nation. So far, each of our elections held has reaffirmed our commitment to democracy—no mean feat particularly when we are witnessing constant attempts at extinguishing democratic freedoms in many parts of the world. In many countries that obtained freedom at around the same time that we did, elections have actually served to provide autocratic regimes with a veneer of respectability.

If India is to continue to be a global benchmark for democracy, every decision of the Election Commission must be informed by integrity, transparency and autonomy, for that alone can confer legitimacy to the electoral process.

---

2 *T.N. Seshan vs Union of India and Others* (1995) 4 SCC 611.

1

The Great Indian Election

Of the 834,999 polling stations set up for the 2009 general election (GE 2009), one was located in the village of Banej in Junagadh district of Gujarat. By itself this would not be extraordinary but for two little-known facts. One, that it was located in the heart of India's only lion sanctuary where the rare Asiatic lion roams free and two, that it was set up for a single voter. Every vote counted!

Pujari Bharatdas Darshandas had refused to abandon his temple, dedicated to Lord Shiva, when the village was relocated away from the lion sanctuary. Nor was he prepared to travel 20 km to the nearest polling station to cast his vote. Instead, for all elections since 2002, the Election Commission sent forth a team of officials to set up a polling station in the nearby one-room outpost of the forest department.

One presiding officer and two other officials travelled through almost 40 km of dense jungle, accompanied by a couple of policemen, presumably to keep the lions at bay! The station was set up the day before polling; our officials stayed overnight and opened for business at 7 a.m. The pujari arrived to cast his vote in the afternoon. Because there was no other voter, and as a special case our station was closed before the mandatory eight hours were over. The lone voter, who enjoyed being in the limelight, would disclose that no candidate *ever* ventured into the jungle to canvas for his vote, '... but I do vote without fail ... sometimes even one vote is crucial'.[1]

~

Two questions are invariably asked of me when people learn that I served in the Election Commission of India and conducted the fifteenth general election to the Lok Sabha in 2009.[2] The first, asked with varying degrees of awe, is how we are able to conduct so gigantic and complex an exercise so flawlessly. The second, which follows in quick succession is why the rest of India's governance is quite so dysfunctional. Let me attempt to answer the first question in this chapter.

The five years I spent in the Commission, first as commissioner and later as chief election commissioner (CEC), were the culmination of a varied career as a member of the Indian Administrative Service that spanned thirty-seven years. I consider myself fortunate that I could contribute towards the growth of a constitutional edifice held in high esteem. I also had the good fortune of being able to conduct a general election—not all CECs get to do so.[3]

My path to becoming CEC was, however, strewn with innumerable obstacles and difficulties. It also did not help matters that there was a significant lack of trust and harmony within the Commission at that time. This caused loss of time and energy that could have been put to far better use to strengthen the Commission and, through it, the larger polity. I will elaborate on this in a separate chapter.

From my earliest days in the Commission, it was clear to me that I had left behind my freedom as a civil servant. As secretary to the

---

1 *The New York Times*, 'India Ink', 6 December 2012.

2 Three state assembly elections were conducted simultaneously, viz., in Sikkim, Andhra Pradesh and Odisha.

3 The 2014 general election was conducted under CEC V.S. Sampath; the 2004 general election was conducted under CEC T.S. Krishnamurthy; and the 1999 general election was conducted under CEC M.S. Gill.

Government of India, first in the Department of Consumer Affairs and later in the Ministry of Information and Broadcasting, my remit had been to transmit the government's policies and schemes to the country at large. This involved constant interaction with colleagues in different ministries and with the media. For instance, as the official spokesperson of the government when the tsunami struck our coastal areas on 26 December 2004—a national disaster of epic proportions—I spent several weeks engaging with the press on a daily basis. In the Commission, however, such interactions were frowned upon in an unstated way. I found myself immediately distanced from the 'outside' world in a job that was equivalent in status to that of a judge of the Supreme Court. It was an altogether more restrictive existence. Very soon my official life became confined to the Commission and Commission-related activities.

This chapter and ones that follow attempt to provide a brief snapshot of how the Commission has evolved, its independence, inner workings, difficulties and contradictions. With space constraints in mind, I have tried to explain the nuts and bolts of conducting elections, as well as some significant happenings in my term as election commissioner and finally as chief election commissioner.

A Daunting Exercise

The Great Indian Election[4] is, without doubt, the largest electoral exercise in the democratic world. It is largest in terms of the sheer numbers involved as well as in terms of the administrative apparatus required to conduct the polls. In 2014, the electoral register had grown to 834 million (an increase of a humungous 100 million voters over the 2009 general elections). Close on 66.38 per cent of that number had cast their votes in as many as 927,553 polling stations. The numbers on the rolls exceeded the entire population of North

---

4 Also see 'Election Commission of India: How the giant polling machine pulls it off', *Hindustan Times*, 6 January 2017.

America or Europe and Russia combined. Numbers in themselves do not usually add up to efficiency or to good electoral practices; they often lead to confusion, lack of proper oversight, delays or worse. The fascination of the Indian elections lies in the manifest ability of the Commission to get this complex process right with seeming ease, delivering each time a set of results within a matter of hours that is acceptable to political parties, candidates and to the country at large. Most Indians have now come to take fair elections for granted, while the Election Commission has emerged as the keystone of the democratic arch.[5]

Indeed, if one were to ask of the average Indian in which public institutions she reposes the most faith, the Supreme Court and the Election Commission are likely to be mentioned in the same breath. Past surveys have shown that a majority of Indians put their trust in the Commission.[6] Because these institutions are trusted, their verdicts enjoy public acceptability. When elections are ongoing they are not just routinely discussed, they are passionately analysed.

A remarkable development of the India story has been that, from the start, electoral results have been accepted by winner and loser alike, leading importantly to orderly transfers of power—no mean achievement for a country that obtained its independence and proclaimed itself a sovereign democratic republic only seventy years ago. In many ways India has emerged in the global consciousness as a role model for plural democracies and more especially amongst those countries that gained freedom from colonial rule at about the same time in the late 1940s and through the '50s. Some electoral management bodies which are increasingly grappling with the

---

5 Although a large body of constitutional and legislative enactments owe their inspiration to Britain's (unwritten) constitution and laws, the UK's Election Commission does not have the powers of its Indian counterpart. Each UK county has its own returning officers (county laws can vary) who report ultimately to the Home Office.

6 Alfred Stepan, Juan L. Linz and Yogendra Yadav, *Crafting State-Nations: India and Other Multinational Democracies,* Baltimore: Johns Hopkins University Press, 2011, p. 77.

challenges of religious diversity, ethnic conflicts and multiculturalism are beginning to look at India's Election Commission on how it handles its manifold complexities.

Over the last two decades, the Commission has successfully evolved, drawing upon new strengths and skills, as it has striven to widen its ambit and egalitarian framework. In encompassing traditional values with newer integration processes, this has often meant confronting social tensions with innovative measures developed to constructively resolve them. These have included bringing together often conflicting strands within the electoral mainstream. The Commission has emerged as a wholly autonomous body—independent of the government—that has strengthened the democratic fabric of the country. The right to vote has evolved into an instrument of political awakening. There has been a steady movement towards enfranchisement and participation by those sections that were hitherto either disinterested (such as the youth), or who had been deliberately excluded for a host of complex reasons.

Early History

So, what makes India's general elections a focus of attention? Is it the magnitude, the unfathomable diversity, the form or content or a mixture of all these? It would be too simplistic to attempt to answer this in terms of size and volume alone, for even when the first general election was held in 1951–52, India's population stood at 361 million,[7] making it the largest democratic country in the world. At that time, it was certainly about the boldness of the democratic exercise, for there was no shortage of sceptics who were convinced that India's experiment with democracy could not last.

Among them were (predictably) the exiting colonials, who believed that it was the Raj that had kept India together despite its many

7 The 1951 Census of India, the first after Independence and Partition placed the figure at 361,088,090.

fissiparous tendencies. This was exemplified in the Churchillian view of the superior race and his contemptuous dismissal of India as a geographical expression, best compared to the Equator.[8] Notwithstanding the success of a largely peaceful movement that culminated in the country's independence, there remained many who were convinced that the erstwhile British and Princely India would pull in different directions. Although some conceded that the 'steel frame' of the Indian Civil Service (ICS) comprised many outstanding Indian administrators, they believed that the inherent contradictions would surface as soon as the British government (and its administration and army) left India's shores.

Therefore, the announcement of the first general election[9] (spread over four months) was viewed through this prism as the first step towards India's impending failure. However, the prophets of doom were to be proved wrong. Prime Minister Jawaharlal Nehru's choice of Sukumar Sen as the first chief election commissioner was a very sound one. Inducted from the ICS into the mint-new Indian Administrative Service (IAS), it became his task to devise and create an electoral architecture without the benefit of precedent—the British Raj had felt no need for an independent election commission for the elections of 1937.[10]

An interesting problem lay with many voters belonging to the princely states who had never been exposed to elections and were bound by feudal ties to their former rulers, may well have been apprehensive about voting for an altogether new dispensation. No comprehensive study has yet emerged on this subject except, perhaps, in respect of the erstwhile princely state of Jodhpur.[11]

---

8 In a speech Churchill delivered at London's Constitution Club in 1931. See Banyan, 'Is India a country or a continent?', *The Economist*, 9 Febraury 2017.

9 See Chapter 2, 'India's First General Election 1951–52'.

10 Ibid.

11 See Dhananajaya Singh, *The House of Marwar*, New Delhi: Roli Books, 2005 and L.S. Rathore, *The Untold Story of Freedom Struggle in Marwar*, Jodhpur: Books Treasure, 2012.

The Constituent Assembly drafted the longest written constitution in the world, seeking a balance between Britain's Westminster system and the American Constitution's checks and balances. Laws passed by India's parliament under the Union List would be subject to the judicial process, unless especially placed by parliament under the Ninth Schedule of the Constitution.

During the lengthy and historical debates in the Constituent Assembly, there arose the most fundamental question of all—whether or not to provide universal adult franchise. Its seeds had been sown much earlier. The leaders of the freedom movement had been committed to this since 1928. On 19 May 1928, the Report of the All Parties Conference chaired by Motilal Nehru (with stalwarts such as Subhas Chandra Bose, Sir Tej Bahadur Sapru, Sir Ali Imam and M.R. Jayakar as members) stated that the Conference was opposed to any artificial restrictions on the right to vote and pressed for universal adult franchise as well as equal rights for women. On 23 October 1928, B.R. Ambedkar—brilliant jurist, politician, Dalit leader and social reformer, who campaigned against social discrimination of India's depressed classes—too supported this in his deposition before the Simon Commission. The 1931 Karachi session of the Indian National Congress adopted a resolution that encapsulated this.

Thus, freedom fighters and national leaders were committed to the ideal of universal adult suffrage almost two decades before Independence. The Constituent Assembly reiterated this resolve, thereby striking a blow at separate electorates and the limited franchise that the British Raj had offered. This would prove to be arguably the greatest leveller of India's heterogeneous society.

The debates in the Constituent Assembly echoed the sentiment that although we were an unequal society, each vote was of equal value. By that argument, every person, irrespective of gender, race, region, religion or social status were sought to be placed on the same footing. Age-old inequalities would not be eliminated at one stroke, but they would diminish gradually by the conferral of political equality. This reflected a particularly bold vision, especially if we recall that in the elections conducted under British rule, franchise had been restricted to the educated and propertied classes, while in many other countries women as well as other marginalized groups had to struggle long and hard to get the right to vote.

Constitutional Provisions

A formidable challenge—then, as now—is that India continues to remain a society with deeply rooted social hierarchies. Identities of caste, religion, community and region remain deeply entrenched, particularly in rural areas. Yet, from the first general election on, the newly emerged polity offered the traditionally marginalized groups a democratic route towards empowerment. Indeed, this process of democratization of castes turned out to be the most significant social development of twentieth-century India. With universal adult franchise in place, political parties and individual candidates would gradually come to accept a policy of reconciliation rather than confrontation.

The other great initiative of affirmative action lay in the constitutional provision for reserving seats for the Scheduled Castes (SC) and Scheduled Tribes (ST), which came into effect with the promulgation of the Constitution in 1950. This ensured that those who had been sidelined and depressed for centuries were now offered a minimum guarantee of participation in governance. With every passing election thereafter, be it to the Lok Sabha or to the state assemblies, the participation of the Dalit and backward castes was set to grow. In 1951–52, the preponderant majority of MPs in north India belonged to the upper castes. Out of the total 489 seats, seventy-two seats were reserved for Scheduled Caste candidates and twenty-six for Scheduled Tribe candidates. The expectations of the upper castes that the lower castes could be coerced into voting for them began to change with the emergence of leadership from within these sections. By 2004, the share of the 'depressed classes' had grown to 25 per cent. Over time, SC and ST leaders would come to occupy key elected positions in the states and at the Centre.

The framers of the Constitution armed the Election Commission with enormous powers. Under Article 324, the Commission was conferred wide-reaching powers for the 'superintendence, direction and control of the preparation of electoral rolls' for the first and future elections. These would be exercised in the conduct of elections to the post of president and vice-president of India, to parliament, as well as to the state assemblies (and Union territories with legislatures).[12] Article 325 placed on the Commission the responsibility of maintaining a unified electoral roll that is free of bias. Article 326 enunciated universal adult franchise and gave voting rights to those who were over twenty-one years of age. (In March 1989, through the Constitution [Sixty-first Amendment] Act, parliament reduced the voting age to eighteen).

Article 329 which ensures that no one can interfere in the electoral process until the results are declared lies at the heart of the Commission's effective delivery. Even the courts cannot interfere in electoral matters, except by an election petition *after* the election process is over. The courts have the right to decide on the fairness of elections and malpractices, if any, with respect to laws and rules that exist at that time. This proved to be a well-thought-out decision on at least two counts: one, any judicial interference during the brief period of elections would necessarily slow down the election process, if not altogether impede it. And two, this served to highlight and protect the independent powers that were conferred on the Commission.

Legal Provisions

From the promulgation of the Constitution on 26 January 1950 to the first national election—to the Lok Sabha and the state assemblies simultaneously—lay a gap of nineteen months. This was needed to put enabling legislation in place. The Representation of the People Acts of 1950 and 1951 (RoPA) provided for the

---

12 The Constitution created a separate constitutional entity of state election commissions to conduct local-level elections including those to the municipalities and panchayats.

preparation of electoral rolls and the procedure of electoral conduct.[13] It spelt out the qualifications and disqualifications for the membership of the Houses, what constitute corrupt practices related to elections as well as rules regarding delimitation of constituencies. Section 123(2) of the RoPA, 1951, also defined direct or indirect interference in the free exercise of any electoral right as a corrupt practice.

In a bold move towards positive social affirmation, special provisions were included to safeguard the interests of voters belonging to the Scheduled Castes and Scheduled Tribes. Therefore, forcing or intimidating a member of the Scheduled Caste or a Scheduled Tribe to vote for a particular candidate, or the reverse, was made an offence under Section 3(1)(v) of the Scheduled Castes and Scheduled Tribes (Prevention of Atrocities) Act, 1989. The RoPA was notably amended in 1966 by which the jurisdiction to hear election petitions was transferred to high courts and, by appeal, to the Supreme Court. Barring some amendments, this Act remains the fulcrum of electoral legal management.

Anticipating that iniquitous hierarchies would play a restrictive role in ensuring the equality of citizenship rights, our lawmakers had gone a step further. Undue influence at elections was made an electoral offence under Section 171-C of the Indian Penal Code (which was inserted as early as 1920). Any interference or attempt at interfering with the free exercise of any electoral right would constitute the crime of undue influence in an election.

Political Parties in India: The Genesis

An oddity in the Indian Constitution, otherwise one of the most elaborate documents of its kind in the world, is that it makes no

13 In *Jyoti Basu vs Devi Ghosal,* (1982) 3 SCR 315, 318, pp. 326–27, the Supreme Court pointed out that the right to elect, to be elected or to dispute an election is a statutory right. It is not a fundamental right, and therefore subject to statutory limitations.

mention of political parties—surely one of the most important pillars of electoral democracy. Conscious of the many challenges that lay ahead, the drafters dedicated a full chapter on matters concerning elections, but there was a curious constitutional silence regarding political parties. This was all the more surprising because democracy cannot function in a vacuum. Political parties are necessarily that vital instrument that link governance with elections, in the process also representing different societal interest groups. The manifestos of political parties spell out their agendas for governance, whenever they acquire power through elections, held at regular intervals to test the political preferences of the electorate. It was, in fact, not until 1985, when the Tenth Schedule of the Constitution was added by the Constitution (Fifty-Second Amendment) Act, 1985, where political parties first found mention. Even then there was no precise definition of a political party.

It was left to the Election Commission to decide if an association or body of individuals could be registered as a political party under rules and regulations drawn up by it. From the first general election onwards, the Commission began the task of identifying political parties, which were recognized either as 'all-India' / 'national parties' or 'state parties'. After due consultation, the Commission eventually recognized fourteen political parties as national or multi-state parties and fifty-nine as state parties for the purposes of the first general election. The entire process of identifying political parties and according them recognition was done by the Commission in the absence of any specific legal provision, using instead its plenary power under Article 324 and Rule 5 of the Representation of the People (Conduct of Election) Rules 1951. Rule 5 importantly provided that the Commission would publish a list of symbols. Here too there was no mention of political parties. As a result, the emergence of political parties in post-Independence India could be traced to the *functional* need for allotting symbols to those parties that the Commission recognized.

Election Symbols

The promulgation, on 31 August 1968, of the Election Symbols (Reservation and Allotment) Order, 1968, thus became a landmark event, not only in the history of political parties in India but also in the evolution of election management. The order had detailed provisions for registration of parties, their recognition and related matters, together with the provision for specification, reservation, choice and allotment of symbols during elections. Under paragraph 15 of the order, the Commission alone can decide disputes among rival factions of a recognized political party staking claim to its name and symbol. In the event of a vertical split, the Commission can freeze the party symbol. The constitutional validity of this order was upheld by the Supreme Court after the same was challenged in 1971.[14] Registered (but unrecognized) parties too were now eligible to get some small preference in the matter of an allotment of 'free' (or unreserved) symbols for their candidates.

Working of Political Parties

The working of the party system in India has since been studied in detail by various committees, including the V.M. Tarkunde Committee (1974–75); Dinesh Goswami Committee (1990); Justice V.R. Krishna Iyer Committee (1994); Law Commission (1998) and Justice Kuldeep Singh bench of the Supreme Court (1996). The problems they identified were, among others, the absence of inner party democracy, the inadequate representation of women, lack of training for party members, problems regarding funding and campaign methods, as well as several negative issues such as regionalism, casteism, communalism, criminalization, growth in electoral violence, fractionalization of parties and the multiplicity of coalition partners. For, over the years, frequent splits and mergers

---

14 *Sadiq Ali and another vs ECI*, 11 November 1971, AIR 187, 1972 SCR (2) 318.

had resulted in fragmentation of political parties, primarily caused by bitter internal disputes. While splits in the legislature groups of the parties and their mergers with one another inside parliament or in a state legislature fall within the jurisdiction of the Speaker or the chairman of the House concerned, questions or disputes relating to splits and mergers of political parties *outside* the legislature continue to be determined by the Commission under its important Symbols Order.[15]

~

The framers of the Constitution, by majority, visualized simultaneous elections to parliament and state assemblies,[16] to be held once every five years, for which they felt that one suitably empowered chief election commissioner would suffice. Should the CEC so wish, he could co-opt one or two commissioners temporarily for the election period. The drafting committee favoured an arrangement whereby the executive (read prime minister in cabinet) would appoint additional commissioners if and when the need arose. While the CEC would have constitutional protection against removal, B.R Ambedkar argued that this need not apply to the co-opted commissioners who were essentially there for a short time. Two members of the Constituent Assembly differed with Ambedkar. Both Prof. Shibban Lal Saksena and Pandit Hirday Nath Kunzru[17] believed that similar protection should be afforded for the commissioners. In the end,

---

15 In a matter recently decided by the Supreme Court, in the course of deliberations, Chief Justice Dipak Misra and Justice Rohinton Nariman asked the Attorney General, 'can we not direct the Commission to frame a rule under the Symbols Order'. See 'Supreme court: Can Candidates tried for heinous offences be denied party symbol?', *The Hindu*, 22 August 2018.

16 See Chapter 11, pp. 294–300; also see author's article titled 'Simultaneous Elections Cannot Happen Without Political Consensus', *Hindustan Times*, 8 March 2018.

17 Details of relevant excerpts are given in an annexe to this chapter.

Ambedkar prevailed. The views of Saksena and Kunzru which I have reproduced in the annexe at the end of this chapter would emerge, in my view, as far more prophetic than was given credit for at the time.[18]

Till 1969, there was no need for appointing additional commissioners. For seventeen years the general and assembly elections coincided. From 1969 this changed dramatically. The long monopoly enjoyed by the Congress party came to an end with power being transferred to other parties in the states. The result was that while the general election would for the most part still be conducted every five years, state assemblies were often dissolved before their term, necessitating mid-term elections. Another reason for expanding the size of the Commission was altogether different. This arose when the executive began to resent the growing assertiveness of the chief election commissioners in the management and conduct of elections.[19] The executive had assumed that having appointed a civil servant to the high constitutional office of the chief election commissioner, the incumbent would be grateful enough to favour the government in power regarding the timing and conduct of elections. The earliest attempt to bridle the chief election commissioner was made when two additional commissioners were appointed in 1989.[20] This move would soon run afoul of Deputy Prime Minister Devi Lal in the subsequent government of V.P. Singh, who in a fit of well-documented pique had the posts abolished. However,

18 For a detailed discussion of this issue, see Chapter 12.

19 It is not unusual for governments and political parties to resent the power of election management bodies in many countries. Even where autonomy may have been granted (as in the Constitutions of some countries), it is sought to be curbed. In several countries, commission members lapse into political biases. Even in the UK (on which, in part, our Commission is modelled) there is clear reluctance to hand over more comprehensive electoral management to its commission.

20 On 16 October 1989, the president, through a notification, appointed S.S. Dhanoa and V.S. Seigell as election commissioners under CEC R.V.S. Peri Sastri.

the die had been cast. In the years that followed the chief election commissioners and commissioners would become handy punching bags. T.S. Krishnamurthy has observed in his book: 'During my tenure in the Commission, political parties often attacked the Election Commissioners including myself ... It [Commission] has shown remarkable restraint while issuing suitable rejoinders.'[21]

From time to time, a stratagem used by the executive to cow down the Commission was by threatening (through carefully placed leaks in the press) to increase the number of the commissioners, ostensibly to enlarge the body to make it commensurate with the country's size and population. Four years later, in 1993, Prime Minister Narasimha Rao finally decided the time had come to curtail what the political establishment viewed as T.N. Seshan's unbridled power and idiosyncrasies.[22] Rao appointed two additional commissioners, M.S. Gill, a senior IAS officer[23] and G.V.G. Krishnamurthy, a former member of the Law Commission. Incensed, Seshan moved the Supreme Court against these appointments on the plea that they were meant to restrain him and curb the independence of the Commission. The following year and a half was not a pretty period for the Commission, because the tug of war within the Commission and the often-vitriolic remarks made by Seshan about his colleagues spilt into the public domain. During the time that it took to dispose of this petition, Seshan gave the new appointees no work and treated them shabbily.[24]

This unhappy episode finally ended in 1995 when a five-judge bench of the Supreme Court headed by the Chief Justice of India,

---

21 T.S. Krishnamurthy, *The Miracle of Democracy: India's Amazing Journey*, New Delhi: HarperCollins, 2008, pp. 199–200.

22 T.N. Seshan, retired IAS officer of the Tamil Nadu cadre, was the tenth CEC, best remembered for cleaning up elections in India.

23 Dr M.S. Gill, the eleventh CEC, was a former Union agriculture secretary, who subsequently became an MP and minister.

24 'With two more election commissioners, T.N. Seshan's wings likely to be clipped', *India Today*, 31 October 1993.

in a unanimous ruling, declared the appointments of Gill and Krishnamurthy to be legal.[25] In an order that was to have a far-reaching effect and which changed the way that business was henceforth conducted in the Commission, the court not only rejected Seshan's petition but declared that he was only primus inter pares (the first among equals). Noting that he enjoyed the same perquisites in terms of salary, emoluments and term of office, the court declared the powers of all three to be exactly equal. The bench held that the CEC had a crucial role in electoral management but only to ensure that there was no administrative confusion. They held that a majority decision within the Commission would prevail, which, they clarified, meant that two commissioners could overrule the third; indeed, the two commissioners—Gill and Krishnamurthy—who were not given any work so far, could now overrule the mighty Seshan himself. The court was also scathing about his dictatorial ways. From this point on, the Commission began to function as a triumvirate. In fairness to Seshan, he did adjust to the new order of things.[26] Nevertheless, Gill would henceforth play the arbitrator when the other two disagreed, which was not quite infrequent.

The election commissioners have largely been appointed from within the ranks of the erstwhile Indian Civil Service and its successor the Indian Administrative Service.[27] They have traditionally been

---

25 Writ Petition (Civil) No.805 of 1993. Judgement delivered on 14 July 1995.

26 See Chapter 10: 'Electoral Reforms.'

27 Prime Minister Vajpayee had sought to supersede T.S. Krishnamurthy of the Indian Revenue Service in 2004. It became widely known that he wished to appoint the retiring cabinet secretary T.R. Prasad directly as the CEC, but gave up the attempt when T.S. Krishnamurthy and B.B. Tandon threatened to resign. T.S. Krishnamurthy recorded as follows in *The Miracle of Democracy: India's Amazing Journey*, p. 122: 'My appointment was announced after some uncertainty and there had been media reports about an outsider being brought in for the post. In the midst of these speculative reports, I decided to be away from Delhi to isolate myself from the rumours. I had actually decided to put

selected from among the senior-most officers who have achieved the rank of secretary in the Central government and who by the time of their appointments would have gathered over thirty-five years of administrative experience.

Organizational Structure

For a country the size of India, the Commission maintains a comparatively small secretariat of about 300 officials and staff at its headquarters in New Delhi. The keystone of the Commission's arch outside its headquarters is the chief electoral officer (CEO), one for each state and Union territory. The CEO enjoys statutory backing after an amendment in 1956 of the RoPA, 1951. This senior IAS officer is drawn from within the state government and his or her salary is paid by the state exchequer. Yet, he or she is responsible not to the state chief minister or chief secretary, but to the Election Commission of India. This dyarchical role does sometimes lead to problems of differences of opinion between the state government concerned and the Commission. It was often a delicate balancing act, but the Commission does its best to ensure the severance of the CEO's ties of loyalty to the state government. For instance, an effort is made to ensure his office is not within the state secretariat building but independent of it.

During my tenure in the Commission, we chose these key officials very carefully indeed. Whenever a vacancy arose, the state government concerned would be notified by the Commission to send a panel of names: the officers had to necessarily belong to that state cadre to ensure their familiarity with the state administration, its problems and sensitivities. Their names were carefully scrutinized.

---

in my papers in case an outsider was brought in, and had shared this thought with my colleague B.B. Tandon. On 19 January, I was to return to Delhi from Chennai when suddenly a very senior member of the cabinet informed me over the phone that I was being appointed CEC. The communication was made mechanically, without any warmth or congratulations.'

We satisfied ourselves on various criteria—integrity, capability and track record—before we made a selection. If we were not satisfied, we would request the state government to send us a fresh panel, sometimes even a third. The CEO had invariably to be about ten years senior to the district magistrates/district electoral officers (DEOs) in the state concerned. Without such advantage of authority, his or her writ would not run properly. This exercise sometimes stretched to a couple of weeks till we were convinced that the Commission's writ would run without let or hindrance. As a result of this diligence, we hardly ever went wrong in the choices that we ultimately made and the incumbents completed their full terms of five years.

The CEO was assisted by a deputy and a small, practically skeletal, staff. To administer the elections, however, the Commission had evolved a unique administrative model, that of temporarily seconding hundreds of senior officials from within the state government cadres for the duration of the election period. There was, of course, no other choice because if the Commission were to have officers and officials on its own rolls, they would run into hundreds of thousands, which would result in huge redundancies between elections.

The Commission headquarters is manned by just half a dozen senior officers of the rank of joint secretary and additional secretary. The Commission has several times addressed the Union government to permit it to recruit its own officials for the Nirvachan Sadan (the headquarters of the Election Commission of India) secretariat, rather than get officials on deputation. This arrangement would then be similar to the independent secretariats that man parliament, the Supreme Court and high courts which are not dependent on the government for their promotions or benefits, and therefore isolated from any possible pressure.

The Maintenance of Electoral Rolls

The year-round maintenance of electoral rolls is a vital constitutional requirement placed on the Commission. District electoral officers (DEOs), (typically the district magistrates/collectors manning the country's 640 districts) bear this responsibility. Over time, the administrative cadres, even those on temporary assignments, came to be firmly placed under the jurisdiction and control of the Commission, in so far as their electoral duties were concerned. T.N. Seshan,[28] in one of his many face-offs with the government, ensured that the Commission gained the additional power to discipline officials or even replace them, albeit temporarily, during the (comparatively brief) duration of the 'election season'. In due course, this would come to include the power to transfer out any official found 'unsatisfactory'; in rare cases, this would include even the senior-most bureaucrats and police officers, including those at the very top of the administrative pyramid—the chief secretaries of state governments and directors general of police. There is no parallel in electoral management in any other electoral commission in the democratic world.

With experience gained over time, systems were soon strengthened. Duty manuals and compendiums of instructions were created to reduce overlaps. Work allocations became more clearly defined reducing the scope for ambiguity. In the run-up to the elections, the officials concerned were given thorough briefings which included the sharing of 'best practices' that may have developed in the interim. Constant hands-on training on EVMs helped reduce the failure rate to below 0.5 per cent. Similar training is presently being provided to the election officials concerned on the new VVPAT machines.

Administrative Powers

Although for administrative purposes, the Election Commission is under the charge of the Ministry of Law and Justice, the ministry's real power over the Commission has receded over time, becoming more procedural than real. That said, the executive holds on to what it can. For instance, foreign travel by the CEC and commissioners

28 Tenth chief election commissioner in office from December 1990 to December 1996.

require to be 'cleared' by the government while applications for leave, (even for a half-day casual leave) by commissioners, necessitates a formal application addressed directly to the president of India, which ends up on the law minister's desk. The 'executive' in the case of the CEC and commissioners is the president of India. The president's role too evolved into something akin to that of the British monarch in relation to her prime minister who, in Bagehot's words, retains the right 'to advise, to caution and to warn'. The president must be notified about the start of the election process and it is to the president that the final results, once compiled, are presented.[29]

It is well recognized that it was T.N. Seshan who armed the Commission with teeth for the first time. His run-ins with the government soon became legendary. In one of his altercations with Prime Minister P.V. Narasimha Rao, Seshan reportedly told him that there were only three ways that he could be rid of. Resignation was not an option as he would not oblige Rao. There was no question of his death either, said Seshan. So, if the PM wished, the government could impeach him.[30] Seshan was far too shrewd not to know that the government did not have a two-thirds majority in parliament. Any impeachment proceeding is difficult at the best of times but as the government enjoyed at best a simple majority, he would have known that this was likely to fail. Seshan, however, soon found himself checkmated by the prime minister, who was far more the master of the game than any CEC could possibly aspire to be. The prime minister countered him by appointing two additional election

29 However, not once during the course of the 2009 general election, did the then president, Pratibha Patil, ask me about it. Before the start of the electoral process, I had conveyed to the secretary to the president that the Commission would present the results to the president on 18 May 2009, by 5 p.m. The full Commission delivered these only an hour later, at 6 p.m.

30 See T. S. Krishnamurthy, *The Miracle of Democracy*, p. 59.

commissioners.[31] Indeed, such was the timing of this announcement that Seshan learned of this new development only when he alighted at Pune airport.

A game similar to chess ensued. Seshan moved the Supreme Court against the appointment of the two commissioners on the grounds that the independence of the Commission was being compromised. He then proceeded to treat two commissioners as if they did not exist. He called no meeting of the full Commission. He denied them work. No papers or files for information or decision were sent to them. For months, they were barely given any staff. Finding themselves without work, the two commissioners largely stayed away. The judgment of the court took one and a half years to be delivered—a very long time before the Election Commission began to function as a triumvirate—which then finally restored some order at the Nirvachan Sadan.

The history of the Commission will surely have 1990 as its defining moment. Before the advent of Seshan in 1990, there were nine chief election commissioners who were barely known to the public at large. They were brilliant civil servants who gradually built up the Commission though the atmosphere they worked in was somewhat under the shadow of the executive. Seshan was made of sterner stuff. He effectively stamped his authority, and that of the Commission, on the country's electoral system. Dubbed 'alsatian' in the process by his many detractors, he provided an altogether new meaning to the manner in which the Model Code of Conduct (MCC) was henceforth implemented. He made it a far more level playing field than it had hitherto been, ensuring that governments in power could not turn elections to their advantage. His frequent outbursts delighted an ever-hungry press. Many rather intemperate ones such as 'I eat politicians for breakfast' made headlines. It would take the Supreme Court's order, and its scathing comments about Seshan's conduct, for him to finally temper his often-dictatorial ways. The Commission did meet from time to time, but the tension between the commissioners

31 The single member Election Commission had been converted into a three-man one.

remained till the end of Seshan's tenure. Not infrequently, Seshan would 'run' the Commission from his own house, relying on a few officials to conduct day-to-day business.

Although his successor M.S. Gill's manner was more tactful and accommodating, Seshan's idiosyncrasies had sufficiently alarmed the political establishment. This lack of trust would continue to manifest itself even two decades after Seshan, especially in the realm of electoral reform.[32] Even Gill's more pragmatic approach failed to get the political establishment to react positively on a number of suggestions he made to the government. His efforts to seek an amendment of the law to disqualify anyone accused of a criminal offence (punishable by imprisonment for five years and more) from contesting an election were rebuffed. His argument that once elected they could well find themselves in ministerial office, which would, even more ironically, entitle them to protection by the police was similarly ignored.

There were other reform proposals made to successive governments over the years. Amongst them was the Commission's request that parliament should amend the law to bar a candidate contesting from two constituencies simultaneously. To move towards transparency in political funding, the Commission sought that accounts of all political parties be properly audited, not by some fly-by-night company but by such companies as the Comptroller and Auditor General (CAG) might suggest. The Commission has since repeatedly sought more sunlight on the collection of funds by political parties and to make them available for public scrutiny.[33] None of these suggestions have been met with the response that the Commission sought.

Over the years, the Commission, seeking financial autonomy on the lines granted to other constitutional bodies, has repeatedly written to the Central government that its budget should be charged to the Consolidated Fund of India and not voted by parliament, but without

32 See Chapter 10: 'Electoral Reforms'.

33 Election Commission of India, 2004 Compendium of Reforms prepared by CEC T.S. Krishnamurthy, 30 July 2004.

success. These are only a few of the many recommendations made to the government. The quietus with which they have been received is reflective of the subterranean tension between the government of the day and the Commission. The one significant reform that I sought and on which I myself wrote to Prime Minister Manmohan Singh in 2010 was to take the spirit of the Supreme Court order in the Seshan case to its logical conclusion by according the same constitutional protection to the members of the Commission as is accorded to the CEC. To be sure, my letter was promptly acknowledged by the law minister but, in essence, met with the same apathy.[34]

The Use of Technology

The Commission continues to derive enormous advantage by being amongst the first electoral management bodies worldwide to embrace technology so comprehensively. The use of electronic voting machines (EVMs) was a bold idea that would transform the manner in which polls were conducted. Their introduction was gradual; initially used in bye-elections, then in a clutch of states. The use of EVMs was subjected to quite relentless litigation arising from accusations that they could be tampered with and a host of other complaints. The Commission defended their use vigorously. The result was that the usage of EVMs was supported by a host of judgments from various high courts. The Karnataka High Court even called it 'a great achievement in the electronic and computer technology and a national pride'.[35] In 2004, the then CEC, T.S. Krishnamurthy took the plunge and comprehensively employed EVMs for the 2004 general election. The EVM's manifest advantage was that the results could be finalized accurately in a matter of hours. The scourge of 'booth capturing' and the looting of ballot boxes, rampant in the 1980s and '90s came

34 See Chapter 12: 'Chief Election Commissioner: Equal or Superior'.

35 See the Press Note by Press Information Bureau, the Government of India, dated 16 March 2017.

down sharply, especially after the polling stations were better secured. After several courts and the Supreme Court endorsed the inviolability of the machines, public acceptance grew, in spite of attempts to blame the EVMs, especially by those vanquished at the hustings.[36] It helped enormously that both their usage and their storage are placed firmly in the charge of government officials who are necessarily under the disciplinary powers of the government. Improvements in EVMs have constantly been made. To allay recent criticisms from some political parties, a new generation of machines have been introduced with enhanced safety features. Most recently, the Supreme Court has directed the Commission to deploy the VVPAT machine alongside each EVM to establish a 'paper trail'.[37]

An equally significant example of the use of technology is the computerization of electoral rolls, a massive exercise aimed at greater precision and transparency. To create an integrated electoral register, hosted on the Commission's website, different states prepared language-specific software too. This was followed by the reintroduction of electoral photo identity cards (EPICs), using digitized photo images both on the cards and on the newly created photo electoral rolls. The countrywide application of rolls and cards during GE 2009 were a significant step towards accuracy, which helped prevent to a large extent electoral fraud that was common in the 1980s where duplicate names and names of deceased voters were rampantly misused.

The EPICs

In time for GE 2009, the Commission was successful in commissioning the production and distribution of 518 million electoral photo identity cards (EPICs), covering a whopping 82 per cent of India's electorate. The inclusion of voter's photograph on the

---

36 See Chapter 7: The EVM: A Controversy That Refuses to Die.

37 Ibid.

card for the first time was a significant step towards reducing, if not eliminating, possible voter fraud.

Prior to 2006, the elector's card was a document that was neither sought after nor particularly used. As a case in point, if someone lost a driving licence or passport, they would immediately press the system for its replacement. But no one really valued our card!

I began to inquire of many of our officials as to how we could remedy the situation. I recollect that it was during a visit to Himachal Pradesh that I asked this of the then CEO of the state, Manisha Nanda. Her answer was succinct: reduce its size to that of a driving licence so that it became wallet-friendly and thereafter ensure that it was accepted by the Central and state governments as a document of identification for all government schemes. I discussed these suggestions in the Commission, which concurred. It took a few weeks to finalize a new design. Thereafter the CEOs began the much more arduous task of obtaining the photographs of millions of voters in order to convert our existing election card sans photograph into the EPIC.

After the conclusion of the general election, we held a wrap-up session of our officials in Jaisalmer in Rajasthan in 2010. We swapped stories on best practices and innovations. It was here that we decided that we must move towards ensuring that every voter must have a card as far as our peripatetic population, particularly in the metropolitan cities, would allow. The Commission came close to this goal in time for GE 2014, just three percentage points short of 100.

General Election 2009

As I was the face of the 2009 general election (GE 2009), I remain in a good position to explain some of the inner workings of the electoral machine. The statistics involved are well recognized to be gargantuan. In 2009, there were 714 million voters on the register. Of these 82 per cent, or almost 580 million, had for the first time been equipped with EPICs. This deterrence against impersonation was indeed an epic task. From a total of 640 administrative districts that straddled almost 8,000 towns and 641,000 villages, a mammoth total of

834,994 polling stations had been surveyed, 'mapped' and thereafter provided with the wherewithal to conduct the election. While 1.18 million EVMs were pressed into use, a staggeringly huge force of eight million civil officials and staff and almost three million police personnel were deployed for a variety of election-related tasks. This temporary deployment, interestingly, equalled the entire population of Portugal or Belgium. In fact, our electoral register almost equalled the entire population of fifty European countries (731 million) or the combined electorate of all fifty-four countries of Africa put together (566 million).

Nor was this all. What was arguably as important was the premium that we sought to place on each individual vote, which is why—apart from a polling station set up for a single voter in the lion sanctuary—there were several other stations set up for a handful of voters in other parts of the country too.

In the icy Himalayan ranges of the Zanskar parliamentary constituency in Jammu and Kashmir, we set up two polling stations for just thirty-seven voters. Not entirely surprisingly, bad weather forced the cancellation of the helicopter that had to ferry the election staff and materials. We could well have decided to postpone the election in these two inhospitable stations by a few weeks rather than hold up the entire process in that constituency. It was argued that thirty-seven votes were unlikely to have a major impact on the result. However, we were informed that a handful of young and sturdy officials had volunteered to trek up to these two villages located at about 4,115 metres (13,500 ft). Were they sure, I asked our CEO. For it involved a 45-km-long climb up to a pass located at 5,029 metres (16,500 ft), which also meant wading through knee-deep snow over large parts. However, their enthusiasm overcame the odds. Not only did they reach on time, but also managed to rest half a night in a cave, which was the only shelter they came across. Was it any surprise then that we decided to celebrate the grit of this team by counting the results of these two stations before we took up any other in Jammu and Kashmir?

~

Over the past decade or so, there has been a paradigm shift towards micromanagement of elections. This has often been criticized by political parties and candidates in the fray, who believe that elections have come to be held in an increasingly restrictive regime. Some voters too have felt the same. When I travelled in June 2010 to remote Kalpa in the mountainous district of Kinnaur in Himachal Pradesh specifically to meet the then ninety-three-year-old Shyam Saran Negi—arguably the first person to cast his vote in independent India on 23 October 1951—he lamented that the Commission had now placed too many restrictions in the run-up to elections and on the election day. Elections used to be a 'festival' he said, adding that 'the joy of elections had now gone'. I had to admit that there was more than an element of truth in this. I did try to explain to him that the challenges involved in delivering credible elections had increased manifold, not to mention the exponential surge in population from 176 million voters in 1951 to 716 million in 2009. This had also been accompanied by the explosive growth of the print and electronic media and consequent voter awareness and public expectations. The revolution in technology through social media had resulted in a constant flood of emails, SMSes, tweets and Facebook pages from a much more aware and often aggressive public. But Shyam Saran Negi remained unconvinced.[38]

Model Code of Conduct

If the elections are recognized as having been successful and without too much abusive rhetoric, it was largely because we were able to administer the model code of conduct (MCC) as impartially and strictly as we could.

The code was first devised and mutually agreed upon by political parties themselves in the run-up to the assembly elections in Kerala in 1960. It was essentially a list of dos and don'ts that would govern everything in the run-up to the election. In due course, this code

---

38 A major controversy involving Facebook is detailed in Chapter 11: 'Emerging Trends'.

evolved within the Commission and the political establishment to become an accepted set of non-legislative rules or norms of correct political behaviour. They were strengthened at periodic intervals, prior to successive general elections. It would become a unique instrument of which there is no exact parallel anywhere else. It continues to lay down 'best practices', which are a set of guidelines with respect to speeches, processions and general conduct. The aim is to ensure a level playing field, so that the ruling party at the Centre or in the states do not try to wrest any undue advantage. It seeks to reduce anti-democratic behaviour and seeks to control or minimize vote buying as well as keep voter-behaviour non-sectarian. What is especially noteworthy is that while the MCC is not based on any statute, it has been the subject of judicial pronouncements in important cases, including an overview taken by the Supreme Court in 2001.[39]

Under T.N. Seshan, the MCC came to be enforced by the Commission more strictly than before, especially in the face of violence and fraud which had become rampant especially in the 'badlands' of Uttar Pradesh (UP) and Bihar. His critics, of whom there were many, accused him of using the MCC as a tool to demonstrate his personal power. He stood his ground. Soon the MCC evolved into an important device used to 'name and shame'. The MCC comes into force as soon as elections are announced by the Commission, and in effect continues for the duration of the electoral period. Since we have entered an era of phased elections (stretching over several weeks), the MCC now remains in force for a longer period than originally envisaged.

So all-encompassing has the MCC become that the working of the Central government (or the state government as the case may be) is perceived to come to a standstill as soon as elections are announced. Citing the code, new proposals are not entertained and indeed day-to-day functioning in government departments slows

39 Union of India vs Harbans Singh Jalal and Ors SLP (Civil) No 22724 of 1997 decided by SC on 26 April 2001.

down considerably. During the 2009 elections, practically every project, new or ongoing, was being quite unnecessarily referred to the Commission for approval. This was never the intent of the MCC or the Commission: the MCC only sought to postpone such new initiatives that might influence voters in favour of the government or garner funds for politicians through contractor-driven new schemes. To obviate the obvious difficulties in governance, we set up a mechanism to review, on a day-to-day basis, any new proposal, doing our best to ensure that the everyday work of government could proceed without let or hindrance.[40]

The powers of the CEC, particularly during elections when he is the voice of the Commission as it were, are very wide. This made me the special target of several opposition parties, which were apprehensive that I was biased in favour of the ruling Congress party. However, during the course of GE 2009, it was against the Congress governments in Assam, Rajasthan and Maharashtra, and the Tamil Nadu government led by the DMK, a Congress ally, that I had to take action for violation of the MCC. The Congress chief minister of Assam was so enraged upon receiving a show-cause notice from the Commission during the election process that in a specially convened press conference he threatened to file a complaint against me in the Supreme Court.[41]

---

40 Earlier the MCC came into force after the announcement of the elections. But now the Commission has amended its order after the Telangana Legislative Assembly was dissolved, to enforce restrictions upon the government in the event of an early dissolution of the assembly. Basing its order on the Bommai judgment (*S.R. Bommai and Ors vs Union of India and Ors*, 1994, SCR 644: AIR 1994 SC 1918) that a caretaker government should merely carry on day-to-day work and not to take any major policy decision in the interim. This order now binds the Centre and the states. See 'Election Commission order places Telangana under Model Code of Conduct', *The Hindu*, 27 September 2018.

41 This and related incidents are discussed in the state-wise accounts that follow.

Supervision and Control

Control rooms were necessary not only at Nirvachan Sadan but importantly in state capitals and district headquarters, to establish continuous contact, especially in areas of Maoist domination and in the more far-flung mountainous states. However, once the poll was announced and the model code of conduct came into operation, every single complaint that we received needed to be examined for its veracity, and that too within a few hours. The efficacy of the MCC could only be maintained if this were the case. With the communication network having been established (and tested to ensure that it worked), our swift responses helped create the psychological presence of the Commission even in some of the remotest locations.

I could not help but realize just how continental India is in size when I began state-wise tours leading up to the 2009 general election. Three months or so prior to the general elections, it was customary for the CEC and the commissioners to embark on an extensive tour of the states to conduct constituency-wise reviews of the preparedness of men and machines. We had divided the states and Union territories amongst ourselves, each of us to cover about ten. These were exhaustive (and exhausting) day-long interactions, which were so detailed and meticulous that they often stretched to ten hours at a time. Sometimes they spilled over to the following day. They would primarily encompass those directly concerned—the returning officer (RO)/ district magistrate (DM) and his/her counterpart police official, the superintendent of police (SP).[42] These were the key officials at the cutting edge of the electoral process. Those found severely wanting were immediately replaced, but as this was perceived as a great put-down, we resorted to this sparingly. However, the vast majority of the officials were up to the mark. Despite rigorous protocols in place, which our deputy election commissioners from headquarters reviewed

42 Henceforth referred to as ROs, DMs and SPs (or in the case of senior superintendents of police as SSPs).

before the Commission arrived, it would still take many long hours before we were satisfied with the overall electoral readiness (See Chapter 3: Notes from the 2009 General Election).

Electoral Observers

Over the years, the Commission has evolved an intricate system of electoral observation machinery. Unlike some other electoral management bodies, the Commission does not invite overseas monitoring. Our observers, senior officers of the rank of joint secretary for the most part, are drawn mainly from the IAS ('general observers') and the Indian Revenue Service ('expenditure observers'). However, this distinction was blurred in 2009 when officers belonging to Indian Forest Service were among the 2,500 senior officials,[43] who were 'pulled out' from their normal duties and sent to electoral constituencies for almost a month. Observers were not deployed in either their cadre states or home states and were sent elsewhere largely to protect them from accusations of favouritism.

Their duties were very wide. They would look into any complaint of inaccuracy or omission in the electoral rolls, become available to hear complaints from political parties or candidates, redress these through the respective DMs, SPs and electoral officials, and keep an eye open for violations of the MCC and other malpractices. They advised the DMs/ SPs on police deployment and security issues and decided which electoral stations or areas deserved special attention. In concert with key officials, they positioned the micro-observers at ultra-sensitive stations. They did this and more. Overall, they helped maintain transparency and a level playing field that the Commission sought to ensure in every constituency. In short, they were the eyes and ears of the Commission. That many of them had themselves been DMs meant that they understood the mechanics of the election all too well.

---

43 An extra 500 observers were assigned to the three states where simultaneous polls to their assemblies were also conducted.

As I became increasingly aware that the quantum of Central forces (which had become such an essential part of effective election management) was not being assigned in the numbers that I had hoped for by the government, the role of the observers—many of whom had performed similar duties in earlier elections and were therefore experienced and seasoned—became vital.

Phased Elections

The Commission has sometimes been criticized for the increasingly long duration of the election period. Newspapers have editorialized that the entire exercise should be completed in one go or, at best, in a couple of short phases. Critics have complained that from the date of the announcement of polls to the completion of polling, general elections have tended to stretch up to two months and beyond. We were conscious of this criticism when we planned the 2009 electoral exercise, but soon found that for a number of reasons over which we had no control, we had no option but to conduct the elections in at least five phases. The twenty-eight-day period of actual polling (from 16 April to 13 May) was preceded by a forty-six-day campaign period (from the announcement of the election and issue of our press note on 2 March 2009 to the first date of poll on 16 April 2009). An important reason for phases, then as now, is the Commission's dependence on the quantum of the Central police forces that can be made available at a particular juncture by the home ministry, which of course has its own priorities.

I was most disappointed that we did not get as much force for GE 2009 as we felt we required. Indeed, it was about half of what we had asked for (and half of what was made available for the 2014 general election). There was no alternative but to devise other means to ensure the integrity of the poll process—which was paramount—and the overall need for security as well as the safety of candidates, party workers, poll staff and equipment. Fortunately, because of hundreds of hours of meticulous planning and execution by all the senior district officials, we were (just about) able to manage within our constraints. This involved the timely positioning of the forces and their subsequent movements from one phase of polling to the next. Special trains had to be engaged to move them without disrupting the normal schedule of the railways. It required several days of consultation with the railway top brass before 119 special trains were requisitioned, which would crisscross the country over the five phases of polling, spread over four weeks.

Moreover, all this planning had to be done in a manner that maintained the secrecy of poll dates. That was not all. Millions of civilian polling staff had also to be transported, a day before (or on the poll day itself), to their respective polling stations. This was another gigantic exercise for which thousands of buses were requisitioned and timetables planned. To avoid the suspicion that poll staff might display local loyalties or friendships, poll officials are never assigned their home districts. In fact, they were assigned their responsibilities, at random, by a computer programme, and would learn of their places of responsibilities just a day before. With such detailed micro-management to be completed, not to mention difficulties of distance and insurgency, there was no alternative to phased elections.

Maoist Insurgency

Conducting the elections on schedule in areas affected by Maoist insurgency was among my biggest challenges. Their areas of domination had come to be known as the 'Red Corridor'—as many as ninety 'highly affected' districts spread over several states largely in eastern and central India.[44] The Maoists were ideologically opposed to elections and had in the past variously threatened political parties, candidates, the election machinery and voters alike. Police forces were almost always their principal targets: while striking a blow at the symbol of the state, the Maoists were simultaneously able to steal

---

44 Estimates of the spread of Maoist influence varies greatly and has been described in greater detail in Chapter 8: The Maoist Factor in Elections.

police weapons for their own use. While this guerilla warfare has been going on for almost five decades—since the beginning of the Naxalbari uprising in West Bengal in 1967—their opposition to the electoral process was a part of their ideological struggle against the state. Voters were routinely frightened away by them; they sometimes fired on the voters even as they stood in queues at polling stations. In some particularly gruesome incidents, voters who had defied Maoist diktats had had their index finger chopped off.[45]

Red Corridor

The Red Corridor is a somewhat loosely defined expression to describe a significant number of contiguous administrative districts linking as many as ten states from Andhra Pradesh in the south up to the Nepal border in the north, from the interior districts of West Bengal and Odisha in the east, to the Gadchiroli district of Maharashtra in the west, with the deeply forested parts of Jharkhand, Chhattisgarh, UP and Bihar making up the centre. With a preponderantly tribal population that made up the Maoist force, their jungle habitat also afforded a natural sanctuary to the Maoist militias. In 2009, over a hundred districts—almost one-sixth of India's districts—were affected by left-wing extremism. In the face of Maoist retreat in recent years, this figure has been reduced by the Ministry of Home Affairs to approximately ninety districts, of which thirty-six are designated as the 'worst affected' (in Chhattisgarh, Jharkhand, Odisha and Bihar). While this might be described the traditional Red Corridor, now a new corridor appears to be forming through Kerala, Tamil Nadu and Andhra Pradesh.

---

45 Perhaps their worst attack occurred well after the 2009 general elections when on 25 May 2015 they ambushed members of a political party in the Sukma district of Chhattisgarh. Here Maoist insurgents used both landmines and gunfire on a convoy of Indian National Congress leaders causing at least twenty-nine deaths, effectively wiping out much of a recognized political party in the very run-up to the state assembly elections.

Since I was the face of the Commission in 2009, I also became the special focus of their attention. This happened too because I had more than once publicly announced the determination of the Commission to conduct elections *everywhere* and according to schedule. Towards that end, I made a few well-publicized visits, including one with my colleague V.S. Sampath,[46] to better understand the difficulties faced by our officials on the ground.

The modus operandi used by the armed cadre of Maoists was to spread terror and create large-scale disruption. Their methods varied, but invariably involved the use of lethal weapons. To win the battle, they needed arms, ammunition and explosives. The latter were also needed in mining operations, which is why these were targeted so often. The security forces were targeted mainly for two reasons—they were the 'face' of the enemy, and their weapons would be 'legitimately' seized to arm their own (guerilla) outfits. And since elections had become the chosen path to democracy, attacking poll officials, voters and the security paraphernalia, was conferred legitimacy in their eyes.

Innovations from Within

The Booth-level Officer (BLO) System

Ensuring the fidelity of electoral rolls is the sine qua non of a fair election and we took this 'mantra' very seriously to try and ensure that those eligible to vote would not be left out, either inadvertently, through carelessness, or even by design. The voter registration process and revision of electoral rolls for each of the 4,120 assembly constituencies and for the 543 parliamentary constituencies had already grown into a round-the-year affair. For GE 2009, we decided to adopt a completely new method to ensure as accurate an electoral roll as possible, particularly to counter the effect of people moving between states, cities and within cities, often without informing the

46 He was the sixteenth CEC, in office from 11 June 2012 to 15 January 2015.

election office of their proposed movements. It was equally true that our electoral machinery had still not perfected a system that made it easy for citizens to effect such changes without going through enormous trouble. This is how the booth-level officer (BLO) system came to be born.[47]

The BLO remains a government functionary who is given the task of 'owning' the voters belonging to an average polling station—usually between 1,000 and 1,500 voters. In the run-up to GE 2009, the BLO was given the added responsibility of maintaining an accurate list of voters and to keep these lists up to date. This vitally meant deleting the names of those who had either passed away or shifted out of the neighbourhood. This also meant adding the names of eighteen-year-olds—who were being encouraged, by a new programme, which came to be called Systematic Voter's Education and Electoral Participation (SVEEP) in 2010, and by other means—to enlist and exercise their franchise.

In a country as large as India, this was no easy task. There were plenty of teething problems. The Commission did not have sufficient staff of its own while the state governments were initially reluctant to offer any more hands to the Commission. Many of those who were eventually spared were teachers or revenue officials, leading to some legitimate concerns being raised that these additional responsibilities were detracting them from their principal duties. The numbers we sought were not small. We needed a veritable army of 800,000 such personnel. Such was the esteem that the Commission was held in that the states finally agreed. The BLO mechanism served us well in keeping the electoral register in a far better shape than it had been in previous elections. There were still complaints to be heard: 'Our BLO comes to our homes when we are at work' or 'the BLO spelt our names inaccurately' or 'my wife's photo has been swapped with

---

47 See 'The Importance of being a Booth Level Officer' by the author in *The Hindu*, 28 May 2013.

mine', yet on the whole this innovation went a long way in ensuring far greater accuracy of the voters list.

Communication for Elections Tracking (COMET)

In a country as vast and diverse as ours, we embarked on another ambitious initiative, which was to undertake a mapping of all our communication assets with reference to all polling stations in the country. What this meant was that we created a detailed plan for every one of our 834,000 polling stations. Each of them acted as a hub for as many lines of communication as were feasible. The logistics required to reach man and machine to every polling booth entailed months of detailing by our indefatigable officials at Nirvachan Sadan, working closely with the CEOs who, in turn, supervised the DEOs/ DMs and SPs in each of the parliamentary constituencies. We anointed this formidable network with the acronym COMET (communication for election tracking). Admittedly not everything worked at supersonic speed, especially over those vast tracts that had to be traversed on foot. What gave us added leverage was that by 2009 the mobile phone network had grown exponentially since the 2004 general election, so that it now covered almost 62 per cent of the country.

However, that still left a not inconsiderable gap. These remaining polling stations usually lay largely in inhospitable areas. In much of these areas, mobile connectivity was very poor and landline phones did not work. High- and very-high-frequency communication equipment was pressed into service wherever we could. Where none of these worked—for instance, at very high altitudes or in deep forests where mobile towers had been wantonly destroyed by the Maoists—we pressed other strategies into use, which have been described in a later chapter of the book. Where nothing worked, we had to fall back on 'runners', a leftover from Mughal times and passed on to us by the British Raj.

Vulnerability Mapping[48]

We were conscious of the fact that traditional social hierarchies based on caste identities remained dominant in all but the biggest cities. These were most often translated into problems caused by largely silent threats and intimidation of voters belonging to the marginalized and other vulnerable communities by the upper castes. In the past, incidents of intimidation often went unreported or were ignored or not acted upon. In keeping with the vision of the framers of the Constitution, we took an important step towards affirmative action that did not require any statutory change to redress this situation. Diagnosing this as a socio-economic phenomenon for which an institutional response could be designed, our officials began the task of identifying, with the help of computers, such pockets (both urban and rural), where there had been low, negligible or even an absence of voting in previous elections. With the analysis of the data that became available, a broad picture began to emerge. For example, it would appear that a certain section of a village had not voted for a decade. Was it apathy or anger against a candidate, or was this because of intimidation? Our officials dug deeper by sending observers to inquire from people living in those pockets the reasons that had kept them away. The resultant data led us to create a 'vulnerability area' map, on to which even the smallest areas of exclusion were marked with red dots. Sometimes, a red dot appeared simply because of an infrastructure problem, e.g., a bridge over a river had broken down necessitating voters to walk a much longer distance to find another way to reach the polling booth. The pattern that emerged was that, for the most part, voters belonging to the depressed classes were prevented from reaching the polling station. Intimidated, afraid of violence, they stayed away.

This 'red-dot' approach had proved to be an effective confidence-building measure in the 2007 assembly election in Uttar Pradesh. As

---

48 See 'Vulnerability Mapping, an Electoral Innovation', *The Hindu*, 13 June 2013.

many as 27,831 polling stations had been identified as 'vulnerable' on the basis of past incidents combined with computer-based feedback, which revealed the areas that had not participated in previous elections. We even discovered some 'red-dot areas' that had not voted since Independence. By 2009, we had virtually mapped the entire country. The Commission was clear that it was imperative to create a shield against such hostility. But at the ground level we did not have enough police force to provide comprehensive security. To obviate the need for the vulnerable to walk through 'hostile' territory, the first option that suggested itself was to shift the polling station to a safer middle ground. This was not an easy task. Many political contestants objected; any shift needed the consent of all the political parties in the fray. We decided to leave the established booths alone. Instead, we created the 'auxiliary stations' and sited them near the residential area of the marginalized voters. At the end of the exercise, the district officials had mapped almost a hundred thousand auxiliary locations in the country. The result of this affirmative measure was a matter of enormous satisfaction, especially when we were swamped with feedback that thousands of voters could exercise their franchise without fear.

Transgender Rights

The Commission became the first constitutional authority in India—and possibly in South Asia—to recognize transgender rights. Interestingly, the issue was raised by students in the question-and-answer session that followed the lectures that I delivered in Bhubaneswar (Odisha) and Chennai (Tamil Nadu) within the space of a few weeks. As no statutory amendment was needed, the Commission approved a change in the rules, whereby we added 'O' for Other alongside 'Male' and 'Female' in our relevant documents.[49]

49 ECI Circular No. 22/2/2009/ERS dated 6 November 2009 which used the appellation 'Other'. ECI Circular No 23/2012/ERS, Vol. IV dated 23 February 2013 changed the appellation to Transgender.

The appellation 'Other' was replaced by Transgender by the Supreme Court in an order passed on 15 April 2014.[50]

Disability-friendly Measures

As part of our continuing policy of affirmative action, we adopted measures aimed at helping the disabled or those with problems due to advanced age to vote with relative ease and dignity. I was anxious to go beyond our standard guidelines, travelling the proverbial extra mile if we could. There were already instructions in place for the provision of ramps for wheelchair-bound voters—this having emanated from an order of the Supreme Court.[51] As a direct result, ramps had become an essential feature of the architecture for all electoral stations. However, I had observed during my travels that in the case of additional electoral booths (or 'auxiliaries'), they were yet to be provided with ramps. Even the ones constructed for the past elections were not well maintained. While reiterating the court orders, we tried to make our ramps gentler to traverse. (Some of the photographs in this book testify to the effort the aged and disabled made to exercise their right to vote). For the first time, I had two audits instituted, one before and another during the elections. As a result, some glaring exceptions emerged out of the woodwork. One example that came to notice was in Varanasi where, near the crowded ghats, some polling stations were located on the first floor of buildings. The Commission managed to relocate some of these

---

50 *National Legal Services Authority vs Union of India,* Supreme Court WP (Civil) No. 604 of 2013 decided on 15 April 2014. Judges sitting K.S. Radhakrishnan and A.K. Sikri.

51 WP (Civil) No. 187 of 2004, *Disabled Rights Group vs CEC and another*. The Supreme Court in its order in this writ petition by an NGO, the Disabled Rights Group, directed the Election Commission to undertake disability-friendly measures. The Commission responded by instructions for the provision of ramps at polling stations, separate queues for the handicapped, and the introduction of Braille numerals in all new EVM machines that would be manufactured henceforth.

but had to retain eight polling stations. Any relocation of these stations meant shifting the booths much further afield, which both political parties and local residents objected to. Instead, we made special provisions for the disabled to be carried up. Fortunately, these exceptions were few.

Our efforts to assist the visually disabled to vote independently were not as widespread as I had hoped, but we made a beginning. In our country's ocean of poverty, not every visually impaired person is Braille-literate; we soon found how few were. Nevertheless, with the assistance of the National Institute for the Visually Handicapped (NIVH) headquartered in Dehradun, we successfully printed Braille ballot papers. In NIVH's residential campus, where almost all its residents were visually disabled, a special polling station was created so that voters did no longer need to walk almost 2 km to their designated booth. Nor did they need the assistance of a helper and were able to cast their votes in secrecy. As a result of these and other related efforts, we succeeded in putting mechanisms in place which would gradually enlarge into broader policy initiatives.

Transparency Measures

As the elections drew closer, many candidates, especially those belonging to different opposition parties, became increasingly uneasy about the possibility of the ruling party of the state exercising their power over local officials to their advantage. To allay these fears, we asked all our CEOs to convene frequent meetings with all political parties and candidates and take their concerns on board. Our observers were given the same mandate and through them we opened additional 'windows' to listen to complaints and redress them. Typically, apprehensions related to those candidates (or their supporters) with criminal histories, who were known to unleash violence wherever they could. Fears were also expressed that some areas were more vulnerable to the ruling party's pressures.

To assuage their fears, we introduced new deterrent measures. For the first time, all candidates with criminal cases pending against them would be compulsorily *tracked* by our video camera teams who would record their movements throughout the campaign. This proved to be an important psychological deterrent. The political establishment and the press testified that it contributed enormously towards creating a peaceful electoral landscape. We hired as many as 74,729 video cameras, which were also used to record the proceedings in 'sensitive' polling stations on polling day. We supplemented video cameras with as many as 40,599 still (digital) cameras to 'snap' each voter as he or she entered any designated polling booth.

These out-of-the-box measures were necessitated by the inability of the home ministry to depute sufficient number of Central police forces to maintain law and order during the election process. After three reviews with the Union home secretary, the home ministry informed the Commission that they were unable to offer more than 600 companies (i.e., 60,000 men) of the Central police forces[52] to enforce law and order at sensitive polling stations and counting centres. Although we appreciated the difficulties that the home ministry faced, this did come as a major setback. There was now no way out except to devise other methods that could combine transparency with security. Indeed, a few months before the election, a few officers and I had hit upon the idea of using videography extensively to overcome the eventuality that we may not get the central police forces in the numbers that we had hoped and planned for. When this happened, we resorted to Plan B. As per existing practice, we would have stationed observers in each constituency for almost a month prior to the polling day. We now decided to supplement them with additional hands. This is how the concept of the 'micro observer' was born. They were not dwarfs, as one wag put it, but full-fledged junior government officials. They would be posted on the election day to a vulnerable polling station (or a cluster of polling stations if they were housed in the same complex) to assist the

---

52 The Central Reserve Police Force (CRPF), the Border Security Force (BSF) and the Indo-Tibetan Border Police (ITBP) and the Central Industrial Security Force (CISF).

observers. That as many as 141,000 micro-observers were deployed throughout the country on the polling day contributed substantially towards a sense of greater security. We soon made it widely known that all video film and photographic data had to be secured safely by the ROs in their custody, as these would be needed as evidence in any election petition that might ensue.

Together, these had a major psychological impact.[53] Thus the new measures that we had devised,[54] several months before, to compensate for a possible shortfall in the availability of security forces, proved to be of critical help in what would otherwise have been a very difficult situation. It was a matter of immense satisfaction that when the elections finally ended, there were hardly any complaints across the nation.

Despite the increasing tensions within the Commission, and the unprecedented situation I faced,[55] particularly in the run-up to GE 2009, I had no difficulty in steering the ship through the election. Compared with the general election that followed, GE 2009 might well be remembered for its smooth functioning and absence of acrimony. Many were the encomiums that followed including from several heads of government and electoral management bodies the world over.

~

A postscript to the general election was the 'birthday' celebrations the Commission organized on 25 January 2010 when the Election Commission of India turned sixty. I took the decision to celebrate the Diamond Jubilee in as befitting and dignified a manner as India's

---

53 With observers, micro-observers, video cameras tailing all candidates who had criminal records, cameras recording who entered and exited the polling stations, videographing the entire process on counting day, we successfully built an enormous record of poll-related functioning.

54 Deputy Election Commissioners Balakrishnan and J.P. Prakash assisted me in formulating these measures.

55 See Chapter 12: 'Chief Election Commissioner: First among Equals'.

electoral body deserved. As suggested by M.S. Gill—who was the CEC when he organized the Golden Jubilee celebrations of the Commission—I personally invited the president, vice-president, prime minister, the Speaker of the Lok Sabha, two former prime ministers,[56] leader of opposition in the Lok Sabha, leaders of UPA and NDA, leaders of all the recognized national political parties as well as thirty-six heads and representatives of overseas electoral management bodies. Many of our overseas guests remarked that they had never seen such a galaxy of constitutional authorities at a single event in their countries. Truly this was a celebration of democracy.

On 25 January 2010, the *Hindu* carried this balanced summation in its lead editorial titled 'The Election Commission at 60':

> After overseeing 15 general elections to the Lok Sabha, the Election Commission of India, in its diamond jubilee year, can with justifiable pride claim to have nursed and strengthened the electoral processes of nascent democracy. The successes have not been consistent or uniform, but over the last six decades the Commission managed to make the world's largest democratic process freer and fairer. One of the instruments of this success is surely the Model Code of Conduct. Designed to offer a level playing field to all political parties, it has been used to neutralize many of the inherent advantages of a ruling party in an election. Although the model code was originally based on political consensus and does not still enjoy statutory sanction, it served as a handy tool for placing curbs on the abuse of the official machinery for campaigning. While there have been complaints of excess in the sometimes-mindless application of the model code, the benefits have generally outweighed the costs. Under overreaching Chief Election Commissioner such as T.N. Seshan (1990–96), the Commission did seek to extend its jurisdiction beyond constitutionally

---

56 Pratibha Patil, president of India (2007 to 2012), Hamid Ansari, vice-president of India (2007 to 2017), Manmohan Singh, prime minister (2004 to 2014), Meira Kumar, Speaker of the Lok Sabha (2009 to 2014) and H.D. Deve Gowda, former prime minister (1996 to 1997). I.K. Gujral, former prime minister (1997 to 1998) was unwell and could not attend that meeting.

acceptable levels, but such attempts have been short-lived. After the Election Commission was made a three-member body, its functioning became more institutionalized and more transparent with little room for the caprices of an overbearing personality.

The diamond jubilee is also an occasion for the Commission to look at the challenges ahead, especially those relating to criminalization of politics and use of money power in elections. Neither of these issues is new. What is clear is that the efforts of the Commission to tackle them have generally lacked conviction and have not yielded any significant results. Although the political system and players must take a major share of the blame, and the Commission's powers are constitutionally circumscribed, these will have to be noted as failures. The dominant role of money in elections, which is taking newer and more outrageous forms, is deeply worrying. Instances of politicians paying for news coverage and bribing voters were widespread in the 2009-2010 elections. Another pressing issue relates to the powers of the Chief Election Commissioner vis-à-vis the two Election Commissioners. CEC Navin Chawla has written to Prime Minister Manmohan Singh asking that the Constitution be amended to equalize the removal process for the CEC and Commissions. Against the background of the unseemly controversy over the previous CEC's attempt to have his colleague removed on baseless and subjective grounds, an amendment that makes it explicit that the Commissions too can be removed only through impeachment is an institutional imperative.

ANNEXE

Excerpts from the Debates in the Constituent Assembly of India on the proposed Election Commission of India (1949) (Article 289 of Constitution)

The Honourable Dr B.R. Ambedkar:[57]

57 *Constituent Assembly Debates*, 14 June 1949, Volume/8/1949, paras 8.105.204–214, http://cadindia.clpr.org.in/constitution_assembly_debates/volume/8/1949-06-15?paragraph_number=118%2C120

'That for article 289, the following article be substituted: -

289.(1) The superintendence, direction and control of the preparation of the electoral rolls for, and the conduct of, all elections to Parliament and to the Legislature of every State and of elections to the offices of President and Vice-President held under this Constitution, including the appointment of election tribunals for the decision of doubts and disputes arising out of or in connection with elections to Parliament and to the Legislatures of States shall be vested in a Commission (referred to in the Constitution as the Election Commission) to be appointed by the President.

(2) The Election Commission shall consist of the Chief Election Commissioner and such number of other Election Commissioners, if any, as the President may from time to time appoint and when any other Election Commissioner is so appointed, the Chief Election Officer shall act as the Chairman of the Commission.

[....]

(4) The conditions of service and tenure of office of the Election Commissioners and the Regional Commissioners shall be such as the President may by rule determine;

Provided that the Chief Election Commissioner shall not be removed from his office except in like manner and on the like grounds as a Judge of the Supreme Court and the conditions of service of the Chief Election Commissioner shall not be varied to his disadvantage after his appointment:

Provided further, that any other Election Commissioner or a Regional Commissioner shall not be removed from office except on the recommendation of the Chief Election Commissioner.

Therefore, so far as the fundamental question is concerned that the election machinery should be outside the control of the executive Government, there has been no dispute.

Sub-clause (2) says that there shall be a Chief Election Commissioner and such other Election Commissioners as the President may, from time to time appoint. There were two alternatives before the Drafting Committee, namely, either to have a permanent body consisting of four or five members of the Election Commission who would continue in office throughout without any break, or to permit the President to have ad hoc body appointed at the time when there is an election on the anvil. The Committee has steered a middle course. What the Drafting Committee proposes by sub-clause (2) is to have permanently in office one man called the Chief Election Commissioner, so that the skeleton machinery would always be available. Election no doubt will generally take place at the end of five years; but there is this question, namely that a bye-election may take place at any time. The Assembly may be dissolved before its period of five years has expired. Consequently, the electoral rolls will have to be kept up to date all the time so that the new election may take place without any difficulty. It was therefore felt that having regard to these exigencies, it would be sufficient if there was permanently in session one officer to be called the Chief Election Commissioner, while when the elections are coming up, the President may further add to the machinery by appointing other members to the Election Commission

[....]

It has been brought to the notice both of the Drafting Committee as well as of the Central Government that in these provinces the executive Government is instructing or managing things in such a manner that those people who do not belong to them either racially, culturally or linguistically, are being excluded from being brought on the electoral rolls. The House will realise that franchise is a most fundamental thing in a democracy. No person who is entitled to be brought into the electoral rolls on the grounds which we have already mentioned in our Constitution, namely, an adult of 21 years of age, should be excluded merely as a result of the prejudice of a local Government, or the whim of an officer.

[....]

We have therefore given the Chief Election Commissioner the same status so far as removability is concerned as we have given to the Judge of the Supreme Court. We, of course, do not propose to give the same status to the other members of the Election Commission. We have left the matter to the President as to the circumstances under which he would deem fit to remove any other member of the Election Commissioner, subject to one condition that the Chief Election Commissioner must recommend that the removal is just and proper.

Prof. Shibban Lal Saksena: Sir, I have given notice of an amendment to an amendment to article 289.[58]

Mr President, Sir, I must congratulate Dr Ambedkar on moving his amendment.

[....]

What is desired by my amendment is that the Election Commission shall be completely independent of the Executive. Of course, it shall be completely independent of the provincial Executive but if the President is to appoint this Commission, naturally it means that the Prime Minister appoint this Commission. He will appoint the other Election Commissioners on his recommendations. Now this does not ensure their independence. Of course, once he is appointed he shall not be removable except by 2/3rd majority of both the Houses. That is certainly something which can instill independence in him, but it is quite possible that some party in power who wants to win the next election may appoint a staunch party-man as the Chief Election Commissioner. *He is removable only by 2/3rd majority of both Houses on grave charges, which means that he is almost irremovable. So, what I want is this that even the person who is appointed originally should be such that he should be enjoying the confidence of all parties -his appointment should be confirmed not only by majority but by two-thirds majority of both the Houses. If it is only a bare majority then the party in power could vote confidence in him but when I want2/3rd majority then it means that the other parties must also concur in the appointment so that in order that real*

58 *Constituent Assembly Debates*, 14 June 1949, Volume/8/1949, paras 8.105.218–231, http://cadindia.clpr.org.in/constitution_assembly_debates/volume/8/1949-06-15?paragraph_number=118%2C120

independence of the commission may be guaranteed, in order that everyone even in opposition may not have anything to say against the Commission, the appointments of the Commissioners and the Chief Election Commissioner must be by the President but the names proposed by him should be such as command the confidence of two-thirds majority of both the Houses of Legislatures.[59]

The second point made by Dr Ambedkar was that this commission may not have permanent work and therefore only the Chief Election Commissioner should be appointed permanently and the others should be appointed when necessary on his recommendations. Our Constitution does not provide for a fixed four years cycle like the one in the United States of America. The elections will probably be almost always going on in some province or the other. We shall have about thirty provinces after the states have been integrated. Our Constitution provides for the dissolution of the Legislature when a no-confidence is passed. So, it is quite possible that the elections to the various legislatures in the province and the Centre will not be all concurrent. Every time some election or other will be taking place somewhere. It may be so in the very beginning or in very five or ten years. But after ten or twelve years, at every moment some elections in some province will be going on. Therefore, it will be far more economical and useful if a permanent Election Commission is appointed—not only the chief Election Commissioner but three or five members of the commission who should be permanent and who should conduct the elections. I do not think that there will be lack of work because as I said in our constitution all the elections will not synchronize but they will be at varying times in accordance with the vote of no-confidence passed in various legislatures and the consequent dissolution of the legislatures. Therefore, I think that there will be no dearth of work. This commission should be a permanent commission and all the commissioners should be appointed in the same manner as the Chief Election Commissioner.

59 Italics by the author.

They should all be appointed by a two-thirds majority of Legislatures and be removable in the same manner.

Clause (4) says 'the conditions of service and tenure of office of the Election Commissioners shall be such as the President may by rule determine'. This I think is not proper. The conditions of service and tenure of office, etc., of the Election Commissioners should not be in the power of the President to determine. Otherwise he can use his influence in a manner prejudicial to their independence. Therefore, I want that these things should be determined by Parliament by law and they should be permanent so that nobody will be able to change them and no election Commissioner will then look to the President for favours.

These are my suggestions so that the Election Commission may be really an independent Commission and the real fundamental right, the right of adult franchise, may be exercised in a proper manner. I agree with all that Dr Ambedkar has said I only want to suggest that what he has suggested will not be sufficient to carry out what he wishes.

Pandit Hirday Nath Kunzru:[60] I find, Sir that I made a mistake when I said that the other Election Commissioners and the Regional Commissioners could be removed in consultation with the Chief Election Commissioner. They can be removed only on the recommendation of the Chief Election Commissioner. There two things are noticeable: the first is that it is only the Chief Election Commissioner that can feel that he can discharge his duties without the slightest fear of incurring the displeasure of the executive, and the second is that the removal of the other Election Commissioners will depend on the recommendations of one man only, namely the Chief Election Commissioner. However, responsible he may be, it seems to me very undesirable that the removal of his colleagues who will

60 *Constituent Assembly Debates*, 16 June 1949, Volume/8/1949, paras 8.106.17-26, http://cadindia.clpr.org.in/constitution_assembly_debates/volume/8/1949-06-15?paragraph_number=118%2C120

occupy positions as responsible as those of judges of the Supreme Court should depend on the opinion of one man. We are anxious, Sir, that the preparation of the electoral rolls and the conduct of the elections should be entrusted to people who are free from political bias and whose impartiality can be relied upon in all circumstances. But, by leaving a great deal of power in the hands of the President we have given room for the exercise of political influence in the appointment of the Chief Election Commissioner and the other Election Commissioners and the officers by the Central Government. The Chief Election Commissioner will have to be appointed on the advice of the Prime Minister, and, if the Prime Minister suggests the appointment of a party-man, the President will have no option but to accept the Prime Minister's nominee, however, unsuitable he may be on public grounds.

[....]

I think, Sir, therefore, that the Draft placed before us by Dr Ambedkar has to be modified in several respects, so that the Election Commission may, in reality, consist of impartial persons and the Election Commissioners may be able to discharge their responsible duties fearlessly.

[....]

The Election Commissioners are not on the same footing as the Chief Election Commissioner. I feel, Sir, that the opinion that I have placed before the House, was at one time or other the opinion of Dr Ambedkar too. We have in the List of Amendments, amendment No. 103 which has not been moved by Dr Ambedkar, but has been given notice of by him. Honourable Members who have read this amendment will have noticed that clause (2) provides that a 'member of the Commission shall only be removed from office in like manner and on the like grounds as a judge of the Supreme Court, and the conditions of service of a member of the Commission shall not be varied to his disadvantage after his appointment'. It will be clear therefore that the suggestion that I have made is in accord with the better judgment of Dr Ambedkar which, unfortunately, has not been allowed to prevail.

My honourable friend, Professor Shibban Lal Saksena, moved a number of amendment yesterday, Sir, with regard to the new Draft placed before the House by Dr Ambedkar. It may not be practicable to accept some of them, but I think that he has done a public service by drawing the attention of the House to the glaring defects in the Draft that we are considering. I think it is the duty of my honourable friend, Dr Ambedkar, to consider the matter carefully and to provide such safeguards as will give general satisfaction by ensuring that our electoral machinery will be free not merely from provincial political influences but also from Central political influences. We are going in for democracy based on adult franchise. It is necessary therefore that every possible step should be taken to ensure the fair working of the electoral machinery. If the electoral machinery is defective or is not efficient or is worked by people whose integrity cannot be depended upon, democracy will be poisoned at the source; nay, people, instead of learning from elections how they should exercise their, vote how by a judicious use of their vote they can bring about changes in the Constitution and reforms in the administration, will learn only how parties based on intrigues can be formed and what unfair methods they can adopt to secure what they want.[61]

61 Italics by the author.

2
The First General Election (1951–52)

As India's sixteenth chief election commissioner, I was fortunate to be able to build on an edifice that had already been created and embellished. Yet, I have often wondered how our first chief election commissioner, Sukumar Sen[1] was able to construct a structure from scratch to be able to conduct India's first general election.[2] Sen left no memoir and no notes of his almost nine momentous years at the helm. Indeed, very little is known about him. A member of the ICS, he was appointed by Jawaharlal Nehru to create the electoral architecture, perhaps because he was also a mathematician. Nehru, no great admirer of the erstwhile Imperial Civil Service, also leaves us no clue amongst his voluminous writings on why he believed Sen fit the bill. Tantalizingly, the enormous challenges that Sen faced in devising and implementing the elections are drawn from a single report published in 1954 by the Election Commission of India.[3]

---

1 Sukumar Sen was the CEC from 21 March 1950 to 19 December 1958.

2 The total number of seats in the first Lok Sabha was 489 (today it is 543).

3 The Election Commission of India, *Report of the Election Commission of India*, Vol. 1 and 2, Delhi: Manager of Publications, Government of India, 1954.

Having had the privilege of occupying the same office, albeit five-and-a-half decades later, I believe we owe it to our electoral history to begin to reconstruct how Sen went about this gigantic task. That he designed and conducted almost flawlessly our first two general elections, makes him, to my mind, one of India's 'unsung heroes'.[4]

The historian who has comparatively recently attempted to restore Sukumar Sen's place in history is Ramachandra Guha.[5] More recently, Guha came across an old edition of *Shankar's Weekly*,[6] a respected Indian journal of the 1950s and '60s. In its issue on the eve of India's second general election Sukumar Sen was its 'The Man of the Week'. The *Weekly* wrote:

> Sukumar Sen could easily have been a bit of the Steel frame that rusted, for he was a District and Sessions judge for 19 years. That he brought to August 1947 the resilience and that made him the Chief Secretary to the very difficult Government in Bengal, was due undoubtedly to the fact that he had much more than steel in his frame. Bengal in the war years was almost a lost province and when division rent it, what seems to be wholly ripped off was the morale of the administration. While the White scooted, many a brown saheb collapsed in a din of scandal.
>
> Sukumar Sen's Chief Secretaryship for three years, on the other hand, seem to prepare him for the most unconventional job that ever came to an I.C.S. man. He was chosen to play obstetrician and to deliver Indian democracy's first crop of nearly three thousand elected representatives. Realizing with surprising un-I.C.S. humility that democracy likes its mechanics to be as self-effacing as possible, the Chief Election Commissioner became an unseen, undogmatic

4 Ramachandra Guha, *India After Gandhi: The History of the World's Largest Democracy*, London: MacMillan, 2007.

5 Ibid., pp. 133–34.

6 *Shankar's Weekly* is a currently defunct magazine that ran from New Delhi and was edited by cartoonist K. Shankar Pillai. 'The Man of the Week' figured in its issue of 17 February 1957.

influence patiently judicial in his attitude to parties but insistent in regard to the machine he wielded.

Where nearly two hundred million people, for the most part unlettered but politically conscious nonetheless, are set on choosing between one phenomenally big party and a clutter of many small and new ones, where words have come to be replaced by symbols, where a corps of workers recruited ad hoc from a thousand offices with no experience of applied democracy have to face an army of agents both suspicious and persistent, the actual process of election can be very wearing.

But largely due to Sukumar Sen it can be said that apart from Panch Shila the most impressive gift we have given Asia in the first decade of our freedom is the system of elections that has been perfected in this country. His success was recognised internationally when he was asked to organize the first Sudan elections. As the voters get ready to clutch at the voting papers for the second Indian general election, every political party has reason to remember Sukumar Sen with gratitude for doing a very difficult job very well, indeed.[7]

What is known about Sukumar Sen is that he was born in 1899, graduated from the prestigious Presidency College in Calcutta (now Kolkata) and went on to study mathematics at the University of London. He joined the ICS in 1921 and, as was common in those days, served the customary innings in the districts before being seconded to the judiciary by the British Raj. After Independence he was appointed as the first chief secretary of West Bengal. This was when he came to Nehru's attention who chose him to be appointed as India's first chief election commissioner (CEC). A grateful government would reward Sen with the Padma Bhushan award in 1954. Between the two general elections, he also chaired the International Election

7 Extract from the article 'The Man of the Week', published on the 17 February 1957 issue of *Shankar' Weekly* and reproduced by Ramachandra Guha in the article 'A Forgotten Bengali Hero' in *The Telegraph*, 27 September 2008.

Commission that conducted the election in Sudan. In Sudan, Sen seems to have become acquainted with Mekki Abbas, who was the director of the Sudan Gezira Board and who played an active role in Sudan's constitutional development.[8]

In my quest to learn more about Sukumar Sen, I travelled to Kolkata to meet one of his two surviving daughters. Jayanti Sen, now ninety, shared her memories of her father. She also put me in touch with her younger sister, Purabi Ward, now eighty-four and living in London, with whom I had a long talk on the phone. Both sisters agreed that their father was a fair and just man, quite grounded, and not at all 'imperial', though he was a member of the ICS. 'My father was not a favourite of the British', recalled Jayanti. 'He listened to all but took a decision after listening to all sides. As a judge he was known to be fair, and often ruled against what might have been viewed as "imperial" interests.' She felt that this may also have been the reason why the British government retained him on the judicial side; they were 'wary' of bringing him to the executive. Purabi added with a laugh that although he admired British culture, he was not anglicized to the extent that the other members of the ICS were. 'At home, we always spoke Bengali', she said. When I asked why he did not write his memoirs or even kept a diary, she replied, 'My father was a doer not a talker. No sooner had his job with the Election Commission got over than he went to Sudan to advise the government there on elections. Immediately after that was over he was appointed as administrator of the Dandakaranya Project in West Bengal. He was therefore in the saddle when he died at the [comparatively young] age of sixty-three.'

I asked both sisters how it came about that Jawaharlal Nehru chose their father to be the first CEC. Jayanti recollected that it

---

8 During my research in the Election Commission Library, I came across a book titled 'The Sudan Question' by Mekki Abbas which was gifted by the author to Sen as a gesture of gratitude for Sen's valuable role in the electoral process in Sudan.

was Chief Minister Dr B.C. Roy,[9] under whom Sen served as chief secretary of West Bengal, who recommended her father's name to the prime minister. Purabi pointed out that Dr B.C. Roy was one of India's most respected physicians who was also Nehru's doctor. Both sisters affirmed that it could be because their father was known to be 'sympathetic and just' that Dr B.C. Roy suggested his name. Could his mathematics background have something to do with his appointment, I asked? Purabi Ward felt it was possible. She told me he was a gold medalist twice over from the University of Calcutta, and he had also won awards for mathematics.

Of the two sisters, it was Purabi, who moved with her parents from Calcutta to New Delhi. Although she was only fourteen at the time, she did recall that his small office was located in a hutment. Meanwhile, he travelled throughout the length and breadth of the country organizing mock elections to prepare the people for elections. She recollected that as a schoolgirl, she accompanied him twice on his tours. As it happened, he chose Udaipur for a poll rehearsal on 5 August 1951, which he attended personally. Later such rehearsals were conducted in all states. I was fortunate to obtain from the Sen family a rare copy of a speech he made in Calcutta titled 'Reminiscences of a Civil Servant' wherein he observed:

> We had perforce to be tolerated in the Service [by the British government]. But Authority saw to it that none of the plums of office came to us. There was quite naked discrimination against those of us in particular [who were] believed to entertain nationalistic sympathies. We the 'suspects' in the Service were deliberately kept

9 Bidhan Chandra Roy, MRCP, FRCS, second chief minister of West Bengal, held this office for fourteen years (1948–62). Legendary physician and freedom fighter, exemplary public servant, Bharat Ratna awardee (1961), he established five cities in West Bengal, as also the Burdwan University, where Sukumar Sen became its first vice chancellor in 1960.

> out of the Executive Branch. Indeed, as a Judge, I was always able to follow the dictates of my conscience.[10]

Yet it was only through the report of the Commission, which he closely supervised and for which he wrote the Preface, that his own voice emerges a little. Here he holds the somewhat romanticized view that 'Republican forms of government existed in many parts of ancient India' and in 'some of these republics, every adult male member had the right to vote and to be present in the general assembly which decided all public affairs'. The 'genius of India', he averred, had fashioned 'autonomous and almost self-sufficient village communities' which had 'lasted through the ages', and were 'run on truly democratic lines without, of course, the outward trappings of the vote and the ballot box'. From this point of view, the elections of 1952 were 'like the rejoining of a historic thread that had been snapped by alien rule'.

The first Lok Sabha was preceded by the Constituent Assembly (1946–49). This had been set up to undertake the enormous task of compiling a Constitution for the country emerging into freedom. It took almost three years to complete its task, giving effect to the Constitution which drew largely from the British Westminster model as well as the American system of checks and balances. On 26 January 1950, the Indian republic was born. The Assembly coalesced into an interim parliament but this was of course not the outcome of universal adult suffrage which would have to wait another two years. The RoPA was first passed in May 1950 followed by the amended one in July 1951. While proposing the Act, Nehru expressed his hope that elections would be held as early as spring of 1951. He was giving Sen barely one year to get organized. Sen demanded both time and

10 Sen remained a district judge for seventeen years until 1947. After Independence, instead of being appointed to the high court, he was brought to the executive and appointed the chief secretary of West Bengal.

patience. Placing myself in Sen's shoes, I believe that the organization that he was able to create and the elections that he delivered in such a short span were nothing short of a miracle.

Organizing the General Election

The first general election was spread over four months, from November 1951 to March 1952. Compared to the 714 million voters that were on the rolls when I conducted the general election in 2009 (and over 816 million that stand on the rolls today), Sen's challenges might appear not especially daunting. That was far from the case. Indeed, Sen's task was in many ways more difficult. It is true that there were but a quarter of the voters that I had to contend with in 2009: 176 million over the age of twenty-one on the electoral register. Yet the biggest challenge lay in their enumeration and the creation of an electoral roll for the very first time. As is well known amongst electoral management bodies, it is critical to get the electoral rolls right, without which the elections are flawed from the start. The other obstacle was that most would-be voters could neither read nor write. The average literacy rate was just over 16 per cent; illiteracy among women was considerably higher. Yet another major difficulty was that barring a small section of people who had participated in provincial elections, no one knew what elections meant or entailed.

Sen had before him the unenviable task of identifying and registering an unlettered population. It did not help that a number of women refused to identify themselves by their own names but proffered the names of their menfolk—fathers, husbands or sons. At that time, most people used no surnames. They usually had a given name by which they were known in their families, particularly in rural areas. The concept of a surname had been slowly introduced during British rule. People began to adopt either their caste names or names of the villages and towns to which they belonged, or appended names derived from their occupation as surnames.

Surnames were now demanded by the enumerators to complete the electoral register.

Sen would devise a simple but unique technique that was quickly emulated in the other newly independent nations. With his team of equally brilliant, hand-picked officials (largely drawn from the Constituent Assembly secretariat) he prepared the road map for the elections. Sen allotted to each political party which proposed to contest the elections, a simple but unique party symbol by which it was easy for everyone to identify the party or candidate of their choice. To further simplify matters, he offered each of these parties their own ballot box. This made it much easier for a voter to drop his or her ballot paper in the box of their chosen candidate. It certainly complicated matters that the voter had two choices to make, instead of one, for this was both an election to the Lok Sabha and for the provincial assemblies simultaneously. While there were 489 seats for the Lok Sabha, there were almost 4,000 seats for the assemblies. Sen and his team realized that the vast majority of voters would be visiting a polling station for the first time. They would then face the confusing situation of voting for two elections simultaneously. They would also be faced with a host of newfangled instructions comprising several dos and don'ts. What made this election doubly interesting was that this was not just the voter's first experience, it was also a first for Sen and his team.

There were many interesting sidelights. The story of the ballot boxes that needed to be manufactured was a saga in itself. The numbers needed were staggering: 2,473,850 solid steel ballot boxes. These boxes were supplemented by over a hundred thousand wooden boxes as well. Sen and his team had gone into the design of the boxes meticulously. Twelve companies were shortlisted and five manufacturers were finally selected. Although the preponderant numbers came from the well-known Godrej and Boyce Company in Maharashtra, orders were also placed with companies in West Bengal, Tamil Nadu and UP. Eventually, 8,200 tonnes of steel were used. The boxes had to be of a design which was manifestly tamper-proof and which would come equipped with a seal which would only be broken after all the ballots had been cast, at the time of counting. However, as the election progressed, so did the complaints.

If Nehru could be impatient with Sen, Sen was no pushover. I might say that he was even a little imperious in the manner that he conducted the elections. One of the areas where Sen was perhaps autocratic was when he ordered the striking off of the names of those women who declared their inability to offer their own names. He refused to accept 'so-and-so's wife' or 'this one's mother'. He termed this 'a curious, senseless, relic of the past'. As a result, as many as two million women voters were effectively disenfranchised. When I conducted the general election in 2009 such a peremptory order would have been unthinkable and completely unacceptable to political parties. It is interesting, though, that the number of women Sen struck off in the general elections came down considerably when he conducted the second general election in 1957. Quite clearly, either women had concluded that they wished to vote, or political parties had concluded that they could not afford to lose the votes of their women constituents and ensured the addition of surnames.

The Election Commission in its 1954 report provides valuable data on the first general election. Polling booths numbering 224,000 were equipped with two million steel ballot boxes. As many as 16,500 clerks were appointed on six-month contracts to type and collate the electoral rolls constituency-wise. As many as 380,000 reams of paper were used for printing the rolls. 56,000 presiding officers were appointed to supervise the voting. They were assisted by 280,000 helpers. Even though the law and order situation was much better than what it would be in the lawless 1980s, as many as 224,000 policemen were assigned to guard against violence and intimidation and ensure free and fair elections.

The use of simple election symbols was Sen's master stroke. These symbols were drawn from daily life and were most easily recognizable. A pair of bullocks for one party, a hut for the second, an elephant for a third, a sickle and a sheaf of paddy for a fourth, an earthenware pot for another—representing everyday rural life and the landscape common to most parts of India. Each party, having been given its own ballot box, hoped that voters entering the polling booth could now simply drop their ballot paper in it without too much trepidation. Fearing the possibility of impersonation, the election team developed an indelible ink to be applied on the voter's finger. It was supposed to remain visible for a week although there would be complaints in UP that this was not always the case. In any event, a total of 389,816 phials of this ink were ordered to be used.

The redoubtable Sen and his team did much more. An entry marked in the electoral rolls became both a matter of inclusion as also of identity. It was the gateway to citizenship, particularly for those affected by Partition. Partition riots had displaced a staggering eighteen million people, many of whom found temporary shelter in the many 'camps' that dotted Delhi, Calcutta and other cities. The role of Sen and his fellow bureaucrats was, therefore, all the more praiseworthy. For those living in the princely states where land records varied between one state and another, entry into the electoral rolls was also important. The prodigious body of work put in from the time the Constituent Assembly was set up to 26 January 1950 is an immensely important story of procedural equalities, of inclusion (and exclusion), of citizenship, of a chance to be part of a new order and a leap towards social equality. Sadly, Sen has not left us any papers that sheds light on this hugely important body of work.

Nonetheless, the Commission was the first major institution to use the media (film and radio) to educate the public about this novel exercise in democracy. The Films Division (set up in 1948) made a documentary on electoral franchise and its functions, as well as the duties of the electorate. It was shown in over 3,000 cinemas throughout the country. Many more people were reached through All India Radio, which broadcast numerous 'educative programmes' on the Constitution, the purpose of adult franchise, the preparation of electoral rolls and the process of voting. Sen himself participated in a number of radio talks on these subjects.

Hitherto, participation by Indians in elections had been limited to the educated and generally landed, English-speaking elite. Under the watchful gaze of various provincial governors, they had been permitted to participate in the limited suffrage offered in the provincial assembly elections of 1937. Not only was it a limited franchise; it was also on the basis of a divided polity based on separate electorates. It was again from this narrow elite that the members of the Constituent Assembly had been selected.

Given this background, and the population's lack of electoral experience, it was a stupendous feat for the Commission to organize such a massive election without too many glitches. For it succeeded in grafting a system of universal adult franchise on to a largely undemocratic social system. It was, barring a few notable exceptions, also completely feudal in the vast swathes ruled by the princes. This feat was all the more remarkable when one realizes that universal adult franchise came to the UK as late as 1928 when women were finally permitted to vote. In the United States of America, where suffrage was extended to the non-white population, after years of struggle, often violent, as late as 1965.

A Unique Exercise

The events leading to the elections were, of course, an unprecedented experience for both voters and political parties. Never before had a *nationwide* election on the basis of *universal adult suffrage* been conducted. Never before had so many millions actually stepped out of their homes clutching a piece of paper to participate in direct national elections.[11] The Commission's report was to recall[12] that

11 Ornit Shani observes: 'Turning all adult Indians into voters over the next two years against many odds and before they became citizens with the commencement of the Constitution... was India's stark act of decolonization. This was no legacy of colonial rule. Indians imagined the universal franchise for themselves ... and made it a reality.' Ornit Shani, *How India Became Democratic: Citizenship and the Making of the Universal Franchise*, Cambridge, UK: Cambridge University Press, 2017, p. 1.

12 Report of the Election Commission, 1954, The Election Commission Library.

it was 'a great and fateful experiment, unique in the world in its stupendousness and complexities'. For the marginalized could take the giant stride forward towards a place in the new order of things based on a new polity. There were plenty of sceptics, not least amongst them the relics of the Raj. However, the magnitude of the exercise also ensured worldwide attention. Journalists and observers descended from numerous countries to study its working at first hand. 'In fact, every country desiring to adopt parliamentary elections on adult franchise but faced with difficulties in the shape of illiteracy, ignorance and undeveloped communications evinced the utmost interest in the Indian elections.'[13] Indeed, this was the story of how a vast majority of newly enfranchised voters brought up in a far-from-democratic social milieu set about establishing a new political system.

The only princely state of size and distinction that threw itself into the first elections was Jodhpur. The then maharaja, Hanwant Singh, 'encouraged among others by Winston Churchill, had publicly announced that he would contest India's first general election'.[14] Throwing himself into the election with gusto, he contested as an Independent candidate. He supported several candidates for the thirty-five state assembly seats as well as the four Lok Sabha seats that made up the former state of Marwar. He stood from the Jodhpur parliamentary seat. The maharaja's candidates (contesting as members of the Ram Rajya Parishad) won thirty-one out of the thirty-five assembly seats and all four parliamentary seats. Not surprisingly, the maharaja who was both venerated and popular, won his seat with ease. He could not, however, savour his triumph, for on the very day of counting, the small aircraft that he was piloting crashed, killing him on the spot.

Regarding Hanwant Singh's participation, L.S. Rathore has written:

---

13 Ibid.

14 Dhananajaya Singh, *The House of Marwar*, New Delhi: Roli Books, 2005, p. 195.

> The first general election in India under its new Constitution were held in January 1952. At the time the Congress was the single dominant party at the national level. Because of its active participation and successful leadership during the freedom struggle, the Congress leadership, especially Pandit Nehru, had acquired a halo. ... The Congress had emerged as a giant-sized organization. Against its dominant position, the rest of the political parties in India, which were in the election fray, appeared pigmies. ... It was very difficult for a rival organization or an Independent candidate to win a seat in the Assembly against the Congress. ... Unmindful of the consequences, Maharaja Hanwant Singh took up the gauntlet against the Congress in Jodhpur region.[15]

In an important recent study, borne of extensive research from the archives of the Election Commission and elsewhere, Ornit Shani has challenged the assumption that India's electoral democracy was somehow inherited from the colonial infrastructure. She seeks to establish that it was an 'ingeniously Indian enterprise', powered by Indian bureaucrats themselves, conducted almost immediately after Independence, until the Constitution was adopted two-and-a-half years later, on 26 January 1950. The colossal task of creating voters from a mass of 173 million poor, largely illiterate people became the mission of a handful of bureaucrats drawn from the secretariat of the Constituent Assembly itself. Working under such stalwarts as Sir Benegal Narsing Rau, who played a key role in drafting the Constitution, they were the ones who designed the instructions for the preparation of the electoral rolls from as early as November 1947 itself. For there was hardly any time to lose. This necessitated a huge body of interaction between a handful of bureaucrats and a vast citizenry. Universal adult franchise was a giant step forward from an exclusionary regime permitted under the Raj. For a place on the

---

15 L.S. Rathore, *Life and Times of Maharaja Hanwant Singh*, Jodhpur: Books Treasure and Man Singh Pustak Prakash Research Centre, 2012, p. 311; see also the Annexe to this chapter.

electoral roll ipso facto invested that person with citizenship as well, a means to secure membership of the new nation. As Ornit Shani says:

> Indians were voters before they became citizens.
>
> In making concrete their democracy through the preparation of the first draft electoral roll over the two years that preceded the enactment of the constitution, Indian bureaucrats and the people did not make a leap to catch up with the Western democracies. ... The measure and tenacity of inclusion that drove the making of the universal franchise in India at the inception of establishing its edifice of electoral democracy ... was also unsurpassed.[16]

The bureaucracy worked assiduously to ensure eligible persons were enrolled even if they did not meet the qualifications as to residence. To provide one instance, the collector of Bombay took proactive steps as early as November 1948 to ensure the voting of vagrants, servants and footpath dwellers.[17] Those on the margins of society could now claim a place in the new structure of universal adult franchise and thereby for the first time participate in electoral politics.

Setting Standards

Nehru and the Indian political leadership were acutely aware of the importance of this election in setting standards for the future and as indicators of the strengths—or weaknesses—of India's fledgling democracy. 'Nehru pointed out that it was the first election in India on a colossal scale and the standards set up would set a precedent and

16 Ornit Shani, *How India Became Democratic: Citizenship and the Making of the Universal Franchise*, Cambridge, UK: Cambridge University Press, 2017, p. 251.

17 Ibid., pp. 208–10.

influence future elections and coming generations.'[18] The campaign preceding the voting was as much a massive effort to educate voters as it was to win their allegiance to particular parties and candidates. Nehru was particularly active and effective in this respect.

It was, therefore, not surprising that the campaign was fought out on the basis of personalities rather than on issues. In a sense there were no real national issues, except the issue of support for, or opposition to, the ruling Congress party and its charismatic leader, Jawaharlal Nehru.

In its report the Commission went on to say: 'The successful completion of the general elections in India can be said to constitute an important landmark in the history of democracy. Never before has such a vast electorate gone to the polls. The future of the democratic way to life in India depended very largely on the success of the experiment as also on the extent to which these elections would evoke public enthusiasm and satisfaction.' Most observers seemed to be convinced that India's 'act of faith', its 'tremendous experiment' in democracy, had paid off, and had demonstrated the soundness of the decision of the constitution makers to adopt the system of universal adult franchise immediately.[19]

There were, however, those who were doubtful about the wisdom of this decision. Ironically even Nehru had doubts, strange as this seems for one who had been one of the strongest champions of universal adult suffrage and direct, secret elections. Nehru's misgivings arose largely during the election campaign when he saw enough evidence of communalism and provincialism, against which

---

18 Indeed, the first election was the story of how a vast majority of newly enfranchised voters brought up in a far-from-democratic social milieu were enrolled and encouraged to help establish a new political system. See, ibid., pp. 21–24.

19 The Election Commission of India, *Report on the First General Election in India, 1951-52*, Vol. I, Delhi: Manager of Publications, Government of India, 1954, p. 208.

he repeatedly spoke and wrote. He worried about these early signs. In an address at a UNESCO symposium in New Delhi on 20 December 1951, while the elections were underway, he publicly expressed his doubt whether the masses were likely to select the right leaders through the electoral process.[20]

Given the paucity of documentation during these early years after Independence, we are fortunate that there is a report prepared by Indian Political Science Association (IPSA)[21] which contains a vary informative account including some interesting vignettes of the elections. Of considerable interest was the very first electoral exercise that was conducted at Kalpa in Mahasu, Himachal Pradesh, on 25 and 27 October in order to beat the onset of snow. The polling in Mandi followed on 19 and 25 November. Himachal Pradesh (HP), then a much smaller state, had an area of 27,169 sq. km and a population of 983,367.[22] The state had been formed by the merger of twenty-one former princely hill states and a few hill stations. Interestingly and somewhat ironically, Simla (now Shimla), the Raj's summer capital and presently the capital of HP was then part of Punjab, which is the reason why the bulk of the state employees were excluded from participation. That year, Himachal Pradesh offered three seats to the Lok Sabha and thirty-six seats to the state assembly.

Then as now the organization of polling parties, the transportation of ballot boxes and other materials to the inaccessible tehsils required meticulous administrative planning which was conducted under the charge of Captain I. Sen, chief electoral officer for the state. Indeed,

---

20 See *Jawaharlal Nehru's Speeches*, Vol. 2, New Delhi: Publications Division, 1954, p. 385.

21 S.V. Kogekar and R.L. Park (eds), *Reports on the Indian General Election 1951–1952*, Indian Political Science Association, Bombay: Popular Prakashan, 1956.

22 Irene Tinker-Walker, 'Himachal Pradesh: The Elections', in S.V. Kogekar and R.L. Park (eds), *Reports on the Indian General Election 1951–1952*, Indian Political Science Association, Bombay: Popular Prakashan, 1956, p. 299.

the field parties that he would have dispatched continue to echo in the practices the Commission still follows in the mountainous regions of India including Himachal Pradesh. The difference is that poll parties now carry EVMs and not heavy ballot boxes. If the weather is not inclement, helicopters are pressed into service. But for many of the high and inaccessible parts of mountain areas, election officials continue to traverse long distances on foot.

Irene Tinker-Walker gives us a most interesting account of the election in Himachal Pradesh. She informs us that while the polling officials were given fairly adequate training, the voters themselves did not really know what to do or indeed what to expect, particularly in the more remote areas of the state, which were isolated from mainstream political developments. The officials were not equipped with detailed manuals on voter education. These would come much later. 'The administrative machinery felt it was the duty of the political parties to explain the process. However, there was hardly a political system to speak of. And even the local Congress party, by far the best known and organized, was not able to sufficiently reach out to people in the villages. The hill states had always been somewhat removed from the raging politics in the plains. It is doubtful whether the average voter even understood who the parties were and what they stood for. Most of them had heard the name of Nehru but that was it.'[23] Most people, simple and trusting, did as the village headmen or elders advised. Since times were still quite feudal, it was probably the local raja's writ that ran.

In all the chaos of a first-ever election, there were plenty of newfangled things to confuse voters. For a start, there were double-member constituencies at both state and national levels. That meant a plethora of ballot boxes which the voter had never seen before, boxes for the MP's election; boxes for the assembly election; boxes for individual candidates and parties. 'Frequently he would place his vote on the top of the box, or put both ballot papers in one box. Apparently, candidates instructed their supporters to put both papers

23 Ibid., Chapter 22, pp. 299–301.

in their box in order to prevent the voter from inadvertently casting his second ballot paper for a rival candidate.'[24]

India's First Voter

To listen first hand to the experience of (arguably) India's first voter (in October 1951), Shyam Saran Negi, I decided to travel to the remote Kinnaur district in Himachal Pradesh on 1 July 2010. He had been a schoolteacher in Kalpa village. The Commission had honoured him as a part of its Diamond Jubilee Celebrations earlier that year. I spent an exhilarating few hours with him as he took me down memory lane. He was then a spry ninety-three and still agile.[25] He told me that he had never missed casting his vote, having participated in every election. He described the very first vote he cast in 1951. He had already made up his mind for whom he was going to cast his vote. It was such a festive occasion. There was a local band, a lot of music and noisy electioneering. It was truly a festival, he added. Then pointing his finger at my chest, he remarked that the Commission had now taken the 'fun' out of elections. 'No band-baazi', no festivity, no excitement, it was now akin to a funeral. What had elections been reduced to, he lamented. The local press, present in large numbers, lapped up his stories and a photograph taken togethe made national news. Negi was conferred his much-deserved celebrity status during the 2014 general election when the, HP State Election Commission appointed him as their brand ambassador. Google too ran an ad campaign featuring Negi asking the people to cast their vote.

There were many other interesting stories that emerged from the first election. The elections in UP, the largest state, had even then to be staggered into phases. In its first phase (January 22) almost 9.1 million voters went to the polls in as many as eighty-eight assembly and forty-four Lok Sabha constituencies. In the second

24 Irene Tinker-Walker, 'Uttar Pradesh: The Elections', in ibid., p. 302.

25 Negi celebrated his 100th birthday on 1 July 2017.

phase (January 24) polling was held for eighty-eight assembly seats. The third phase (January 28) saw polling in seventy-three assembly seats and the fourth (January 31) in eighty-six assembly seats. The remaining constituencies which were located in the hill districts went to the polls on 18, 19 and 21 February.[26] It was reported that there was 'not much rowdyism' although rival party workers clashed at a few places. In Lucknow, voting was suspended for twenty minutes in one booth. However, 'order was quickly restored by the police'. Repolling was ordered at a dozen polling stations.

Shortcomings and Malpractices

There were other complaints. It was reported from UP would come reports that the ballot boxes could be opened without tampering with the seals. The *Statesman* wrote of 'a deep-rooted conspiracy' in their manufacture, but offered no proof.[27] The *Times of India* (11 February 1952) said 'there have been cases of ballot boxes found broken although every care was taken to make them strong, light, durable, portable, safe and easily packable.' There were complaints about indelible ink as well. A correspondent noted that the indelible ink could be 'easily erased'. Ram Manohar Lohia, chairman of the UP Socialist Party, said after the elections: 'A conspiracy was hatched in Lucknow to distort the electoral verdict in UP.' The Communist Party of India made allegations of 'use of every possible device, including coercion and intimidation of voters, bribery, unfair utilization of the government machinery and other corrupt practices to nullify the verdict of the people'. None of these charges has been supported with adequate proofs.[28]

---

26 S.V. Kogekar and R. L. Park (eds), *Reports on the Indian General Election 1951–52*, Indian Political Science Association, Bombay: Popular Prakashan, 1956, Chapter 8: Uttar Pradesh, pp. 160–61.

27 Ibid., pp.163–64.

28 Ibid.

It is noteworthy that even though this was the first election immediately after Independence, caste and religious feelings were exploited to influence voting choices. In the eastern districts, Congressmen organized a mammoth movement called 'Shoshit Sangh' of downtrodden castes.[29] Muslim voters numbering about 14 per cent of the total mostly voted for the Congress party. Most of the 20 per cent Scheduled Caste voters also voted for the Congress party. Nehru was alarmed by these early tendencies.

Delhi too had its share of interesting sidelights.[30] With a population of 1,744,072 and an electorate of 744,668, it was one of the smallest political units, but its importance was enhanced being the capital and the seat of the Central government. Of the 1.744 million population, almost half a million were refugees from West Pakistan. Voting took place in Delhi on 14 January 1952 in 896 polling booths for four parliamentary seats and forty-eight seats for the state legislative assembly.

With the towering presence of Prime Minister Jawaharlal Nehru in Delhi, the Congress was clearly recognized as the dominant party. 'With few exceptions, Nehru's campaign turned the tide in the Congress direction.'[31] There was plenty of colour in the campaign. The candidate from the Reading Road Constituency, D.R. Kulkarni, who had been given the camel as his election symbol, managed to organize a procession of camels, naturally perching himself on the leading animal. In the Manakpura constituency the candidate from the Congress party was a local astrologer. Needless to say, he brought out posters prophesying a Congress (and his own) victory.

---

29 Ibid., p. 164.

30 Richard L. Park and Gopal Krisna, 'Corrupt Practices in the Election' in S.V. Kogekar and R.L. Park (eds), *Reports on the Indian General Election 1951–1952*, Indian Political Science Association, Bombay: Popular Prakashan, 1956, pp. 279, 281.

31 Ibid.

But in this instance the stars failed him; his Socialist Party rival won the seat![32]

There were other glitches that would today have been violations of the model code of conduct. The provision of the election law that no election poster should be displayed within a distance of 100 yards of a polling booth was observed in the breach. On polling day, a number of polling booths were plastered with election posters of various parties and candidates. In one constituency two persons were arrested for impersonating voters. Interestingly, the maximum election expenditure then allowed under the law was Rs 200 for a state assembly seat and Rs 7,000 for a Lok Sabha seat. 'It is an open secret that these limits on election expenditure were not observed by most candidates', said the report.

The elections were marked by the near-absence of local issues, except in so far as reference to internal autonomy of the state was concerned. National issues, such as communalism, the secular state, unity of the nation, nationalization of industries, redistribution of land, a 'tough policy' towards Pakistan, integrated national culture and the Hindu Raj, were the slogans and issues most commonly discussed during the election.

A significant observation in the IPSA report was as follows:

> A large number of refugee voters could not exercise their franchise because polling booths happened to be too far from their places of residence. At the time of enrolment of voters, these refugees were entered as voters in the constituencies in which they were then living. But before the elections arrived, many of these refugees were shifted to new colonies. As a result, the distance between the place of their residence and of their registered polling booths was in some cases as much as 10 miles. In the areas where educated middle classes predominate, the polling was rather dull.[33]

---

32 Ibid., p. 286.

33 Richard L. Park and Gopal Krishna, 'Delhi', in S.V. Kogekar and R.L. Park (eds), *Reports on the Indian General Election 1951-52*, Indian Political Science Association, Bombay: Popular Prakashan, 1956, p. 291.

A report on the elections in a remote constituency in Himachal Pradesh perhaps captures the real beauty of what was achieved by India. A personal note[34] in the report reads, 'The number of people who did understand what they were doing—however vaguely—was impressive. They realized that in some way their vote did count. Why else would anyone be wooing them. Even a twenty-eight-year-old woman understood that her slip of paper would help send the Raja "to see after our troubles". She and her bent old mother walked two miles to vote, and both of them were carrying a pink card which bore the Raja's symbol. The headman had given it to her so that she could remember for whom she was to vote. For a day at least, she too knew she was important. Even that is a beginning.'

ANNEXE

Hanwant Singh on participation of princes in the democratic process:

> Showing great courage and resilience the Maharaja on 6 December 1951, in an interview to a correspondent of an English daily *Hindustan Times* gave the following quick and critical rejoinder to Pandit Nehru. The Maharaja said: 'There is absolutely no ban on the participation of the Princes in the political activities. There is hardly any need for them to be panicky about the privileges granted to them by agreements or covenants or constitutional guarantees. At any rate when the States have been obliterated from the political map of India, what is the use and importance of privileges—they are no more than hollow promises, appearing tinsel like the shiny toys of the children. After the collapse of the feudal structure, the only path open to the Princes is that they have to rebuild themselves completely and to

---

34 Irene Tinker-Walker, 'Himachal Pradesh: The Elections', in S.V. Kogekar and Richard L. Park (eds), *Report on the Indian General Election 1951-52*, p. 302.

reassert in the new order of a representative democracy. They should rise to the occasion and meet the aspirations of the people ... Let the Princes merge their identity with the main current of the nation, and win peoples' confidence ... The Princes should not forget that the ultimate source of authority is the people and them they should cultivate. The privileges are mere husks; the Princes should not be worried about them.[35]

35 L.S. Rathore, *Life and Times of Maharaja Hanwant Singh*, pp. 312–13.

3

Notes from the 2009 General Election

THE fifteenth general election of 2009 was a watershed one. The electoral register had swelled to a new record of 714 million voters. The number of candidates in the fray stood at an all-time high at 8,070, the highest ever since EVMs were comprehensively used in 2004. For the first time as many as 556 women contested the polls.

Unusual too was the fact that for the first of the five phases of polling, held on 16 April 2009, N. Gopalaswami headed the Commission. I took over as CEC on 20 April 2009. V.S Sampath assumed office that day as the third commissioner. These midstream changes caused considerable comment both in the national and the international press. No one could recollect any election in any country where the head of an electoral body changed midstream.

The election threw up new challenges. A six-year long judicial exercise to reshape the country's constituencies according to population growth had critically changed India's electoral map. The last delimitation exercise had been undertaken three decades earlier, from 1973 to 1975. The freshly redrawn constituencies were based on the latest available census of 2001. The Delimitation

Commission,[1] set up in 2002, completed its task in 2008. By then it had redrawn boundaries, in smaller or larger measure in 499 of the 543 constituencies. This also resulted in a 20 per cent increase in the number of polling stations, a staggeringly large figure that translated itself into almost 167,000 polling booths. What this also spelt for political parties and candidates alike was that in some cases earlier 'general' constituencies now became 'reserved', and vice versa. Where this happened, candidates who may have nurtured their constituencies for years, were now faced with the prospect of a completely new constituency with a new electorate with whom they would have to begin to work anew. In almost all cases, existing boundaries were altered, which meant that parties and candidates would have to accept that the contours of their electorate too had altered in smaller or larger measure.

Third, it was for the first time that electoral rolls were created bearing the voter's photograph. These now matched the voters photograph on the electoral photo identity cards (EPICs) (except in the states of Assam, Nagaland and Jammu and Kashmir). It reduced the scope for impersonation sharply, for election officials in polling stations now only needed to match the two sets of photographs with the voter's face in order to detect fraud.

What was also remarkable was that it was an election marked by minimal violence (except in the Maoist-affected states),[2] minimal complaints and minimal repolls. This was also generally acknowledged to be a peaceful election—the sheer size of India's general elections attracts enormous national and international attention. To ensure transparency and fairness that would be

---

1 Delimitation Commissions have been set up four times in the past—1952, 1963, 1973 and 2002—under respective Acts of parliament. The present constituencies, carved out based on the 2001 census, shall continue to be in operation till the first census after 2026. Recommendations of the 2002 Delimitation Commission chaired by Justice Kuldip Singh, a retired judge of the Supreme Court, were approved by the then president, Pratibha Patil, on 19 February 2008.

2 See Chapter 8: 'The Maoist Factor in Elections'.

apparent to voters, contestants and political parties alike, we had employed some measures never used before. We made use of enhanced mobile connectivity to cover over half a million polling stations. This made instant communication possible in almost two-thirds of India. GIS (Geographic Information System) mapping was used to prepare more accurate electoral rolls in the cities, while satellite technology enabled penetration into hitherto impregnable areas with relative ease. We supplemented and strengthened our internal observation machinery by stationing 151,000 additional observers ('micro-observers') to enable closer oversight in as many 'sensitive' parliamentary polling stations.

If elections were to be conducted fairly and transparently and perceived to be so, the application of the model code of conduct had to be effective, strict and impartial. Because the time period of elections was necessarily compressed, our actions had to be swift, for prolonged deliberations would defeat its very purpose. The importance of maintaining a level playing field was perhaps best described by Harish Khare, a respected columnist when he wrote in 2017: 'The challenge before the commission is to be vigilant and watchful against the collusion at the lower level of civil society and police bureaucracy in favour of the ruling party of the day. Such collusion is a perennial possibility, just as it is a constant threat to the very idea of a level playing field. All political parties end up trying to use unfair means; it is the commission's job to create the necessary conditions and caveats to prevent unfairness.'[3]

In the course of my research for this book, I searched for material that the early commissioners may have left behind—memoirs, diaries, notes. Sadly, little was available in the public domain.[4] Therefore, I am glad that I had kept notes of meetings in the run-up to the polls, especially those that I made during our reviews. These were in the

---

3 'Honest Elections, Honest Democracy' by Harish Khare, editor-in-chief, *The Tribune*, 14 April 2017.

4 I interacted with both daughters of Sukumar Sen who gave me some insights as detailed in Chapter 2. With K.V.K. Sundaram's son, I drew a blank.

nature of observations, sometimes succinct summaries, sometimes a scribble and at other times more detailed notes. These have come in useful now as they revived memory and threw light on the wide range of issues that become crucial in the run-up. In my reviews I followed our compendium of instructions for all levels of electoral officials, the MCC—our bible of *dos* and *don'ts*—as also our detailed checklists. While these were uniform for the smallest islands to the largest states, each review threw up its own set of problems which necessitated their own solutions. I have endeavoured to provide a glimpse in this chapter.

Nor was this all. After the elections got over, I convened a meeting of all our CEOs in Shillong to analyse our performance and create a repository of best practices to add to the nuts and bolts of election management. We shared some of these in a publication that we specially brought out to celebrate the Diamond Jubilee of the Commission on 25 January 2010.

The reason I have not covered all the states and Union territories in this chapter is that my colleagues and I had divided our responsibilities between ourselves. The country was too large and we had barely a few weeks to undertake these reviews. While my notes do not suggest any particular methodology, they do take into account the special challenges that varied from state to state and which arose because of geography or distance or sometimes due to problems unique to that state. These include the importance of the MCC, instances of money and muscle power, the problems we faced because of poor communication in certain parts of the country, our encouragement to NGOs, and the special challenges that emerged. Important too were how our officials faced these challenges. For the problems that we encountered in areas affected by Maoist insurgency, I have devoted a separate chapter. This first-hand account offers a glimpse of some aspects of electoral management. Through my observations, recollections and some amusing anecdotes, I hope I have been able to capture the enormity of conducting a general election and in the process, record a valuable period of our electoral history.

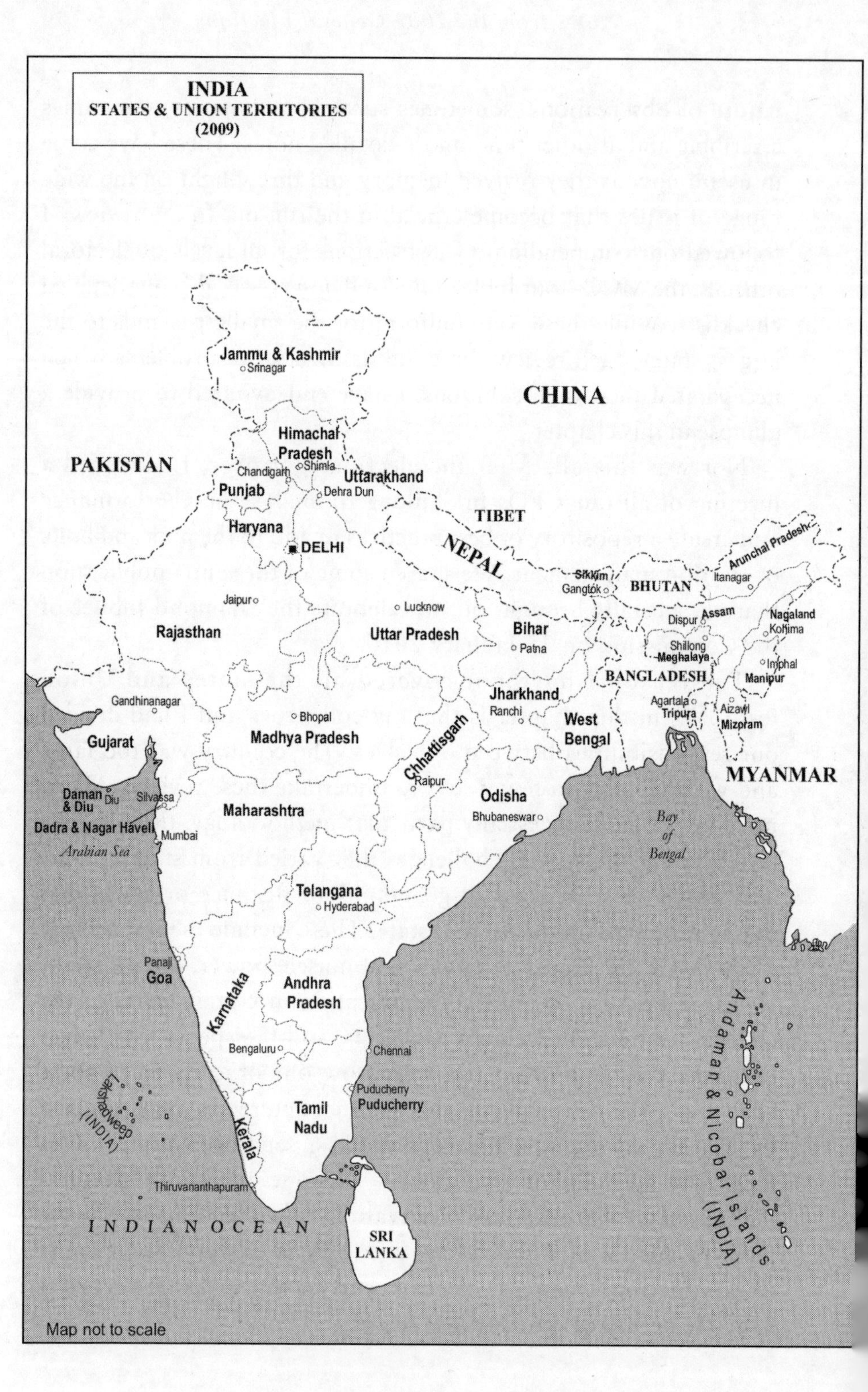
INDIA
STATES & UNION TERRITORIES
(2009)
CHINA
PAKISTAN
TIBET
NEPAL
BHUTAN
BANGLADESH
MYANMAR
SRI LANKA
Jammu & Kashmir
Srinagar
Himachal Pradesh
Shimla
Chandigarh
Punjab
Uttarakhand
Dehra Dun
Haryana
DELHI
Jaipur
Rajasthan
Lucknow
Uttar Pradesh
Bihar
Patna
Sikkim
Gangtok
Arunchal Pradesh
Itanagar
Assam
Dispur
Nagaland
Kohima
Shillong
Meghalaya
Imphal
Manipur
Agartala
Tripura
Aizawl
Mizoram
Gandhinanagar
Gujarat
Bhopal
Madhya Pradesh
Jharkhand
Ranchi
West Bengal
Chhattisgarh
Raipur
Odisha
Bhubaneswar
Daman & Diu
Diu
Silvassa
Dadra & Nagar Haveli
Mumbai
Maharashtra
Arabian Sea
Bay of Bengal
Telangana
Hyderabad
Panaji
Goa
Karnataka
Andhra Pradesh
Bengaluru
Chennai
Puducherry
Puducherry
Tamil Nadu
Lakshadweep (INDIA)
Kerala
Thiruvananthapuram
Andaman & Nicobar Islands (INDIA)
INDIAN OCEAN
Map not to scale

Andhra Pradesh

This being the country's fourth largest state in 2009,[5] with a total population of eighty-six million, it became necessary to hold these elections in two phases (16 and 23 April). This encompassed not only the forty-two Lok Sabha seats but also 294 assembly seats. Forty-five million voters, more than the entire population of Argentina or Canada, exercised their franchise. After the 2008 delimitation, seventy-four new assembly constituencies had been carved out, which necessitated creating 416 additional polling stations. There were, therefore, problems aplenty. In addition, the state had the longest coastline of 970 km as well as 64,000 sq. km of forest cover. This largely abutted Maoist-affected Chhattisgarh.[6] Its border districts had witnessed many years of Maoist-led confrontation causing great difficulties in conducting elections. In recent years, the state government had succeeded in containing the Maoists by pushing them into Chhattisgarh and effectively sealing state borders with the help of its especially enlisted force called the Greyhounds.

Since this was one of the three states[7] where simultaneous polls to the Lok Sabha and legislative assembly were to be held, our micro-management began months earlier. It was quite usual for us to divide constituencies into broad categories. Some were classified as 'communally sensitive', others had witnessed law and order problems in past elections. It was also customary for our officials to prepare detailed backgrounders. Clear parameters were laid down and lists of items to be ticked off drawn up. As a result of such intensive preparation, we were able to put in place the precautionary measures that a state of this size demanded. These included a wide range of security measures, precautions against known troublemakers, accounting for licensed weapons and keeping vigil for unlicensed ones; cracking down on illicit distillation of liquor and its distribution

---

5 Telangana was carved out of Andhra Pradesh, making the latter the eighth largest state.

6 See map (as in 2009) on page 208.

7 The other two states were Orissa and Sikkim.

before polls as an inducement to voters, not to mention the movement of illicit cash and freebies. The mining lobby had created pockets of enormous wealth and some of the richest people in the state contested the polls. As a result of heightened vigilance there were not too many incidents involving law and order and repolls were confined to sixteen polling stations in all.

As I look back, three distinct strands stand out for special mention. The first was that this was the largest of the three states where simultaneous elections to the Lok Sabha and legislative assemblies were conducted. The sheer size and diversity were a challenge in themselves. Second, the involvement of NGOs and election watch groups was at its most vibrant. The third, sadly, was a negative factor: the blatant misuse of money power that sought to make a travesty of electoral law and practice.

First, the best. The involvement of NGOs and citizenry, albeit for a couple of weeks, showed up the best of electoral practices. In order to equip eligible voters with their place on the electoral register and a corresponding EPIC in their hands, CEO, I.V. Subba Rao brought on board a number of NGOs bearing names like 'Election Watch', 'Jaggo Re', 'Lead India', 'Melukolupu' and 'Lets Vote', all of whom helped in varying degrees in building bridges with various communities. They gave of their time freely, with many young people taking leave from work for a few weeks to contribute to democracy. Some worked in villages, others preferred to work in cities and towns, many of them set up voter facilitation desks at their own expense. Some assisted BLOs to update the rolls with correct data. Others helped voters to locate the new polling stations.

Unique to this state, a week-long campaign called 'Yuva Tarang' was spearheaded by a host of vice chancellors and college principals to draw out on their respective campuses, young, often first-time, voters. This successfully contributed to almost 600,000 students enrolling themselves. What helped this to gain traction was the option to register on campus or at their native villages if they so wished.

The participation of civil society facilitated voter awareness, voter registration and even helped towards the peaceful and orderly conduct of polls. This partnership model was strengthened in most districts by the collectors setting up facilitation desks or assisting in other ways. For instance, 'Election Watch' volunteers were constantly on the move, tracking happenings on the ground and reporting these to election headquarters. 'Jaggo Re' was more successful with voter registration amongst rural and backward communities. 'Let's Vote' encouraged almost 40,000 people from the corporate world to register. Members of the NGO 'Let's Vote', largely young professionals, took unpaid leave of absence from their jobs for almost a month. 'Lead India' worked to motivate parents through their school-going children. Corporates like Big FM (which ran radio channels) gave free air time.

In some rural pockets, where EVMs were still seen as newfangled machines, an initiative was undertaken to make the elections more people-centric by allowing groups of rural people to watch demonstrations on how EVMs worked as a part of massive village-level publicity campaigns. They were encouraged to sample machines hands on. As many as 200,000 posters describing the procedure for using EVMs were produced in different dialects of Telugu, the state language. A TV spot was produced in Urdu for the Urdu-speaking people of the state.

Polling officials did ensure that physically challenged people and senior citizens did not have to wait long in queues. Women police personnel escorted them directly to the presiding officers. This was quite a task in so large a state. One newspaper reported as follows: 'Gangamma, 65, was surprised when she was sent directly into the polling booth, bypassing the long queue, when she came to vote at the polling booth at AV College in Domalguda. "This is something I never expected. I voted many times, but this is the first time that I did not have to stand in queue. Even my voter ID card was delivered to my house."'[8]

---

8 'Senior citizens did not have to queue up to vote', *Deccan Chronicle*, Hyderabad, 17 April 2009.

In many places, urban voter apathy triumphed. Despite the involvement of civil society and the enthusiasm shown by the educated middle class to cast their vote,[9] what was disappointing was that the Hyderabad Lok Sabha constituency would register a low turnout of 54 per cent, while its twin city of Secunderabad was not much better at 56 per cent.

Much more disheartening was our inability to control the hydra-headed monster of 'money power' which reared its ugly head. It is not that our observers and senior officials were lacking in their efforts. There were frequent raids by mobile police squads whenever they or the observers received tips or even anonymous calls. But illicit liquor, black money and 'freebies' made their clandestine way into 'buying' votes, usually in the dead of night.

Fortunately our other bane—'muscle power'—was better controlled because of many preventive measures the DMs and SPs had taken, with the result that the ugly incidents of yore involving violence, intimidation and 'booth capturing' became a thing of the past. Tough measures were taken: almost 200,000 people (who had police records, under security sections of various enactments), were 'bound down' to good behaviour. Central police forces were stationed at all sensitive booths. A staggeringly large number of 77,754 unauthorized liquor shops were closed.

As a result of this heightened vigilance, huge amounts of black money, almost Rs 39 crore, were seized by watchful officials. Predictably, no one came forward to claim these sums which were duly deposited in the state treasury. Rumours would circulate that some candidates had spent in excess of Rs 10 crore each to make sure they had 'earned' their seat in parliament, reminiscent of the 'robber barons' of nineteenth-century America. These experiences would help reinforce the Commissions determination to devise tighter controls and also to press for urgent electoral reforms. I have outlined this in a later chapter.

9 'Middle classes come out to vote', *The Hindu*, Chennai, 16 April 2009.

Arunachal Pradesh

Once a part of undivided Assam and a separate state since 1987, Arunachal Pradesh straddles the north-eastern-most shoulder of India. From the perspective of electoral security, it draws three international borders: a long 1,080 km border with China on its north and comparatively smaller borders with Bhutan on its west and Myanmar to its south-east. To these are added two domestic ones (Assam and Nagaland) to its south. A huge land mass of 83,743 sq. km, with a sparse population of less than 1.4 million (an electorate comprising 732, 000 voters), it sends only two members to the Lok Sabha and sixty members to the state legislature. By comparison the national capital Delhi—a tiny fraction in size, but with a population of almost 18 million—sends seven members to parliament.

Border 'sealing' is an important part of security management. States with several borders invariably need sufficient forces to 'seal' them from the inflow of criminal and unruly elements, illicit funds, freebies and liquor. In earlier elections, some of these would flow in from across international borders too, often ill-defined, thick jungles without clear markers. Some of these issues were settled bilaterally and in other cases the Indian side of the border was strengthened at least for the duration of elections.

During my tenure in the Commission, I visited Arunachal Pradesh several times, partly because of the attraction that I had for the north-eastern states. This is our own 'Land of the Rising Sun' with its mountainous terrain surging upwards to meet the Himalayas. Divided by the Brahmaputra and its tributaries, covered in many parts by dense forests, our major problem lay in trying to create a communication network that would work with reasonable efficiency. The absence of an airport at Itanagar, the state capital, or even a railway line to connect the state to the rest of the mainland (the railway line would reach close to Itanagar only five years later in April 2014), was a major drawback. I was fortunate to travel by helicopter—there is a daily commercial service from Guwahati in Assam to Itanagar, barring days of inclement weather. Without this, road travel over potholed roads is a nightmare. The infrastructure is appalling and mobile connectivity is absent for the most part. There are difficulties in even making a telephone call. There was some improvement in telephone connectivity between 2004 and 2009, but this was still a far cry from the progress made by other hill states, principally Himachal Pradesh and Uttarakhand. In 2009, it still meant up to eighteen hours of travel to cover the distance of 465 km between Tezpur and Tawang, and easily over nine hours from Guwahati in Assam to Itanagar.

Our poll officials who were dispatched to set up and man the polling stations had to travel over mountainous terrain covered by deep rainforests, on foot. We had hoped that while sitting in our headquarters, poll information from the state's 2,057 polling stations might reach us at reasonably frequent intervals; the reality was that as many as ten polling stations required (what our official manual quaintly described) a day's 'foot march', sixty-five stations needed a two-day trek, while at least thirteen polling stations required a 'three-day foot march'. Nor was that all. Thirty-two polling stations needed a day's march from the nearest helipad if the weather was clear, while thirteen polling stations needed two days' march. If the weather was inclement, it needed up to nine days to establish a station. Such long distances were an everyday challenge to the people living there, as it was for the candidates, their supporters and the voters.

We desperately needed satellite phones but after considerable effort (and I personally made a few calls too), we managed to procure less than 100 satellite phones for the whole country. While we employed a few in the remotest areas, vast areas still lay outside easy reach. There was no choice but to go back to the age-old 'runners' for dissemination and collection of information. But such was the terrain that it would take our runners up to three days before they reached the circle headquarters where telephone or wireless connections were available. From then on progress was somewhat speedier. With the help of police wireless, our officials could transmit staccato messages to subdivisional headquarters, from where the magic of mobile connectivity took over.

The problem of communication, and its deft solution, was best tackled in this state by the husband-and-wife duo of Ankur Garg, deputy commissioner (DC) of Tirap district and Swati Sharma, DC, West Kameng district during the assembly elections that followed on the heels of GE 2009. A report in the *Asian Age* detailed the problems and explained the out-of-the-box solutions Garg and Sharma used to mitigate these problems:

> Characterized with a very difficult terrain comprising high mountains, deep gorges, dense forests and fast free-flowing rivers, ... there are places which are accessible only after six to eight days of foot-march and there are three polling stations which have only four voters each. Poor physical connectivity, insufficient security forces and lack of electronic connectivity, coupled with unforgiving weather conditions make the task of conducting elections in the state, one of the most challenging tasks for the administration. ... Of the 5,612 habitations in the state, only 1,134 are connected by all-weather pucca roads. The problems are compounded by frequent and severe natural disasters like floods, landslides, etc., which often lead to long-term disruptions. ... The existing low-voltage power transmission networks are prone to frequent break-downs; it requires several days to locate and repair the fault in thick forests under heavy rains. The distance between habitations is large, and often one has to travel for more than 100 km before reaching the next habitation which often consists of only about 20 or 25 households.... The total police strength available in the district to cover these '162 critical' polling stations was only 225....
>
> The topography of [West Kameng] district is mostly mountainous, consisting of a mass of tangled peaks and valleys. Covering an area of 7,422 sq. km, the altitude of the district varies from 650 ft. to 13,714 ft. There are 150 polling stations in the district of which forty-three can be accessed only by 'foot-march' ranging from two to four days, involving crossing of suspension bridges at many points. There is a polling station in the district which has only four registered voters. The husband and wife duo made up for the lack of security forces by using technology to prevent bogus or proxy voting, booth capturing and violence. As a part of this initiative, poll proceedings

> from several selected hyper-sensitive polling stations were telecast live over the internet (webcasting) in the open domain by installing laptops connected to ordinary webcams at these polling stations.... Political parties and citizen forums got the impression that *all* the polling stations were covered with webcams for live telecast. In fact, in several polling stations, we installed dummy cameras to give an impression of the feed being telecast. This made up to a great extent for the lack of available hardware.... As soon as information on use of cameras for live webcast was made public, there were frenzied efforts from certain quarters to ensure that this was not done. The Tirap district election office received threats warning against the use of cameras at these polling stations. ... Wherever polling was covered live, it passed off peacefully without a single incidence of disturbance or disruption. Also, in spite of the large number of voters, polling concluded in time as the voters were exceptionally well-behaved in queues. The feeling that you are being watched serves as a deterrent to law-breakers.[10]

Assam

I have never quite understood why the states of the north-east are quaintly called the Seven Sisters. Historically, some of these states were carved out of the erstwhile united Assam in view of problems of ethnicity among others. The mighty Brahmaputra river cuts through the middle of the state of Assam. Brahmaputra, which at the best of times is difficult to cross becomes a veritable sea during the monsoon rains. The state is large and populated enough to return fourteen members to the Lok Sabha. Elections here were conducted in two phases (16 and 23 April).

Not unlike Arunachal Pradesh, some of our senior officials proved to be particularly innovative, devising new and inexpensive communication techniques. They cleverly connected web cameras with their laptops and computers and with wireless Internet connectivity and wherever this was available, sent real-time images

10 Manoj Anand, 'Arunachal Webcast Inspires EC', *The Asian Age*, 5 June 2010.

streaming through the Internet. The results were spectacular. We could see the actual polling process while sitting at our Commission headquarters over 2,000 km away. Using these techniques, our review of facts, figures and instructions became easier. Since mobile connectivity had improved enormously since GE 2004, we could now avail of SMS text messages (except in those heavily forested areas or tea plantations or in the small islands formed amidst rivers and rivulets, where mobile towers had not yet been erected). Later, at the stocktaking meeting convened in Shillong (Meghalaya), the Arunachal Pradesh and Assam 'models' became de rigueur to overcome management difficulties in remote regions.

One of our standard measures that came to define security management in the last decade or so, was the requirement that some weeks prior to the election day all licensed arms were to be deposited in the concerned treasuries for the duration of the election. Unfortunately, some states which had either witnessed insurgencies or had 'flourishing' criminal gangs in some pockets had seen the resurgence of illegal weapons, which were either manufactured locally by the underground militants or mafias, or else were smuggled across porous borders. During my review in Guwahati on 18 April 2009, I expressed my unhappiness to the district authorities that as many as 18,175 non-bailable arrest warrants were pending action,[11] particularly in a state which had seen its fair share of sectarian violence. I was more concerned with those against whom there were non-bailable warrants for heinous offences such as murder, rape, kidnapping and dacoity. To make matters worse, just a few days earlier (on 8 April), our central observers were fired upon in the insurgency-hit North Cachar Hills district. This was a startling incident, as this had seldom, if ever, happened before. Fortunately, no one was injured. It had been a close call.

Prompted by this incident, I gave a rather stern warning to the officials that if they failed to act promptly, especially in serious

11 'Arrest absconding accused within seven days, says EC', *The Sentinel*, Guwahati, 26 March 2009.

criminal cases involving violence (as opposed to civil cases) they would be transferred from their charge. This resulted in double-quick action. Almost 6,000 absconders were soon apprehended. My warning, given to the officials in a closed-door meeting, leaked out, for it was carried prominently by the local press. Newspapers also pointed out that the state police only needed a warning from the Election Commission to energize them and arrest accused people and wondered why the state police did not do their duty always. Since it was not the function of the Commission to pursue matters of governance after the election period was over, I was not aware of any subsequent action. Some sporadic incidents apart, where EVMs were damaged by miscreants in three polling stations, the election passed off peaceably. Our extensive reviews ensured that even minute details were taken care of.

Every state or Union territory had its unique problems. One special problem related to Assam has been that of 'doubtful voters'. This first arose during an intensive revision of the electoral rolls in 1997. The Commission had then ordered the letter 'D' to be affixed against those voters who failed to provide proof of citizenship, or whose citizenship had been challenged. Their cases were to be decided with regard to the Citizenship Act, the Assam Accord, the Foreigners (Amendment) Act, 2004, and finally the Foreigners Tribunals. The All Assam Students' Union (AASU) had led a six-year movement against illegal migration of Bangladeshi nationals. This had become a sensitive and controversial issue in Assam: some feared that large-scale migration from Bangladesh would pose a threat to the identity of indigenous communities. In 2009, there were as many as 143,000 recorded doubtful/disputed voters who were not included in the electoral rolls. A body called the 'Association of the Disputed Voters' met us during our pre-election visit to press for the removal of the 'doubtful' tag against their names and demanded that their names be included. Since the matter was sub judice, we could not accede to their demands.

Another issue that exploded on to the front pages of the newspapers concerned Chief Minister Tarun Gogoi. The Commission had received a complaint on 19 March 2009 signed by several opposition parties that he had violated the MCC by seeking to collect funds for the election from the owners of tea gardens. More than one issue was involved. The MCC strictly prohibits misuse of official machinery to further party interests. Equally, employing the services of government officials and official paraphernalia for electoral purposes is also an offence. Far from denying the allegations, the chief minister stated at a specially convened press conference on 23 April that he had visited Kolkata for the purpose of raising funds, that it was only to be expected that funds were needed for the election and that these would be accounted for in the proper manner.

The twin issue before the Commission was whether there had been any misuse of the official machinery in the process. It was alleged that the CM had taken one or more government officials working in his secretariat with him, that his air ticket and that of the officials who accompanied him had been paid out of the state exchequer, that he had availed of government facilities by staying in the Assam House in Kolkata and that he used an official car for election-related meetings. As this was a purely election related visit, the Commission issued him a 'show cause' notice stating that it was incumbent on the CM to have travelled and stayed privately. Moreover, being accompanied or assisted by any official who drew his salary from the state exchequer was a violation of the MCC.[12]

The chief minister was furious. At his press conference, he declared that as chief minister he had always to remain in constant touch with key officials, that this necessitated that he be accompanied by his secretaries even if he travelled on political work. He argued that governance and security concerns were a part of his constitutional responsibility. Without such assistance he declared that he could not run the state efficiently in view of the many security-related concerns. In his reply to the Commission, he wrote: 'Unless any official or private secretary accompanies

---

12 'Don't mix official and private tours: EC to Gogoi', *The Sentinel*, 3 April 2009; 'CM under scanner', *The Assam Tribune*, 28 March 2009.

me during my tours, it will affect in discharging my assigned responsibilities and will also greatly hamper the interest of the state.' With further reference to the MCC, he drew a parallel with other chief ministers whom he believed must also be facing similar problems[13] [at the hands of the Commission] and suggested that he would take this up with other chief ministers too. He added this was not intended to be a confrontation. 'I am against such guidelines in principle', he said. He then threatened to take the Commission and its MCC guidelines to the Supreme Court, seeking relief that would doubtless benefit all CMs.

He did not, in the end, take the matter to the Supreme Court, nor, to the best of my knowledge, convene a meeting with his counterparts. Yet I have chosen to highlight this as an example of some of the difficulties that arose between the Commission and chief ministers and Union ministers in the implementation of the MCC. Although Gogoi was 'reprimanded' by the Commission, I must admit that the MCC did sometimes become an irritant, between the Commission trying to be as fair an umpire as possible and the political players in the field who often enough believed that the Commission had become an impediment to their carrying out their constitutional responsibilities. As it happened, I had run-ins with at least three other chief ministers, all of whom belonged either to the Indian National Congress or its allies who were then in power.[14]

Chhattisgarh and Jharkhand

Elections in both states have become synonymous with the difficulties of conducting elections in the Maoist-affected states of India. Carved out of Madhya Pradesh, Chhattisgarh is the tenth largest state in

13 *The Sentinel*, Guwahati, 25 April 2009.

14 In fact, there was a major 'run-in' between my successor S.Y. Quraishi and Union law minister Salman Khurshid, which became sufficiently acrimonious for the Commission to write to the president. Both would subsequently write about this incident in their respective books.

the country with an area of 135,191 sq. km and a population of 25.5 million in 2009. It returns eleven MPs to the Lok Sabha and its EPIC coverage was 64.51 per cent of the electorate. Heavily forested, Chhattisgarh is home to a very large tribal population who mainly inhabit the dense forests of Bastar.[15] In fact, more than 70 per cent of Bastar's population consists of tribals who account for almost 27 per cent of Chhattisgarh's entire tribal population. For the Commission, the predominant problem was that a number of Chhattisgarh districts had come under the influence of Maoists.[16] We decided to conduct elections in Chhattisgarh and most of the Maoist-affected constituencies in the first phase, to restrict the movement of Maoist forces and bind them down to their operational areas.

Jharkhand, which abuts Chhattisgarh to its west, also shares the border with four other states. With a population of 41.7 million in 2009, it sends fourteen MPs to the Lok Sabha. The state was carved out of Bihar on 15 November 2000 and this was the second general election that was being conducted there. Because of its overwhelmingly forest and somewhat hilly districts that run contiguous to the forests of Chhattisgarh, significant parts of this state too had become part of the 'Red Corridor'.

Though ethnically diverse, the population of the state is largely tribal. Because the Maoist cadres had come to dominate several districts, their writ ran parallel to that of the civil administration. At the best of times, communication in these deeply forested areas is poor. But since the extremist challenge to elections had resulted in their dynamiting mobile telecommunication towers wherever they could, the service providers were reluctant to re-erect or repair them. This caused large 'net-shadow' areas. We, therefore, had no option but to set up our polling stations without the benefit of mobile telephony and had to resort to the 'runners' of past eras, with the result that COMET (communication for election tracking) remained

---

15 The Bastar Division comprised districts of Bastar, Dantewada, Bijapur, Narayanpur, Sukma and Kanker.

16 See map of Left-wing-extremist-affected states, p. 208.

a rather grand acronym on paper. Logistics of transportation and the safe movement of our staff and materials became arguably the most serious challenge that I had to confront throughout the entire period.

That we managed to conduct polls in two phases in as many as 23,908 polling stations, videographing the process under the gaze of forty-two observers and 3,879 'micro-observers', was a remarkable achievement. Even more extraordinay was that 51 per cent of the electorate did manage to come out to vote despite threats to life and limb.

The challenge posed by the Maoist extremists in conducting the elections in both these states has been detailed in Chapter 8 titled 'The Maoist Factor in Elections'.

Delhi

I might have thought that the Commission, headquartered in New Delhi, would have made the run-up to elections in this Union territory easier than anywhere else. Quite the reverse. Delhi proved to be rather more difficult than other metropolitan cities and even some larger states. This was largely due to the multiplicity of authorities that has always bedevilled governance in Delhi. Delhi does not defer to any one master. Differing 'landowing authorities' and municipalities, all tugged in different directions. Over the last few decades Delhi has grown exponentially into a much larger entity called the 'National Capital Region' (NCR) that now comprises bustling satellite towns of Gurgaon,[17] Noida, Greater Noida, Faridabad and others. A large peripatetic population and intra-city movement between the satellite towns and Delhi added to the uphill task that faced our enumerators.

In Delhi, as everywhere else in the country, the electoral rolls for various constituencies had to be prepared with effect from 1 January 2009. EPICs (with matching photographs and details on the rolls) had to be completed correctly and distributed to several million

17 Renamed Gurugram since December 2016.

voters before the beginning of March. Delhi is divided into nine administrative districts, each headed by district magistrate (DM). Each of them was assigned a commensurate number of enumerators (BLOs) to prepare accurate rolls. There are several municipal bodies each having its own jurisdiction and staff. But with so much overlap, the DM's writ did not run over several areas and even where it did there was lack of proper detailing and supervision. As election fever rose, so too did the barrage of protests from those whose names were either missing or whose attempts to have their names included had been unsuccessful. Many complained that they had given the enumerators their photographs and other requisite documents, which had apparently got lost. Very soon the local pages of the press were full of these voter grievances.

Since the Commission was based in Delhi, and as I had spent most of my career serving in various capacities in Delhi, I was very soon at the receiving end. People telephoned, wrote and emailed me with their list of woes. Those soon became a flood. With the excitement of elections getting closer, tempers flared and politicians stepped in. The chief minister of Delhi, Shiela Dikshit, accompanied by half her cabinet and several irate MLAs arrived to complain to the Commission about its inadequacies, especially missing names from the electoral register. Not to be left behind, the opposition too descended on us. In view of the Delhi CEO's inability to remedy the situation, the Commission was left with no option than to step in directly, for damage control became the need of the hour in Delhi.

We convened several meetings that began in August 2008 calling the various layers of authority—the commissioner of Delhi, (which post I had occupied briefly) the DMs and a host of other concerned officials to help overcome their hurdles. Finally, after several weeks a staggering 6.5 million EPICs (more than the population of Singapore or Denmark) were distributed just in time for the polling day.

While the Commission was inundated with complaints, the CEO of Delhi was running a campaign to galvanize Delhi's generally blasé and apathetic voters. The 'Pappu campaign' was aimed at the lazy voter. 'If you did not come out to vote', claimed the campaign jiggles, you would be dubbed a 'pappu' (a euphemism for a lazy and pampered child). The press lapped this up and carried stories of renewed enthusiasm. However, the campaign achieved marginal success at best. Voting did go up somewhat, from 47.09 per cent in GE 2004 to 51.79 per cent in GE 2009. Urban voter apathy had scored again.

Elections have traditionally spawned a huge demand for the manufacture of flags, buntings, posters, banners and hoardings. Businessmen and traders make tidy profits at election time. Nevertheless, since 2006 the Commission had begun to clamp down on the pasting of posters and painting of graffiti on government as well as private property. This was because the municipalities and residents alike complained that their walls were being defaced, causing them to repaint their walls at their own expense after the elections were over.

While house owners wholeheartedly approved of the ban, some political parties protested. The answer was not far to seek. For some of the parties it was the cheapest form of publicity through which their candidates could reach out to the public and yet remain within their financial ceilings. The Commission's strict guidelines also hit small businesses badly. The lament of Delhi's traders echoed as far away as Assam: 'The ban has ruined our business this time. The sample posters that we have printed have not been sold. Our workers are short of work', complained a printer. 'In the last elections we used to get orders of more than 20,000 copies. We have made posters for Congress, BJP and many regional parties. Now politicians have turned towards the electronic media', said another.'[18] This trend was even more true for 2014 which saw a sharp shift towards social media as a tool for campaigning.

While some candidates privately welcomed the ban because it levelled the field and saved the poorer candidates from splurging money on costly electoral materials, the absence of flags and banners,

18 'No business for artists, printers in Lok Sabha polls', *The Asian Tribune*, Guwahati, 19 April 2009.

posters and buntings did reduce the atmosphere of gaiety of elections that Shyam Saran Negi, our oldest voter, had complained to me about. Or as a senior politician Margaret Alva complained bitterly to the Commission when it visited Goa on an election-related tour. In the context of the Commission not even permitting a party flag to be displayed, came her angry outburst, 'You have converted the elections from a festival to a funeral!' In 2009, after I took over, the Commission relaxed some of these onerous restrictions.

Haryana

In Haryana, comparatively compact, with excellent communications, we scarcely faced any security-related problems. With ten parliamentary constituencies, it was easy to conduct elections in a single phase (7 May 2009). The worry lay elsewhere, in an unexpectedly large number of contestants. So many, in fact, that we ran out of EVMs! It became necessary to borrow 3,000 EVMs from Chhattisgarh. With names of new candidates pouring in, we borrowed another 2,500 from the state election commission (the constitutional body distinct from the Commission which had been established in 1993 to conduct elections to the local bodies).

The other problem lay with a summer election. People often asked why we could not hold the elections in cooler months, but our schedule was almost always circumscribed by factors beyond our control. For a start, a new government had to be constituted before 1 June, as the previous government's term was coming to an end on that day. School examinations are almost always held from March to early April and, as the polling stations are mainly in school buildings, elections are not scheduled during this time.

By early May, it had become worrisomely hot. We requested our officials to do their best to provide some relief for those who stood in long queues braving the merciless sun. Many provided 'shamianas' and tent coverings wherever they could. Others arranged for drinking water facilities. After the elections were over, we got letters thanking us for shade and water but some mothers asked us to provide crèches at the poll stations where mothers could leave their babies while they waited in the queues the next time.

With Haryana's proximity to New Delhi and the national press, many complaints regarding violations of the MCC reached us, either through delegations calling on the Commission or by emails and letters. A couple of examples from Haryana might illustrate how seriously the Commission took these complaints. The first representation was made against the ruling party in the state, the Indian National Congress (INC), by the main opposition party, the Indian National Lok Dal (INLD) which alleged that on or about 11 March, the chief minister (CM) had misused his official vehicle to attend a political rally. As the election duration is a short one, notice to 'show cause' was immediately served on the CM. We received a rather unsatisfactory reply, upon which we conveyed our 'displeasure' and directed him to deposit a sum of Rs 4,050 (calculated to be the fuel expense) from his own pocket into the treasury. This was complied with in three days. The health minister received a similar notice. After considering her reply, the Commission's 'displeasure' was conveyed to her too, and fuel costs for Rs 2,350 were recovered from her personal account as well.

An unexpected complication that arose, surprising for a comparatively compact state, was the large number of missing names from the electoral registers. Many people who turned up at their booth and found their names missing, were understandably furious. They gave vent to their anger through the press. We faced a great deal of public criticism. Later when we analysed what had gone wrong, we learned that many areas, particularly in Gurgaon[19] district, had witnessed an enormous spurt of building activity since GE 2004. A large number of high-rise buildings and 'gated' communities had sprung up. These usually had their own security systems with guards manning entry gates instructed to deny entry to strangers. The result was that our hapless BLOs, who had no appointment with any particular resident, were not allowed entry and therefore could not

19 The name was changed to Gurugram on 27 September 2016.

verify and update their registers. Those residents who had not noticed the election-related instructions advertised in the press, or had not searched for their names on the election websites, were at a distinct disadvantage. Most of them were unaware that the electoral registers are updated every year, and their cards, bearing their previous address would not ensure their names on the new electoral list.

To remedy the situation for the assembly polls that were to follow, I visited Chandigarh, the joint capital of Haryana and Punjab, and convened a meeting with a number of Residents Welfare Associations (RWAs). Many were still very angry and did vent their rage on me. What fortunately resulted was a formula whereby henceforth the RWAs would work closely with our sectoral officers to enable the BLO's access into 'gated communities' so as to update the registers.

Himachal Pradesh

Almost entirely mountainous with a comparatively sparse population, Himachal Pradesh (HP) sends four MPs to the Lok Sabha. It was logical to conduct the election in the last phase to enable the winter chill to recede. In our terminology this was a 'peaceful state' from the point of security management. Unlike some of the states of the north-east, where security remains an issue and where infrastructure is still somewhat basic, HP prospered after it became a separate state in 1971. Its various elected governments ensured construction of roads and encouraged the growth of telecommunications, which became the life blood of commerce, industry and its famed fruit exports. Our directions regarding logistics management, material management and security management, therefore, worked relatively smoothly.

But the higher Himalayan ranges remained snowbound for most part of the year. In these very remote villages and hamlets, villagers had no option but to trek for almost all their needs. At election time, this meant that many voters had to walk sometimes up to 20 km through the rugged, largely inhospitable and still snowbound terrain to the nearest polling station. Over 50,000 voters in the tribal belt of Kinnaur in the Mandi constituency had done so in election after election, for the most part with enthusiasm. Kunnu-Charang village in Kinnaur's Pooh subdivision was an example of a faraway polling station in the state with as few as 169 registered voters. It was with great difficulty that a booth was set up at an altitude of 3,700 metres while the villagers trekked almost 10 km to cast their votes.

Kinnaur legislator Tejwant Negi was quoted as saying: 'During polls, the tribals are excited about exercising their franchise. Some of them prefer trekking a day before polling to reach the venue (polling booth) where they spend the night.'[20] In fact, there were almost twenty isolated hamlets with a total of about 2,000 voters who needed a full day's march to reach the polling station.

Meanwhile, the tribal residents of Kinnaur had already secured a special place in our hall of fame to become the first ones to vote in the general election of 1951, four months ahead of the rest of the nation. Shyam Saran Negi,[21] arguably the oldest who voted in Chini (renamed Kalpa) village on 25 October 1951, was already a celebrity. Kinnaur district also laid claim to a polling station with the least number of voters. Kaa, near Yangthang, had nineteen voters—down from twenty-one during the 2004 elections.[22] Jai Ram Thakur, a retired schoolteacher from Komik village in the Sangla Valley, said: 'We used to walk miles to cast votes. Now things have changed a lot. Better road connectivity has made most of the polling stations accessible.' In 2009, we managed to arrange helicopter sorties to transport electoral officials and materials thereby covering almost a third of the district's polling booths, most of them at altitudes above 13,000 feet. To clear a vital artery to the gateway to the Lahaul Spiti valley, the Rohtang Pass was cleared of snow by the Border Roads Organization (BRO) officials who worked valiantly to ensure that

---

20 'Tribal voters of Himachal brave weather, trek 10-20 km', *The Asian Age*, 11 May 2009.

21 See reference to S.S. Negi on pp. 27 and 70.

22 *The Asian Age*, 11 May 2009, quoting the then CEO of Himachal Pradesh, Anil Khachi.

our election officials could reach Hikkam—the highest polling station in Mandi constituency at over 4,500 m.

Amongst the stories that the local press enjoyed reporting was the case of Shri Bhadaru, whom they dubbed (arguably) India's oldest voter. Belonging to the village of Juggar, he claimed to be between 127 and 150 years old! Be that as it may, he said he had affirmed his lifelong commitment to elections by voting in every election: national, state and local. 'I will vote this time too', he told the *Times of India*.[23] He added that in the first election of 1951, there had been only one issue that dominated the election: Nehru.

The Commission's policy to assist the disabled found impressive resonance. Several meetings between the Commission officials and those of the local social justice and empowerment department with various associations of visually impaired persons, helped give publicity to Braille signage features being used for the first time, on any significant scale, in an election in the state. Numeric stickers in Braille denoting the serial number of candidates were prepared and pasted to the right of the blue voting button on the balloting unit of the EVM and this was given wide publicity.[24] The local press played a very constructive role in generally highlighting this, which helped generate a new-found awareness on disability issues.

Jammu and Kashmir

Having held elections to the state assembly in December 2008, elections for the six Lok Sabha seats that followed in May 2009 were conducted with relative ease. The people were still in 'poll mode' and the bona fides of the Commission for having conducted a fair and transparent election had been largely established in the minds of most

---

23 'At 127, India's oldest voter has seen it all', timesofindia.com, 6 May 2009.

24 Election Commission of India, *Lok Sabha Election 2009: Reinforcing Indian Democracy*, New Delhi: ECI, 2009, pp. 102–03.

of the voters. During an earlier fact-finding mission that our officials made, some interesting general points emerged. In earlier elections, a high voter turnout, normally a cause for celebration elsewhere, had been met in the Kashmir Valley with suspicion about its credibility. Announcements made by All India Radio and Doordarshan were seen by many as a part of government's propaganda machine. There were hardly any private TV channels, and the local newspapers had a strong anti-government stance, which enveloped the Commission too.

From the Commission's standpoint, there had been no communication strategy to speak of. In the interregnum between the assembly poll of 2008 and GE 2009, we sought to initiate a dialogue for the first time. There was not enough time to make this multi-faceted, so we concentrated on giving credibility to the EPIC. With the feedback that we received, we tried hard to promote their 'utility' aspect in the state. Since 2006, our success lay in making them all-purpose identity cards, that could be used to apply for identification purposes for any government schemes. This effort had succeeded in gaining popular acceptance, and people who had earlier not been particularly interested in obtaining the EPIC now came forward in large numbers, as evidenced from the high percentage of EPICs distributed in the country.

Once the election process got under way, this state became the cynosure of more eyes than perhaps any other. It was a magnet that attracted diplomats, foreign and Indian journalists and observers of every hue. My own office received more requests to visit Srinagar than perhaps any other city. My answer was uniform: Do please visit but don't expect the Commission to make any special arrangements as our hands are full. Having said this, and despite the security considerations, our CEO issued as many as 900 passes to local, national and international journalists and allowed complete access to diplomats and visitors who wished to travel anywhere they wished to in order to 'cover' the elections. Several ambassadors, based in New Delhi sought permission to witness the run-up to the polls and the polling itself. A few ambassadors got in touch with me personally and I advised them that they were free to travel anywhere at will.

Many did. In fact, the Venezuelan ambassador at the time, Mme Milena Santana Bolivar, who had served in India for over ten years, would later tell me that she 'covered' not just Kashmir but practically the entire country, travelling by plane, car and even riding pillion on a motorbike, to see for herself the unfolding of the panorama of India's elections.

Karnataka

The Commission's problems in Karnataka ironically arose not for reasons of poverty but because of its wealth. The inordinately rich candidates, many of them mining barons with a propensity to win the elections—quite literally at any cost—presented the Commission with an administrative challenge. Nowhere did I find this exemplified better than in the district of Bellary, their stronghold. The *Deccan Herald* would report as follows: 'With the first of the two-phase parliamentary elections in the state just five days away, cash and liquor continues to flow in many Lok Sabha constituencies.' By the time the Commission made its review, the seizures of unauthorized cash were to the tune of a whopping Rs 18.5 crore. Together with the value of the unauthorized liquor that had been seized by flying squads, the amount exceeded Rs 23 crore. The local election office in Bidar would report that '... we found seventy-three envelopes in a car. Each envelope had a different amount ranging from Rs 10,000 to Rs 5 lakh. On each envelope, the name of the *caste* to which it should reach was written.'[25] Not less than 600 cases of malpractice had already been registered by the time the Commission made its review. The upshot was that we transferred a number of officials out of Bellary and elsewhere for either partisan behaviour or plain inefficiency.

The toll may have been considerably higher but for several innovative measures introduced by the CEO and the dynamic Special Officer Manoj Ranjan. He launched a drive to stop the lavish feasts

---

25 *The Deccan Herald*, Bangalore, 19 April 2009.

organized by candidates, ostensibly to felicitate 'newly married' couples where there were no brides and grooms and the 'birthday parties' which had mushroomed in such large numbers that one could not help but wonder how these were all being celebrated during election season. It also appeared that candidates had become more religious than ever before as they thronged temples, where there was a propensity to offer liberal donations to the temple as well as sarees and dhotis for distribution to the 'devotees'. Even more ingenious were the coloured tokens that could be encashed for half a bottle of liquor (a yellow slip) or a full bottle (a pink slip). There was no dearth of inventiveness: our officials learned that some candidates had roped in local moneylenders to liquidate the petty loans of voters. Learning perhaps from neighbouring Tamil Nadu, currency notes of Rs 500 and Rs 1,000 denominations were slipped in with envelopes bearing voter slips, or were neatly folded into the morning newspapers. In some places, cash coupons were distributed that could be encashed at specific shopping malls and retail outlets. The 'big boys' had no qualms about renting private helicopters to ferry cash. As each 'new' method was uncovered, Manoj Ranjan introduced a 'susceptible area management scheme', narrowing down areas which were particularly 'vulnerable' on the basis of earlier experience. Because of these measures, was it any surprise that cash and liquor worth almost Rs 40 crore were seized by vigilant officials? Of such seizures, the richest district of Bellary contributed the lion's share of Rs 16.12 crore (see the following table).

A considerable part of the wealth seized during GE 2009 was from the mining barons, amongst others, of Bellary district. A number of show-cause notices were issued to the Reddy brothers asking why they should not be disqualified.[26] Several cases were registered later including against some ministers. The state government decided to oppose the Commission tooth and nail. At this point the state cabinet

---

26 'EC serves notices on 3 Karnataka Ministers', *Business Standard*, New Delhi, 28 June 2010; 'Commission notice to Reddy brothers', *The Mail Today*, New Delhi, 28 June 2010.

SEIZURES OF MONEY AND LIQUOR DURING GE KARNATAKA 2009

Dist No	Dist Name	Total Cash Cases	Total Cash Value Rs	Total Liquor Cases	Total Liquor Value Rs	Total Goods Cases	Total Goods Value Rs	Total Cases	Total Value Rs
1	BELGAUM	2	6604470	160	2353050	0	0	162	8957520
2	BAGALKOT	1	10670	37	145840	0	0	38	156510
3	BIJAPUR	0	0	10	511163	0	0	10	511163
4	GULBARGA	2	1484264	264	7049603	0	0	266	8533867
5	BIDAR	14	3142356	0	0	18	11918800	32	15061156
6	RAICHUR	0	0	116	1705216	0	0	116	1705216
7	KOPPAL	2	2060400	22	138690	1	6900	25	2205990
8	GADAG	0	0	11	401247	0	0	11	401247
9	DHARWAD	0	0	30	1124483	1	15000	31	1139483
10	UTTARA KANNADA	0	0	67	953409	0	0	67	953409
11	HAVERI	3	1101000	36	484823	10	2164700	49	3750523
12	BELLARY	28	147174850	243	4948512	32	9102700	303	161226062
13	CHITRADURGA	1	530000	41	215842	0	0	42	745842

SEIZURES OF MONEY AND LIQUOR DURING GE KARNATAKA 2009									
Dist No	Dist Name	Total Cash Cases	Total Cash Value Rs	Total Liquor Cases	Total Liquor Value Rs	Total Goods Cases	Total Goods Value Rs	Total Cases	Total Value Rs
14	DAVANAGERE	3	8500000	1	9810	1	160000	5	8669810
15	SHIMOGA	3	9095300	154	4600362	6	2595000	163	16290662
16	UDUPI	0	0	20	497390	0	0	20	497390
17	CHIKMAGALUR	0	0	40	200677	0	0	40	200677
18	TUMKUR	0	0	39	66696	1	45560	40	112256
19	CHIKKABALLAPUR	0	0	19	240373	0	0	19	240373
20	KOLAR	2	1011600	58	1744939	0	0	60	2756539
21	BANGALORE	4	4212470	1	1000	1	10000000	6	14213470
22	BANGALORE RURAL	5	782930	31	59060	5	15000	41	856990
23	RAMANAGARAM	0	0	0	0	0	0	0	0
24	MANDYA	2	185000	166	1125041	0	0	168	1310041
25	HASSAN	0	0	0	0	0	0	0	0

SEIZURES OF MONEY AND LIQUOR DURING GE KARNATAKA 2009									
Dist No	Dist Name	Total Cash Cases	Total Cash Value Rs	Total Liquor Cases	Total Liquor Value Rs	Total Goods Cases	Total Goods Value Rs	Total Cases	Total Value Rs
26	DAKSHINA KANNADA	1	2300000	18	372357	0	0	19	2672357
27	KODAGU	6	4023710	31	736791	0	0	37	4760501
28	MYSORE	3	1211855	44	546260	6	3961240	53	5719355
29	CHAMARAJANAGAR	0	0	141	536710	0	0	141	536710
34	BANGALORE URBAN	2	7518810	2	1300	0	0	4	7520110
	TOTAL	84	200949685	1802	30770644	82	39984900	1968	271705229

Compiled by the office of the Chief Electoral Officer, Karnataka, 2009.

scheduled a meeting wherein its main agenda was to withdraw, by executive order, all cases registered on the Commission's directions. We challenged this by sending a top legal counsel to appear before the Dharwad Bench of the Karnataka High Court to appeal against the order of withdrawal that had been passed by a district court. Our counsel argued that this interfered with the jurisdiction of the Commission. Our petition also questioned the jurisdiction of the government to withdraw the cases. We maintained that the closure of any registered case would have to be declared by a court of law after hearing the Commission. The Karnataka High Court upheld our view. This was a major breakthrough and thereafter became a settled practice.

Kerala

Kerala, comprising fourteen districts and 140 legislative assembly constituencies, elects twenty MPs to the Lok Sabha. We conducted the election in a single phase on 16 April 2009. Kerala had notched 98 per cent EPIC coverage as early as 2005. By 2009, this has risen to 100 per cent. With a fully literate population with high awareness levels, it was not surprising that Kerala's DEOs had provided touch screens in all district and even taluk headquarters to enable electors to verify their names on the rolls. Additionally, Voter Awareness Booths were established wherever there were more than two polling stations at a single location. During polling day, separate queues were arranged quite methodically for senior citizens and the physically challenged. Not surprisingly, it was in Kerala that EVMs were tried for the first time in the bye-election to the Parur (now renamed Paravur) constituency in 1982.

Unique to Kerala was the demand made by several political parties to enfranchise the large number of persons from this state who had obtained employment abroad. A broad estimate puts the figure at about 1.65 million, representing about 5 per cent of the total population. This was (and is) a powerful vote bank that could tilt the balance in any election. This 'demand' would also reach the Commission when the then prime minister, Manmohan Singh, publicly endorsed it as a move that his government would support.

We faced several practical difficulties in conceding this. The election rules do not permit for overseas voting. They permit only a person who is ordinarily resident, in any one constituency to be included in the electoral register. In the case of those working overseas, if their names were not already on the electoral register, they would have to return to India and reside for a minimum of six months in the constituency from which they hoped to vote. If their names were on the rolls, they would still need to return home to cast their votes on election day. It was not possible for the Commission to enable them to vote at our respective embassies (a recurring demand) because our elaborate measures—including the application and supervision of the model code of conduct, the presence of observers, the management of electoral stations, indeed the whole electoral 'bandobast'—could simply not be set up in any other country. To give just one instance, some countries do not allow a large assembly of people to congregate in a public space rendering electioneering impossible. Nor could prospective candidates easily travel to those countries to campaign and address rallies, without a plethora of permissions from the host country. Moreover, it was not possible for the Commission to monitor the process overseas. If the prime minister's statement had to be taken to its natural conclusion, it would also mean important legislative changes. It would require parliament to re-examine the RoPA of 1950 and of 1951 and move for necessary amendments in consultation with political parties and the Commission, for which there was , in any case, not enough time.

Our denial for overseas voting raised the issue of e-voting. Attractive as it sounded the Commission had hitherto been unable to devise any form of computer-based voting which would be compatible with EVMs, (and now the additional VVPATs) which are stand-alone machines not linked to any computer. The stage had not yet been reached where the Commission could initiate e-voting even within the country, let alone overseas. In a scenario where every single vote would be crucial to victory or defeat, it is essential to ensure the maintenance of a secure framework with several firewalls that would prevent even a single accusation of error or manipulation since such suspicion would lead to unnecessary complaints and litigation. The future introduction of e-voting would necessarily presage the endorsement by the political class as a whole for it will need legislative amendments. As a result, the present system remains intact.

Madhya Pradesh

Elections in large states are always complex. With an area of 308,245 sq. km, and a total population of 69,896,998,[27] Madhya Pradesh (MP) administratively comprised fifty districts it had 47,210 polling stations in 2009. It sent twenty-nine members to the Lok Sabha; their constituencies comprised 230 assembly segments. Bordering five states meant a number of security and sealing issues. Our redoubtable CEO, J.S. Mathur, had also pushed hard to achieve a very high EPIC coverage of 93.66 per cent.

The size of the state necessitated the election in two phases, (23 and 30 April). Accompanied by our officials, I went to Bhopal on 13 April to conduct a review. As was customary in all such reviews, we began by meeting representatives of all recognized political parties to take their concerns and complaints on board, followed by a meeting with the chief secretary, police commissioner and inspectors general of police, together with the DMs/ ROs and SPs.

Since I kept personal notes of these deliberations, it might be interesting to share a few of my jottings. The districts had been broadly categorized into 'Maoist affected', 'communally sensitive' and 'with problems of law and order'. For instance, I had noted that the district of Jabalpur was 'communally sensitive' and that although the SP was new (in the sense that he had been recently posted there), fortunately the RO/ collector was 'very experienced'. Balaghat district, was not only a problematic 'Maoist area', but that a number

27 Projected population number for 2009.

of non-bailable warrants relating to electoral offences were still pending execution (never a good sign in security management). My notes reminded me that the requisite training given to junior police officials was, 'less than adequate'. To further complicate matters, there were an inordinately large number of candidates in the fray.

In an adjoining district, I thought a key official was 'laid back' and needed 'to be replaced quickly by a more experienced' officer (which we did). Seoni district presented problems of communication, with large parts under the 'shadow' of deeply forested parts where there was no mobile connectivity. Some polling stations were so inaccessible that they could only be reached by boat. 'Something needs to be done very quickly to get COMET going,' I observed. Chhindwara district was 'problematic' because it was 'politically sensitive'. It also had a large number of polling stations having more than our standard norm of 1,500 electors. To compound matters, there were more than sixteen candidates in the fray, which meant we needed two EVMs per booth.

The Satna review revealed that there was an ongoing problem caused by warring dacoit gangs, particularly in its ravine areas of Manikpur. These brigands included the dreaded Shiv Kumar Kol alias Hariya with a bounty of Rs 50,000 on his head, who had been killed by the police two years ago. The ravines of Chambal and Chitrakoot were home to these gangs, who for years had terrorized scores of villages. Twenty villagers had only recently been shot by them, so we needed to station Central forces here. In adjacent Sidhi, there was a shortage of micro-observers, which was redressed. Nearby Singrauli had 'poor communication' and needed 'its mobile towers to be repaired urgently if the situation was to improve in time for the polls' Meanwhile, Reva district, famed for its white tigers, had a deeply forested and 'porous' border with UP, which needed more rigorous 'border security measures'. However, I noted with satisfaction that the collector, a lady officer, was 'strong and experienced'.

Chattarpur district had a maximum number of 'vulnerable pockets', which bordered the once fearsome dacoit-ridden Bundelkhand area of UP. Fortunately, I found it reassuring that the key officials here were 'very experienced'. Panna, once famed for its diamond mines, had several polling stations with poor communication. And so, it went on: 'shadow areas', 'communally sensitive areas', 'Maoist areas', 'difficult communication areas' with the words 'dacoit-infested' coming up every now and then. Was it any surprise then that my appraisal took over twelve hours?

The phenomenon of 'dummy candidates' were not new to MP but it appeared to have more than its fair share. Dummies usually campaigned for mainstream candidates under the guise of being 'independents'. By this stratagem the 'real' candidate could also lay claim to twice the share of election expenses. When we became conscious of this, the dummies became easier to identify, because the giveaway arose at the end of their meetings when they would exhort the gathering to vote for the *actual* candidate in question. This was also a clever way of spreading the candidate's net much wider. When we decided to add their expenses to the expenses of the 'real' candidate, this put an end to 'independents' who fled the cluttered field. There were at least two other kinds of dummies. There were the 'spoilers' who were set up by rival candidates to eat into the vote share of their opponents. Then there were those who often had identical or similar names to the principal candidates and were in the game to cut some votes, which could be particularly damaging in seats which had been won or lost by small margins.

As in Karnataka, our observers noticed a sudden rash of marriage feasts and birthday parties. Sometimes, hundreds of guests were invited to these feasts; on occasion whole villages attended. As biryani was the most popular dish, we dubbed these 'biryani parties'. When expenditure observers decided to add the per-plate cost to the candidate's expenses, this caused the biriyani-party-syndrome to diminish considerably. But human ingenuity being what it is, other forms of felicitation sprung up. A popular one was a puja in the local temple where the candidate was blessed and people contributed sums of money for the occasion. However, with our observers keeping an eye open for such disguised expenditure, the rash of parties and pujas decreased.

Maharashtra

Maharashtra, one of India's larger states with a population of almost 97 million (2001 census), returns forty-eight MPs to the Lok Sabha. Spread over 307,713 sq. km, bearing one-tenth of India's total population, Maharashtra also has the country's second largest urban population with forty-three out of every 100 living in cities and towns. It also has a large migrant population. Its size dictated that the polls had to be conducted in three phases, on 16, 23 and 30 April 2009. Here too, we were faced with multiplicity of candidates. As is well known, one balloting unit of an EVM can take up to sixteen contesting candidates. However, in as many as twenty-five parliamentary constituencies, there were more than sixteen candidates. In one constituency, there were thirty-two contestants. In these constituencies, we had to deploy two EVMs per polling booth. Once again, we had to borrow EVMs, this time from Rajasthan, Gujarat, Andhra Pradesh, MP and UP. The state election commission[28] of Maharashtra too loaned us 35,000 EVMs. This involved the burden of additional planning for the moving of thousands of EVMs in safety and security to any and all 'EVM-deficient' states with something akin to military precision.

No sooner had nominations opened came the deluge. We opened our Maharashtra innings with as many as 1,309 candidates who had thrown their hats in the ring. We simply had no machines to spare. Fortunately, the nomination papers of 209 were rejected by the returning officers for various reasons. Another 282 candidates, mainly independents, 'cover candidates' or 'dummies', withdrew before the last day of withdrawals. The number in the fray now

28 The SEC is an altogether different constitutional body that is mandated to conduct only local body elections.

came down to 819 candidates, but this was still an inordinately high number. The EPIC percentage, meanwhile was 73 per cent, which meant that the electoral registers were not in very good shape either. As I noted, not a brilliant commentary for so progressive a state.

After GE 2009 ended, the press asked me what had disappointed me the most. My answer lay in a single word: Mumbai. The low polling percentage in Mumbai city, where only 41 per cent of Mumbaikars bothered to turn out to vote, (6 per cent less than GE 2004) was difficult to fathom. Indeed, it was the lowest recorded vote since 1977.[29] The press, however, went into a frenzy of analyses. 'It sent a powerful message to politicians that they must not take the voter for granted', went one refrain. The *Asian Age*[30] summed it all up in its headline, 'Mumbai Votes for Weekend Off'. It would appear that Mumbaikars did, in fact, choose to avail of a long weekend coupled with two additional midweek holidays to leave the city for an extended holiday. Learning from this experience, we would choose poll dates that would avoid the possibility of the 'long weekend syndrome'.

As the Commission prepared for the big election, we were all too conscious of the security climate in the state, coming as this did just five months after the terrible terrorist attack that shook India. Away from media glare, the Commission had quietly been keeping itself abreast of all the security measures that the Central and state governments had in place. Any repeat attack would not only come as an enormous blow to 'maximum city', it would certainly deal a severe blow to the body politic and to the people of India. It could possibly disrupt the general process in the country as a whole. Fortunately, the security forces were on very high alert. The Commission and the security agencies worked closely together and ensured the absence of any untoward incident. The *Hindustan Times*[31] reported as follows: 'It was for the first time in the election history of the state that the

29 Maharashtra saw 49.17 per cent polling in 1977.

30 *The Asian Age*, New Delhi, 1 May 2009.

31 *Hindustan Times*, New Delhi, 13 October 2009.

Mumbai Police have sought help from the air force and navy for maintaining the state's internal security during the assembly polls. .... [T]he Navy has already endorsed the proposal and agreed to move some of their warships from deep waters to the coast on patrolling duty, the air force, which had been asked to provide helicopters for a real surveillance, has not responded yet.'

The significance of this election must also be understood in the context of the domestic and regional situation prevailing at that point of time, especially in regions perceived to be under higher risk of threat. The backdrop of the terrorist attack on Mumbai in November 2008 became an integral part of our planning.

Punjab

With thirteen parliamentary constituencies spread over twenty districts covering an area of 50,362 sq. km and a population of 16,815,362 (16.81 million), Punjab shares boundaries with four states and a union territory and also has an international boundary with Pakistan. Its EPIC coverage was excellent at 94.54 per cent. Elections were conducted in two phases, which I reviewed together on 30 April.

Punjab's candidates were every bit as feisty as the electorate from which they were drawn. There was large election spend and much of this showed up as surrogate advertisements, or 'paid news' in the garb of articles and news coverage. As in Madhya Pradesh and elsewhere, there were also a large number of 'dummy candidates'. Once again, no sooner were the legitimate candidates saddled with their dummy's expenses, this problem diminished considerably.

Elections in Punjab almost always threw up concerns about the partiality of the police forces towards whichever party was in power. As soon as the election was announced, this manifested itself with opposition parties voicing their suspicions not just against officials at lower or middle levels but against very senior officers too. It was one of the many ironies that those who complained against local police forces were often at the helm of affairs when these very policemen were recruited. Expressing their lack of faith in the state's police forces, they now wanted the Commission to bring in Central police forces and position them at thousands of polling stations that they held to be vulnerable.

The litany of complaints did not spare the state's senior-most police officer, the director general of police himself. The opposition parties alleged that he was likely to favour the Congress government in power.[32] They wanted the DGP removed for the duration of the election period.

When the Lok Sabha polls were declared, the Commission had already reiterated existing instructions that any official against whom disciplinary action had been recommended in the past or who may earlier have been transferred out on the Commission's orders may not be assigned any electoral duties. Indeed in 2007, the DGP concerned had been removed prior to the assembly polls.

Nevertheless, to shift out the head of the force was not an easy decision to take. He was the head of the force. Any shift, even temporary, would be viewed as being 'shunted out' which could demoralize the police force. I provide this account here as an example not of the power of the Commission but of the responsibility that rested with us to take a correct and balanced decision. Personally, I believed that the officer was unlikely to behave in a partisan manner because he was now the focus of press attention. However, the view in the Commission was that he be shifted out for the election period only.

Rajasthan

Rajasthan, with an area of 342,239 sq. km and a population of 56.5 million in 2009 and a poor gender ratio of 917, returns twenty-five MPs to the Lok Sabha. The state did reflect a healthy EPIC coverage of 91.73 per cent. We conducted the election on a single day on 7 May 2009. The state has an international border with Pakistan, and

32 *The Times of India*, 14 March 2009.

my notes reflected several special measures that were undertaken to seal this as well as six state borders.

In our parlance, Rajasthan is a 'peaceful state', barring a few districts where there have been caste-related clashes in the past. Here, old rivalries tended to intensify during election periods. During the past few elections, a major irritant arose from certain communities seeking a slice of the reservation pie for government jobs. As temperatures in the desert state rose to well over 40 degrees Celsius, so too did tempers of many of the 346 contestants and their supporters. The stationing of security forces, observers, micro-observers and the videography teams did reduce instances of violence or malpractice, but nonetheless I had assigned one helicopter to hover over these districts for law and order duties. This introduced both an element of curiosity as well as a 'visible deterrent' and no major clashes occurred. A few minor clashes did break out in a few places and so we annulled elections, and repolls were conducted on 10 May. The procedure for repolls applies uniformly everywhere. After polls are completed in any part of the country, we invariably leave a cushion of two or three days before counting day, just in case repolls may need to be held.

During the thrust and parry of the election day, some amusing incidents surfaced. One concerned an incident at a mobile polling station in Jaisalmer district. (Half a dozen mobile polling stations had been set up in some rather inaccessible parts of the desert—an innovation developed by Vinod Zutshi, one of the Commission's principal officers who had been in charge of Rajasthan earlier.) Apparently, an early voter at one of these stations had cleverly managed to fit a one-rupee coin in a slot against the name of a particular candidate. As it was doubtless intended, this coin fit rather snugly on the button. The result was that some of the early voters felt tempted to wedge out the coin. As they tried to do this, the pressure was sufficient for a vote to be recorded with its distinctive 'ping' sound. It took a little while before a shame-faced voter informed the election officials that mischief was afoot. The EVM was changed and polling started afresh.

In yet another ingenious case in Jaisalmer district, a rumour was spread that one of the EVMs was malfunctioning, that one particular button, if pressed, gave out an electric shock. Now EVMs don't run on electricity; they run on batteries and do not cause an electric shock. Clearly, the rumour had been spread to deter people from voting for a particular candidate. This was detected quite early in the poll and voters who entered that booth subsequently were told by our officials not to fall for this game.

~

In this chapter I have endeavoured to give the reader an overview of the election processes and highlight some of the main challenges that the Election Commission faced. Though dos and don'ts and standard operating procedures were in place, several districts threw up their own specific problems, some of which I have mentioned as examples. This chapter is also a tribute to the district election officers, their police counterparts and the thousands of polling staff without whose dedication, such a mammoth exercise as the general election would not have been possible.

Elections are the most visible and action-packed part of Indian democracy. It is true that the successful completion of general elections in India renews the nation's faith in the democratic system. Yet, there are serious concerns about growing malpractices which will be discussed in the next chapter.

4

Where Is Indian Democracy Going Wrong?

WHILE I was certainly privileged to have been appointed India's sixteenth chief election commissioner (CEC) and fortunate too that I was at the helm of affairs in conducting the democratic world's largest election in 2009, I was also uniquely placed to see the many fault lines that were beginning to fracture our democracy. The exhilaration that came with managing an enterprise of such enormous complexity was tempered by the realization that we were not entirely masters of the game, and that there were subterranean forces that thwarted the electoral rules with growing impunity.

These negative forces had already weakened the democratic structure that I often wondered whether we could ever hope to realize the aspirations of our freedom fighters, who had sacrificed so much for independence from colonial rule. The truth, depressingly, was that foreign domination was in the process of being replaced by a home-grown oligarchy which had placed power and wealth in the hands of a few. In the process, 'money power', 'muscle power' and a partially compromised fourth estate had swept away everything that Gandhiji stood for when he said, 'I understand democracy as something that gives the weak the same chance as the strong'.

Former UN secretary general and Nobel laureate Kofi Annan while addressing the Austrian parliament in 2014[1] called for an urgent public debate on the state of democracy wherein he described clean and transparent elections with integrity as the bedrock of democracy. He added that despite being the root of democracy, clean democratic elections are by no means assured. In his view, media monopolies and opaque political financing obstruct democratic practices and create unbalanced playing fields during elections, compromising electoral integrity.

In the Indian context, former prime minister Atal Bihari Vajpayee once forthrightly remarked, 'Every legislator starts his career with a lie, with the false election return that he files.'[2] He had the rare courage to give voice to a phenomenon widely recognized but very rarely spoken or written about, almost a secret shared amongst its major proponents. Vajpayee was referring to the declarations that must be filed by all candidates (after the elections) before the Commission, certifying that their campaign expenses have been within the limits prescribed by law, when, in fact, they were seriously compromised.

The cancer has now spread beyond money power, to what is referred to as muscle power. Worse, the stench of corruption of 'paid news' has now spread to our fourth estate as well. In the following pages I will try to analyse each of these problems and suggest remedies borne out of my experiences in the Commission.

Money Power

The first two decades after Independence were relatively 'clean' in these respects. As far as political finance went, private donations as well as membership dues were the mainstay. The Representation

1 Kofi Annan's speech in the Austrian parliament in Vienna on 28 February 2014, Kofi Annan Foundation.

2 'Trust in the Law', *Business Line*, 8 October 2018.

of the People Act, 1951,[3] prescribed limits on individual election expenses which were, by and large, adhered to. In the afterglow of the independence movement, many politicians managed to keep their expenses under control because they belonged to the party that was associated in the public mind with the freedom struggle.

Election-related expenses were more manageable then and donations made by the business sector were legal, if declared in their accounts. Corporate donations by cheque were encouraged and 'bucket collections' made up of small donations of a few rupees were widely prevalent. This phase of Indian politics was noted for the unquestioned leadership of Jawaharlal Nehru, and the electoral dominance of the Congress party both at the national and state levels. True, there was some electoral overspend even then. All this was soon to change.

In 1968, Prime Minister Indira Gandhi's government banned corporate donations, for many reasons. It was alleged by some that the Congress party was increasingly apprehensive of the ideology of the right-wing parties and more particularly it viewed the Swatantra Party as the party of ex-rulers and wealthy industrialists, who represented the antithesis of the socialist approach of the Congress party. The ban on corporate donations created a perhaps unintended vacuum. In retrospect, this should have been filled by some manner of state funding of elections. Unfortunately, such a move was neither initiated by the government nor pressed for by the political opposition. As a major source of legitimate funding dried up, political parties and candidates resorted to alternative sources of resource

3 The Representation of the People Act, 1951, provides for the conduct of elections to parliament and state legislatures, qualification and disqualification for membership, describes corrupt practices and other election-related practices. Act number 43 of 1951, it applies to the whole country, commencing on 17 July 1951. (Related legislation is the Representation of People Act, 1950). It was introduced in parliament by the then law minister B.R. Ambedkar. It was enacted by the provisional parliament under Article 327 of the Constitution, prior to the first general election.

mobilization. The scourge of 'black money'—cash payments made clandestinely—was born.

The 1970s also coincided with price rise and inflation which were triggered by the expense of the war with Pakistan (1971) and the influx of the refugees from the former East Pakistan (now Bangladesh). The sharp upward spiral of prices, which also stoked public restiveness, inevitably had a domino effect on the electoral process. As prices rose, so too did election-related costs causing parties to court big donors. The only exceptions were those political parties that had retained strong cadres loyal to their ideologies.

The structure of politics also began to change leading to a more fragmented polity. It became an era of coalition politics where elections became increasingly drained of ideological content. The period also witnessed the arrival on the scene of a new breed of politicians who had little or no respect for democratic values, and for whom the freedom movement was just a passing phase of history. They saw politics as their livelihood rather than as service to the people. As ideological moorings weakened, indiscriminate electoral alliances mushroomed. Opacity entered the political arena. Pervasive rumours spread (and were widely believed) that government policies were beginning to be influenced by the quid pro quo demanded by those who contributed significantly to party coffers.

Candidate and party spending went up further when in 1974 the Supreme Court ruled that electoral expenditure made by a political party on behalf of a candidate would have to be included in the candidate's personal election expenses.[4] The political establishment struck back. On 19 October 1974, the government issued an ordinance, which was followed by the tabling of a bill in parliament on 7 November which sought to amend the RoPA to circumvent the

---

4 *Kanwar Lal Gupta vs Amar Nath Chawla and Others,* 3 October 1974, 1975 AIR 308; 1975 SCR (2) 269. The court set aside the election of Amar Nath Chawla to the Lok Sabha on the grounds of corruption, in that he breached the ceiling of expenditure prescribed by law, as the court chose to include the expenditure made by his party in the candidate's expenditure.

court's order. The bill was passed by parliament in 1975. Just as long as the candidate concerned had not *specifically* authorized party expenditure or that by their supporters, it would not be included in the candidate's poll expenditure. Moreover, as long as the candidate was not named, party- and supporter-funding could now take care of most major expenses—on publicity for instance, or the expense involved in arranging meetings.

It would be almost two decades later (in 1985) that corporate donations were once again legally permitted, but by then it was a case of too little too late, because the 'black money syndrome' had become deeply entrenched. The advantage for both sides of this trade was manifest; this was surreptitious funding which was both secret and anonymous. The persons making these donations were 'invisible' and, therefore, could not be targeted by any political party, group or individual, particularly by those towards whom such largesse was not directed. They also remained below the radar of the tax authorities. The amounts 'donated' also remained secret, known only to a few party bosses.

As the increase in the costs of conducting and participating in elections continued to outpace the rate of inflation, the political parties, cutting across party lines, continued to devour vast amounts of money to keep their engines running. In 2003, the NDA government amended the RoPA, which made company and individual contributions to a political party 100 per cent tax exempt. The government also made it mandatory for political parties to declare all amounts *above* Rs 20,000 received by them to the Commission, to avail of tax exemptions. It also plugged the 1975 loophole wherein candidate expenditure had excluded party and independent support. These were wholesome steps. However, this amendment also raised the ceiling of declaration from the earlier Rs 10,000 (1999) to Rs 20,000. Significantly, it also permitted nationally recognized political parties to submit the names of forty 'star campaigners' (and twenty in the case of registered unrecognized parties) to the Commission whose entire expenditure on travel (easily the single most expensive segment of expenditure) stood exempted from being added to the candidate's expenditure.

Another significant exemption made was for party propaganda. This meant that while a political party might organize a mammoth rally in the constituency of candidate 'A', where many 'star campaigners' may descend, just as long as the candidate was not on the dais and was not mentioned by name, the expenses were billed to the party account.

There was another fallout. While sums of Rs 20,000 and above were to be declared, sums less than that (say, Rs 19,999) would ensure anonymity. In the absence of disclosure, it was widely accepted that these amounts were (and are) paid in cash and often in multiples as well. Obviously, the Commission is concerned that such 'small donations' would involve quid pro quos. The Commission's demand for the details of such donors (which would require a further amendment to the Act) have been stonewalled. The parties claim it is difficult to detail 'small amounts' under Rs 20,000, and they aver that in any case those contributing small amounts can hardly be accused of 'lobbying'. Yet it is widely believed that over 70 per cent of the party financing is obscure. Some estimates placed this as high as 85 per cent. Political parties, across the board, remain satisfied with this arrangement, irrespective of rivalries or animosity that might otherwise exist between them. It remains for the government to be more articulate in explaining how the collection and disbursal of funds should be cleaned up, instead of rejecting the Commission's efforts to inject greater accountability in the system.[5]

The 2003 amendments had an immediate effect on the nature of electoral campaigns. With expenses on transport and party propaganda no longer charged to individual accounts, planes and helicopters began to crisscross the country, paid for by party funds, not all of which were fully disclosed. Given the reality that an hour of charter charges for a helicopter could be between Rs 2 lakh and 5 lakh, the overall costs during the general elections would run into

5 From January 2018, this amount was brought down to Rs 2,000.

so many millions that this could be the subject of a study by itself. I recall that when I was leaving Lucknow airport after addressing our officials in UP in 2009, there were almost fifteen helicopters parked on one side that the airport manager likened to a taxi stand.

During my five-and-a-half years in the Commission, I began to see the growth of 'money power' as a hydra-headed monster. No sooner would we think that we had cut off its head than others would appear to replace it. For instance, we banned the defacing of public spaces by posters, stickers and banners which would also have the effect of reducing expenditure. Towards this end too we permitted the flying of party flags only on personal dwellings. While some candidates welcomed the decision as it would help bring down costs, some parties complained that we were 'throttling democracy'. It is possible that we went too far.

What was also becoming noticeable was that elections to state assemblies were being fought with even greater manipulation of resources than those for the Lok Sabha. Perhaps the most bitter and fierce contests were, surprisingly, for 'prestigious' bye-elections. The 2009 Thirumangalam bye-election in Tamil Nadu was to gain both national and international notoriety for the novel methods that emerged in the 'art' of bribing voters. This came to be known in Indian election folklore as the 'Thirumangalam formula'.

It happened like this. A relatively simple bye-election, held in January 2009, was converted into a battle royale between the two main parties in Tamil Nadu—the Dravida Munnetra Kazhagam (DMK) and its bitter rival, the All India Anna Dravida Munnetra Kazhagam (AIADMK). Within the DMK too, the rivalries between two brothers, one of whom saw this constituency as part of his fiefdom, added to the intensity and—as it happened—the expenses. While the Commission was busy ensuring that the ground rules were observed and the MCC properly enforced, vast sums of money were surreptitiously slipped under the very noses of our observers and other officials on duty, to clandestinely buy votes.

We would discover much later that it was alleged that almost every voter on the electoral roll received an envelope containing the party's voting slip as well as a 500-rupee note, ingeniously slipped into the folds of the daily newspapers. Fealty, in some cases, was demanded by almost tribal means—party workers handed cash, or a coupon that could be exchanged for gifts or freebies in the dead of night, in exchange for solemn promises sometimes sworn before the household deity. The *Hindu* had accessed almost five thousand US embassy cables including one regarding this by-election.[6] Sent on 13 May 2009, it quoted a close aide of a former Union minister (and chief protagonist in this battle) that in fact a whopping Rs 5,000 had been paid to every voter.[7] Our observers did from time to time receive 'tip-offs' but those were often in the dead of night and almost always anonymous. Few offered their real names.

While it was usual for the Commission to receive several complaints—in person, by email, or on phone—during the hurly-burly of elections, these almost largely related to transgression of the model code of conduct. There were fewer complaints about 'money power'. A rare case that made headlines occurred in 2013 when a former minister from Maharashtra, the late Gopinath Munde, let slip that he had spent Rs 8 crore for his 2009 election.[8] This was way above the then prescribed limit of Rs 40 lakh. This admission made it to the front pages of the press. When the Commission slapped a notice on him, he quickly retracted and said he was 'misquoted'.

In retrospect, one problem was that we commissioners were all too often constrained while interacting with the political establishment. I,

---

6 *The Hindu*, Chennai, 14 May 2016, 'Cash for Vote: Genesis of the "Thirumangalam Formula"'. This article quoted a US Embassy cable that rather than using the traditional method of cash-by-hand, envelopes containing the party's voting slip also contained currency which was slipped into the folds of the daily newspaper which 'forced everyone to receive the bribe'.

7 In 2011, N. Ram, the editor-in-chief of *The Hindu* interviewed WikiLeaks co-founder Julian Assange and thereafter published cables pertaining to India in the main. 'Revealed: The India Cables from WikiLeaks', *The Hindu*, 15 March 2011.

8 'The Munde moment', editorial, *The Hindu*, 11 July 2013.

for one, was apprehensive of being accused of being partisan by the press or other political players. As a result, there was always a chasm between 'us the umpires' and 'them the players'. This had advantages of maintaining a distance but it also may be said that we seldom understood their side of the game. So great was the divide that it was almost difficult to gauge who was spending what amounts of money, or for that matter, what difficultics they might have faced on the other side of the fence. It was only after I had demitted office in 2010 that I began asking questions more freely. When I ran into a former MP from UP at a diplomatic reception in New Delhi, I asked him what the 'average spending' in that state had been during the campaign of GE 2009. 'Rs10–12 crore', came a hesitant reply, although he was quick to add that he himself had remained within the then prescribed limit.[9] The Centre for Media Studies (CMS), a respected think tank, estimated the total expenditure on GE 2014 in US dollar terms at three times that spent on GE 2009, placing a figure at US $5 billion.[10] This could well be true if I was to believe an MP, who had won from Andhra Pradesh, who openly boasted that he spent a colossal Rs 54 crore to win his seat. Nor, he apparently added, was he the highest spender. He named another MP from the same state who had reportedly spent Rs 72 crore. While these disclosures are impossible to prove, they do strike a mortal blow to public accountability and the realization of democratic rights. Surely, no one needs to spend these amounts if people really want them as their representatives.

---

9 The limit was raised to Rs 70 lakh in time for GE 2014, after the government accepted a proposal made by the Commission to raise the expenditure limit from Rs 40 to 70 lakh for Lok Sabha constituencies, on a sliding scale of Rs 22 to 54 lakh for smaller constituencies. Simultaneously, limits were also enhanced to between Rs 20 and Rs 28 lakh, depending on the size and population of the state, for assembly constituencies. Legislation was passed in time for GE 2014. The enhanced ceiling was still a fraction of real costs.

10 Centre for Media Studies, a Delhi-based think tank that has conducted extensive research on election spending. Its chairman is N. Bhaskara Rao.

Clearly such persons who have been elected through the use of big money must represent nobody but themselves, and doubtless convert their expenses into profits in myriad ways.

There have been other worrying tendencies in our hurtling towards oligarchic tendencies. The former founder of an airline[11] was, upon his election to the Rajya Sabha in 2002, appointed a member of the parliamentary committee attached to the Ministry of Civil Aviation. Upon my inquiring as to how such obvious conflict of interest could have been countenanced, I was told that several members of the House had signed a petition that he would bring valuable 'domain expertise' to the committee, precisely because he had established an airline. The airline became insolvent in due course and several cases of bank loan defaults were registered against him. He resigned from the Upper House in 2016, on the very day that parliament's Ethics Committee was prepared to recommend his expulsion.

Money power has grown into a most vexatious problem to resolve. Throughout my tenure in the Commission, it was frustrating to be taught lessons in human ingenuity in this respect. In spite of the presence of a small army—almost 2,500—of very senior officials whom we deployed as general and revenue observers (drawn from senior ranks of the Indian Administrative Service and the Indian Revenue Service, no less), in the course of GE 2009, candidates and parties managed to successfully distribute money and freebies under our very noses by the most dubious means. These were often concealed or transported in the most unthinkable places: in passenger luggage, within car doors, or even hidden under the chassis of public buses. During the course of the Karnataka assembly elections of 2008, a milk van was apprehended carrying liquor instead of milk, and an ambulance was being misused to ferry cash and freebies.[12] Such was

---

11 Now defunct, its promoter is now a fugitive against whom extradition proceeding are pending.

12 The recently conducted Karnataka assembly polls of 2018 have been termed by CMS as the 'most expensive ever' in terms of money spent by political parties and their candidates, placing it in the range of Rs 9,500

the extent of human inventiveness. When planes and helicopters, allegedly ferrying cash, made unscheduled landings on unauthorized helipads, we banned these until they had obtained proper coordinates so that we could then search them. We threatened pilots with the suspension of their licences. We made extensive use of flying squads and surveillance teams when we received any intelligence reports.

When monies were seized, they usually had no claimants. During GE 2009 campaign, over Rs 200 crore of cash and freebies, liquor and even drugs were seized by vigilant officials. Yet, in spite of all our strenuous efforts, far larger amounts of clandestine sums would doubtless have reached their destinations, as was more recently demonstrated in a bye-election in Chennai's R.K. Nagar constituency on 24 December 2017, which was necessitated by the vacancy caused by the death of J. Jayalalithaa. The corruption involved was evident in April 2017 when the Commission cancelled the bye-election because the stench of bribery was rampant. Despite the postponement and increased surveillance, the Commission failed to prevent a huge overspend, which some political commentators put at Rs 100 crore—and that for a bye-election once postponed for a limited constituency of Chennai. This was less a failure of the Commission and more a triumph for those forces that could devise, it was said, a technique that rewarded its voters *after* the election, upon the production of requisite proof.

~

Some analysts argue that the seeds of this malaise could inadvertently have been planted in the Constitution itself.[13] While borrowing heavily from the UK, our Constitution framers did not take into account the fact that while the average constituency in the UK was

crore to 10,500 crore, twice the 2019 expenditure estimates. According to this survey, this did not include the costs of the prime minister's campaign. See, CMS Website. Also, *Bangalore Mirror*, 15 May 2018.

13 'Where Did Indian Democracy Go Wrong?', Prem Shankar Jha, noted columnist and writer, in *Sunday Guardian*, 7 December 2012.

about 375 sq. km in size with about 50,000 voters, an average Indian constituency would have over twenty times that number, at over 1.3 million voters, spread over a much larger geographical area. An MP in a Ladakh constituency would need to cover 173,266 sq. km which could take several weeks. A single constituency in Arunachal Pradesh with an area of 40,572 sq. km would require many days of trekking to reach its far-flung outposts. To make matters more complex, each constituency, since 1971, has had to vote twice—once for parliament and once for the state assembly. Given the size and the number of voters involved, and earmarking a spend of even a few rupees per voter, the conclusion reached was that unrealistic ceiling limits had been placed from the start. During an election campaign, the average MP in India would need to depend on workers familiar with the terrain. They, in turn, would have to harness a small army of workers, most of whom would require to be paid, fed and possibly housed during the pre-election and campaign periods. Many MPs whom I have since met have complained bitterly about how unrealistic the Commission is about the real costs of a campaign.

I believe the Commission could have been significantly bolder in pressing for raising the ceiling for candidate expenditure. Prior to GE 2009, the Commission proposed to the government that the ceiling be raised from Rs 25 lakh to Rs 40 lakh. Again, just before GE 2014, the Commission had suggested another upward revision, from Rs 40 lakh to Rs 70 lakh. Herein lay a dilemma for the Commission. It was widely recognized both by the Commission and privately acknowledged everywhere across the political spectrum that actual spending dwarfed the proposed ceiling. Instead of asserting itself boldly and seizing the bull by its horns, the Commission adopted a more prudent approach, instead suggesting a ceiling on the basis of the indexation formula in line with earlier revisions. A more realistic approach might have been to confer with all the recognized political parties at both national and state levels and arrive at a figure by consensus that was closer to actual spending. This has remained a serious error of judgement, in turn necessitating the retention of an army of officials to keep a watch on candidate spending levels, all the while with the underlying apprehension that corners would be cut, surreptitious spending would continue undetected, and accounts undervalued.

Other worrying trends surfaced. Surveys conducted by the Centre for Media Studies (CMS) in 2008, 2009 and 2014 revealed that nearly one-fifth of the voters across the country were offered *and received money*.[14] In its cash-for-vote surveys, the CMS sample of voters was random, covering 75,000 voters between 2007 and 2014. In 2007, CMS sampled 23,000 below poverty line (BPL) voters. This survey revealed, to give a few instances, that 94 per cent of BPL voters accepted money in Andhra Pradesh, 78 per cent in Tamil Nadu and 73 per cent in Karnataka. In 2008, the sample size was smaller at 18,000, but this time included voters drawn from as many as nineteen states. This sample indicated that money was accepted by 47 per cent in Karnataka, 34 per cent in Tamil Nadu and 31 per cent in Andhra Pradesh. This sample indicated 25 per cent for Delhi.

CMS also sampled voter *expectation* levels just prior to GE 2014. By now, the note-for-vote syndrome had become much more settled. According to CMS, it was no longer a casual affair but had become a conscious decision. Of the states sampled, Karnataka 'polled' a high of 50 per cent. Maharastra followed at 43 per cent, Punjab at 25 per cent, MP at 25 per cent and Delhi at 14 per cent. Moreover, with each passing election, the assets of our MPs and MLAs continued to rise. The increase in the total assets of the members jumped from Rs 1,273.07 lakh in the fourteenth Lok Sabha (2004) to Rs 3,641.30 lakh in the fifteenth (2009). The Association of Democratic Reforms

14 CMS Transparency Study – Lure or Money in lieu of Voters in Lok Sabha and assembly elections. The Trend: 2007-2014. 'Note for Vote' is no longer a casual affair according to their study. Their surveys show that in the assembly elections of 2008, 53 per cent of the voters in Andhra Pradesh acknowledged that money was distributed. The figure for Delhi was 20 per cent. In 2009, 10 per cent acknowledged receiving money in Jharkhand. In 2013, 24 per cent accepted money in Punjab. In 2014, 22 per cent acknowledged this in Maharashtra.

(ADR) report[15] documented that in the 2004 general election, 13 per cent of all candidates were multi-millionaires. By 2009 the corresponding figure had jumped to 16 per cent and by 2014 to 27 per cent. The average wealth of candidates from the two principal national parties, the INC and the BJP, rose to Rs 16 crore. The single richest winner belonged to the Telugu Desam Party (TDP) with a declared wealth of Rs 683 crore. However, these figures need to be tempered by the fact that general prosperity has risen over the past two decades and with it, property prices—urban and rural. It needs to be clarified that a house bought two decades ago in any city for a few lakh rupees would have grown enormously to several crore, thus making the candidates a 'crorepati'. Such unintended increases in wealth needs to be declared candidly by supporting certificates from the relevant authorities.

Another disquieting situation has arisen in recent years from the mushrooming of political parties, most of which have never participated in an election. Under existing laws, the Commission has no option but to register those that comply with the basic criteria demanded. When I was the CEC, I had a list of over 1,300 so-called parties drawn up which revealed that two-thirds of them had never contested an election. The Commission wrote to the government seeking permission to deregister the non-serious ones. There was no response. The total number of registered parties continued to climb. Most of them remain politically dormant, but it is believed that they do accumulate large funds, possibly black in colour. Parliament has not yet given the Commission the power to deregister them.[16]

~

15 Association of Democratic Reforms (ADR)—a non-partisan, non-governmental organization—works on electoral and political reforms. National Election Watch (NEW) is an umbrella organization of NGOs and other organizations seeking to bring transparency and accountability in Indian electoral scene.

16 See Chapter 10: 'Electoral Reforms'.

I might summarize electoral financial transgression into two broad categories. The first lies in the violation of statutory limits governing candidate expenditure. This is almost invariably breached, although candidates are careful to reflect figures that are well within the prescribed limits. The second lies in the opacity of funds collected by political parties. Interestingly, studies drawn from the affidavits that must be submitted by candidates on their wealth and criminal antecedents are constantly analysed by election watchdogs. They reveal that political parties have a marked preference to choose candidates who are wealthy enough to finance their own election and thereby not strain party funds. Several studies also reveal that richer candidates are much more likely to win than their more modest counterparts. More worryingly, candidates with criminal antecedents are even likelier to win if they combine money power with muscle power. Some studies even suggest that the more heinous the crime, the greater the chances of success.

The Commission can hardly be accused of laxity when it comes to trying to bring about transparency in the realm of political finance. In fact, it has been nothing if not persistent. A number of reform proposals had been sent to the government since 1996. In 2004, pending and new proposals were compiled into a comprehensive list of twenty-two reform proposals (seven pending and fifteen new proposals). Amongst them, the Commission recommended compulsory maintenance of accounts by political parties and regular audits by companies duly approved by the Comptroller and Auditor General of India.

The Commission also pressed on with efforts to reduce illicit expenditure. In 2010, a special expenditure monitoring division was established under P.K. Dash, a senior official drawn from the Indian Revenue Service. Under his aegis, a number of proposals were sent to the government. Many of these required laws to be enacted, which has yet to happen. As recently as 19 May 2016, the Commission held a consultation with thirty-five recognized political parties and proposed that candidates disclose the sources of the money they had declared in their affidavits, as well as the sources of income for acquiring properties, which found mention in their declared assets. But this was shot down. More than one attempt has been made to tally the assets of the candidate as declared to the Election Commission with those declared in their income tax filings. We had written to the Central Board of Direct Taxes (CBDT) in my time in 2007 and sought the views of the revenue secretary, but no noticeable headway was achieved. However, it was a beginning. In November 2017, the Commission addressed the CBDT again and pursued it in April 2018. However, the Right to Information (RTI) Act and Section 138 of the Income Tax Act place restrictions on disclosures of personal income tax, and these remain stumbling blocks at reconciliation between two possibly varying declarations of accounts.[17]

Muscle Power

If a fault line that has developed over the past three decades is even more worrying than the blatant misuse of money power, it is that a large and growing number of parliamentarians (as well as legislators in state assemblies) have criminal antecedents. Both the fifteenth as well as the present Lok Sabha have approximately 30 per cent (one in every three) of their members with one or multiple cases registered against them. Some of these are for heinous offences such as murder, attempt to murder, extortion, rape, dacoity and kidnapping. This is an astonishingly huge percentage. What is disquieting is the acceptance of this situation by even those parliamentarians who hold completely unblemished records. Our intelligentsia too has come to accept this in resigned silence. Sadly, so have 'we the people'.[18]

---

17 'EC writes to CBDT, seeks uniform format to report asset discrepancy of candidate', *The Indian Express*, New Delhi, 12 July 2018.

18 A recent ADR report with reference to the Karnataka assembly elections in May 2018 reveals that of the 222 newly elected legislators, 71, (or 35 per cent) have criminal cases registered against them, up from 34 per cent in 2013 and 24 per cent in 2008. The richest legislator declared a wealth of Rs 1,015 crore.

The Commission has proposed several times to the government of the day that if charges are framed by a court of law for offences for which the punishment would be five years or more, such an MP/legislator must step down, or not be allowed to contest.[19] The Commission believes that this would be a reasonable restriction. However, this has not yet been accepted by parliament.

This growing phenomenon has had its own chequered past. Broadly speaking, in the late 1970s and early 1980s, many contestants began to rely on musclemen and local mafias to 'persuade' people into attending their public meetings and ensuring that the crowds they mustered would vote for them. Intimidation and threats became the norm. In many parts of the country, particularly north India, they simply stormed into remote polling stations, threatened the staff with dire consequences, 'captured' the ballot boxes, stuffed them with votes for their nominee and sealed the boxes again. Hapless local officials and policemen on duty were often too terrified to report these occurrences. Local armies such as Ranvir Sena—an upper-caste landlord militia, which had originated in Bihar with the aim of wiping out Dalit organizations and Maoist groups—served the needs of the wealthy landowners and politicians and became one of the groups that spread terror during the elections, suppressing the Dalit voters in particular. As the Commission began to assert particularly after T.N. Seshan (CEC from 12 December 1990 to 11 December 1996) declared war on electoral malpractice with the deployment of Central police forces (as opposed to the local police, viewed by many as compromised), the role of overt muscle power gave way to its more covert uses: outright booth capturing and violence was replaced by less explicit forms of voter intimidation and crowd gathering.

Meanwhile, these 'mafias' had their own expectations: that the politicians whom they helped to win would in turn help them 'settle' their criminal cases or enable them to carry on with their criminal activities unhindered. In due course, these local warlords came

---

19 'Poll chief seeks bar on those jailed for 5 years. Keep our politicians indicted by inquiries too: Chawla', *Hindustan Times*, 27 June 2009.

to realize that helping others to win was not the solution to their problems. From the 1980s on, they now began to offer themselves as candidates. Astonishing as it may seem, many were welcomed into the political fold because they demonstrated to the party bosses that they enjoyed the halo of 'winnability'. They still had mafias under their control, and had grown to dominate strongholds much like the 'rajas' and 'zamindars' of the past.

Some of these 'warlords' were even treated with a degree of veneration, for they demonstrated that they could dispense a rough-and-ready, Robin Hood–style justice, saving those who sought their help the cost of prolonged and expensive litigation. The case of Phoolan Devi is a well-known one of a bandit who joined politics and was elected to parliament (1996–2001) from UP.[20] The badlands of UP and Bihar were then replete with local fables such as hers. Stories of their tyranny also created fear. Another don had only to have his flags strung up in 'his villages' which marked out his territory. Perhaps the most chilling case that was reported in sections of the press was that of a powerful political figure whose word no one dared to cross. Whether stories of his detractors being thrown into a lake full of crocodiles in his palace grounds were exaggerated or not, such legends helped him maintain both an aura of fear and a degree of public acceptance against the backdrop of what was seen as an often unfair and compromised criminal justice system.

Power and criminality now began to feed upon each other, with the result that criminality within political ranks, instead of lessening for fear of being named and shamed, actually increased. Their demonstrated capacity to win elections made them increasingly more acceptable as candidates. While the Commission has been successful in outlawing many of these blatant excesses, it is still worrying that some NGOs, such as Association of Democratic Reforms (ADR) and Election Watch, who have analysed these trends, have shown that when muscle power is combined with money power, the chances of winning increase dramatically. Their analysis has revealed that candidates with criminal cases had a 23 per cent chance of winning,

20 The film *Bandit Queen* was made on her life.

as compared to a 12 per cent chance for a 'clean' candidate. This is also depressingly brought out by Milan Vaishnav of the Carnegie Endowment for International Peace who has highlighted in earlier studies and in a recent book the appeal of rogue candidates who bring in both illicit funds as well as a loyal brigade of supporters. For the parties concerned, the additional advantage is that they are self-financing candidates. In line with the ADR's conclusion, Vaishnav holds in his study that those candidates who face charges of committing heinous crimes such as murder actually improve their chances of victory by margins as huge as 25 per cent.[21] What a sad commentary for any parliamentary democracy!

When I was the chief election commissioner, I ran into the leader of a major political party at an airport lounge. I buttonholed him, asking why his political party chose criminal candidates. I pointed to the high figures nominated by his party for assembly elections. I named a legislator with several criminal cases pending of which at least ten were for the most heinous offences. Another had over twenty cases, again mainly for heinous offences. I asked him too whether there is any solution to this growing problem. He replied frankly, 'When elections are on the horizon, our only mantra is "winnability".' He added less convincingly, 'If there is no election on the horizon, I will attend any meeting on this issue convened by you and sign on the dotted line.' When I put the same question to other leaders, they expressed similar views.

What I continue to find surprising is that even those political leaders who have publicly spoken against giving party tickets to those with criminal backgrounds are, nonetheless, strangely silent in the face of this growing malaise. After all, what can be stranger than the fact that 30 per cent of our lawmakers are lawbreakers? 'Winnability', in the final analysis, is what matters.

But why would voters wish to vote for 'criminals' instead of 'clean' candidates? Could it be that voters are not aware of their

21 Milan Vaishnav, *When Crime Pays: Money and Muscle in Indian Politics*, New Haven: Yale University Press, 2017.

criminal antecedents? It would perhaps be that the findings of NGOs such as ADR and NEW are confined to urban pockets and are not disseminated to the vast rural areas or small town. The more likely explanation is that the widespread mistrust of 'the system' which fails to deliver justice in time leads many voters to trust a criminal who can deliver 'justice'. There could be a variety of other reasons to vote for criminal candidates: party affiliation, ties of caste, religion, region or ethnicity. Many perceive that the institutions of state have broken down (or are outside their reach), when it comes to the settlement of their problems relating to land, water, power and even social structure. What else might help explain the fact that criminals have been known to win elections even from jail? Witness what happened in September 2016 (widely reported in the national and local press), when the four-time MP from Siwan in Bihar was released on bail: thousands of his followers crowded into over 300 buses and expensive vehicles to form a triumphant procession as he proceeded to his home after a long term in jail. He had been convicted in an assortment of heinous cases, including that of murder. This former MP was one of the many accused of serious crimes, who became a lawmaker and enjoyed Z-plus security cover provided by the state. A reader has simply to go to the Internet to read chapter and verse on India's criminal legislators who in some form or the other preside over our destinies.

The Commission has time and again written to the government of the day to halt this disturbing trend. In 2006, the government's response was to set up a standing committee of parliament to examine the Commission's suggestions. In its report dated 27 February 2007, the committee concluded that debarment of those charged with heinous offences, instead of being a panacea, could become an instrument of tyranny at the hands of the political parties in power, seeking vendetta against their rivals. The committee unanimously turned down the Commission's proposal and instead offered the appointment of special courts and day-to-day trials. Given the situation of clogged courts and a vastly understaffed judiciary, the conclusion was inescapable. Till date, no special courts have been set up though notification have been issued for setting up twelve such courts. Privately, discerning parliamentarians accept that the 'winnability factor' continues to prevail.

From my meetings throughout the country, I have to add that the figure of criminality in politics is probably higher than 30 per cent. During the course of my many informal, off-the-record conversations with district and police officials, politicians and other functionaries, I found that criminal elements were known to use their considerable clout with local officials to ensure that cases were simply not registered, even after complaints were filed against them. At the cutting edge, cases would either be 'hushed up', or 'compromised' or simply brushed away in favour of the local muscleman politician. It is not possible to put a figure to these occurrences but were a serious study to be conducted, I would not be surprised if the total figures of such suppression would raise the bar higher.

However, there is one caveat that should be further examined. While the political establishment often cites possible misuse as the principal reason against any exclusionary move, not all cases filed against politicians represent heinous crimes. Medha Patkar could well typify that social rights activist whom many ardently admire, while others love to hate. It must be admitted that the host of cases filed against her are not on account of criminality of any kind at all, but for being arrested on purely civil rights issues. Similarly, there are others who have had cases filed against them for having participated in democratic protest. One, therefore, needs to differentiate between a crusade against criminals in politics (with the aim to deny entry to candidates with criminal charges) and political activists like Patkar who have often risked life and limb for social causes.[22]

The abhorrence of criminality in politics is a common thread running through educated civil society and youth. Practically every university audience I have addressed in India in the last decade

---

22 Christophe Jaffrelot and Gilles Vernier, 'Lawmakers and law–breakers: Why crime data on legislators and electoral candidates must be carefully unpacked', *The Indian Express*, 2 July 2014. In this article the authors call for caution in the manner data is handled. It is necessary to supplement the counting of cases in numbers with qualitative inputs.

have demanded that the Commission should do more to eliminate criminality from the body politic. Students are all too aware of this growing trend from the figures compiled by NEW and ADR from the affidavits by candidates, which are compulsorily submitted to the Election Commission by contestants. In two separate orders passed in 2002 and 2003, the Supreme Court has made it mandatory for all candidates to file information regarding any and all criminal cases pending against them. In addition, declarations of their wealth and their educational qualifications were also mandated. With this information, the court hoped that voters could make informed choices.

In my private interactions with a number of constitutional authorities and opinion makers, it is clear that this alarming trend has worried them enormously. As citizens, judges too are as deeply disturbed. When on the bench, they have almost invariably supported the Commission in its quest for electoral reforms, and more particularly to debar criminals from contestation. However, the judges privately lament they can step in only when matters are ripe to be heard by them. Nonetheless, the apex court has done so emphatically in several important cases recently. Apart from the important 'disclosure orders' of 2002 and 2003, the court has in the last few years passed other significant orders. These relate to the distribution of 'freebies', the installation of 'NOTA' (None of the Above) button in the EVMs and by another significant order of 10 July 2013 (*Lily Thomas vs Union of India*) where they consciously ended the unfair privilege hitherto accorded to MPs/MLAs, which had enabled them to retain their memberships even upon an order of conviction by simply filing an appeal within three months. It was this decision that sent Lalu Prasad Yadav to jail and debarred him from contesting an election for eleven years.[23]

23 Section 8(4) of the RoPA, 1951, provides relief from immediate disqualification if an appeal was filed within three months after date of conviction. The Supreme Court vide WP No. 490 of 2005 *Lily Thomas vs the Union of India and Others* declared RoPA Section 8(4) to be

In spite of these hard-hitting pronouncements of the apex court, the despair felt by the Election Commission was reflected by no less a person than the former chairman of the Law Commission, Justice A.P. Shah, a retired chief justice of the Delhi High Court. In his report to the government (and his public utterances thereafter), he made his disappointment manifest that the entry of criminals into politics has subverted the judicial process. He echoed the Commission's recommendations that persons against whom criminal charges have been framed and which are punishable by more than five years of imprisonment, should be disqualified during the pendency of trial. To buttress his argument, he also pointed to their abysmally low conviction rate of 0.5 per cent. In an interview to *The Times of India* on 19 April 2014, he was quoted as saying, 'The right to be elected is not a fundamental right, so how can one claim that it is against criminal jurisprudence? What we have recommended is disqualification for only six years and that too if charges have been framed by a court one year before elections. That way if the trial is not complete, by next elections the candidate will be free to file his nominations and contest elections.' These recent recommendations, as indeed those made earlier by the Commission, have so far been met with deafening silence from the government and political parties.

In a recent judgment, the Supreme Court has put the onus of enacting appropriate legislation debarring politicians with criminal charges from contesting elections for parliament. The Court in its order dated 25 September 2018 declined to intervene on a petition that had sought to bar lawmakers facing criminal charges from contesting elections.[24] However, the Bench said that citizens have a

---

unconstitutional. See 'Lalu Prasad faces 11-year electoral exile after fodder scam ruling', Live Mint, 3 October 2013.

24 Five-Judge Constitution Bench, headed by the then Chief Justice Dipak Misra, consisted of R.F. Nariman, A.M. Khanwilkar, D.Y. Chandrachud and Indu Malhotra. SC Writ Petition (Civil) No. 536 of 2011, *Public Interest Foundation and Ors vs Union of India and Another* with criminal appeal Nos. 1714–1715 of 2007, Writ Petition

right to be informed about the criminal antecedents of candidates, and ordered that political parties and candidates must release their criminal records, if any, on at least three occasions before the elections, both in newspapers and TV channels after the filing of nomination papers. During the hearing, the Union government had in its affidavit of March 2018 admitted that a total of 1,765 MPs and MLAs—representing a little over one-third of all elected representatives—faced criminal charges. It was only last year that the apex court asked the government to set up twelve special courts across eleven states and Delhi to deal with cases against MPs and MLAs.

This verdict was the result of a PIL filed in 2011 by the Public Interest Foundation, an NGO which had sought the disqualification of candidates who have been charge-sheeted for heinous offences attracting a sentence of five years and more. The Commission in its affidavit to the court had endorsed the suggestion made in the PIL and sent a similar proposal to the Ministry of Law and Justice.

Soon after the apex court's verdict, on 1 October 2018, I wrote an opinion piece in the *Indian Express*[25] an excerpt of which was quoted by Jagdeep S. Chhokar[26] in the Wire as follows: 'The Supreme Court's recent decision was disappointing in that it stopped short of disqualifying candidates who have alleged criminal antecedents from contesting polls, although I do understand that the Court was reluctant to step into the executive's arena. The Supreme Court left it to parliament to frame suitable laws to decriminalize our body

(Criminal) No. 208 of 2011 and Writ Petition (Civil) No. 800 of 2015, 25 September 2018.

25 'The House not in order', *The Indian Express*, New Delhi, 1 October 2018.

26 Jagdeep S. Chhokar, 'The Supreme Court Seems to Be Vacillating Between Being Progressive and Regressive', The Wire, 13 October 2018. Choker, a former professor at IIM Ahmedabad, is one of the founding members of the Association for Democratic Reforms (ADR).

politic to "cure the malignancy" from within ... Unfortunately, this is something that our parliamentarians have assiduously refused to do for the last two decades, ever since the Election Commission first approached the government to enact a suitable law in 1997.'

Emerging Trends

For three years in a row, from 2011 to 2014, I attended a series of thought-provoking seminars conducted by the Election Commission of Mexico (Instituto Nacional Electoral, INE) on the distortions emerging within Latin American democracies. The participants were drawn from many disciplines—politics, journalism, universities and a host of NGOs. They also included former presidents and statesmen. Many of their countries had emerged into freedom after decades of military rule or other forms of dictatorship. Several speakers chronicled the wide disparities that continue to grow even in countries that have a per capita income in the region of US $15,000 (approximately ten times that of our own). They spoke of the neglected sections of their societies: women whose votes continue to be cast by their men folk, the involvement of organized drug cartels in financing elections, of crime-ridden and overcrowded 'barrios', where poverty and low social status define their inhabitants and of the indigenous peoples in their countries, whose voices are seldom heard. The underlying theme was that true democracy could exist only where individual freedoms were assured: freedom from hunger, unemployment, the lack of shelter and importantly freedom from fear. Yet although their economies were doing well, the questions they repeatedly asked were whether their marginalized communities were being truly represented by those who had won their seats to parliament or state legislatures. How could they, asked some, when their elections were financed often by the power of big money, sometimes assisted by crime and drug cartels and at other times supported by the grace and favour of a clutch of industrialists and media barons.

These reflections echoed my own. How far do those whom we elect truly represent the 300 million of our people who do not have access to clean drinking water or more than 700 million who have no access to any form of social security whatsoever? Our daily newspapers are full of stories where the poor are subjected to untold misery. A very sad case that took place in August 2016, which will haunt India for a long time was that of Dana Majhi of Kalahandi, Odisha, who carried the body of his dead wife on his shoulder for 10 km, with his twelve-year-old daughter weeping by his side. He had been refused a vehicle to take his wife to cremation ground in his village. Or the horrific case that went viral of four Dalit youth being flogged in Una, Gujarat, for skinning a dead cow. In these and other such cases, we seldom read of the local MP, MLA, corporator or sarpanch providing any help.

Clearly, by now the negative influence of money and muscle power has become a serious threat to the foundations of our democracy. It is very difficult, if not impossible, for those without access to large funds, to contest let alone hope to win elections. To make matters worse, illicit finance is seeping through organized crime. Since their interests take priority, relationships of accountability have also become distorted.

~

Solutions can still be found but these require political will. A plethora of recommendations on electoral reforms, emanating from several commissions and committees, gather dust. As early as 1972 the Joint Parliamentary Committee on Amendments to Election Laws suggested that the burden of legitimate election expenses borne by candidates or the political parties be shifted to the state. In 1974, the Tarkunde Committee appointed by Jayaprakash Narayan on behalf of the Citizens for Democracy made important recommendations regarding the role of media during elections. The Goswami Committee on Electoral Reforms (1990) suggested checks on surrogate advertising. The Indrajit Gupta Committee on State Funding of Elections (1998) advocated state funding in kind with many detailed recommendations regarding transparency in party expenditure. The Law Commission in its 170th Report on Reform of the Electoral Laws (1999) backed state funding. The National Commission to Review the Working of the Constitution (2001) and the Second Administrative Reforms Commission (2008) offered an array of detailed recommendations. The Law Commission in its subsequent 244th Report (February 2014) and its 255th report (March 2015) made a further slew of recommendations for electoral reforms.

On 7 June 2004, President A.P.J. Abdul Kalam in his address to the joint session of parliament announced that the government would consider state funding as part of broader election reforms. I have already commented on the February 2014 report by the chairman of the Law Commission headed by Justice A.P. Shah. Meanwhile, the Commission, undeterred by the tepid response of various governments to these recommendations, has continued to press for the implementation of these and other proposals, especially in the face of new challenges, as in the case of 'paid news'. Many of its proposals including measures recommending transparency in fund collection and spending, and empowering the Commission to act in cases of electoral bribery by making such cases cognizable offences, have so far been met with silence.

I sensed over my years in the Commission that the political establishment often viewed the Commission in something of an adversarial role. Each commissioner has necessarily to be appointed by the government of the day and that government cherishes the hope that the appointee will be 'our man'. But India looks up to the Commission as an impartial and unbiased body, and that defines the conduct of its officials. It is well known that Prime Minister A.B. Vajpayee was not keen on elevating T.S. Krishnamurthy as chief election commissioner in 2014 and sought to bring in T.R. Prasad, former cabinet secretary (from 2000 to 2002) directly to the post. While there would have been no illegality in this move, a tradition had by now been set for the senior of the two commissioners to be appointed the CEC. It was only when T.S. Krishnamurthy and the third commissioner, B.B. Tandon, threatened to resign that the government did backtrack.

There is little doubt that the needs felt by the existing, entrenched, privileged classes are self-perpetuating. The political segment is driven to accumulate funds, in part to pay for the next election or to help them tide over a period of uncertainty, were they to lose their election or not be nominated by their party. Governments in power are also involved in collecting funds for their party concerned. The result is that for both political parties and candidates, finance has become the predominant challenge facing our democracy. Public funding of elections is a solution that has been suggested by the reports of several committees. But as Pratap Bhanu Mehta writes: '... public funding presumes that political parties are transparent, well run and considerably democratic in their internal workings.'[27]

Some of the reports referred to above have offered public funding as the solution to money power. Public finance can take many forms. It can be direct or indirect. In a scenario where it is direct, the political parties that have seriously contested elections can be paid in relation to the number of votes they may have garnered in the last election. A form of indirect funding can be provided by the Election Commission ensuring that each political party is assured of a proportion of air time according to an agreed formula, even on privately owned television channels, as is the norm in Mexico.

One of the main causes of expenditure lies in publicity sought by the political parties and individual candidates. While I was in the Commission, we offered some relief to political parties when we implemented restrictions on the defacement of public property and on the number of flags, posters and buntings that could be displayed on buildings. Ending the defacement of walls also brought palpable relief to most people who did not relish their city and town walls daubed with political graffiti. Nor were public buildings permitted to display party flags, advertisements or slogans. Wherever this

27 Pratap Bhanu Mehta, 'Debating Election Finance', *The Hindu*, 17 July 2012.

occurred, the municipalities or candidates were made responsible for cleaning the walls at their cost. A blanket ban was placed on residential dwellings being defaced because we found that in many cases owners were afraid to complain when party workers would daub the walls of their houses with slogans. If householders wished to display party flags, these were permitted but with restrictions. Posters were banned from being splashed on public property including electricity and telephone poles. Some political parties did complain that our orders were too strict, but others privately appreciated them, because it saved both party and candidate enormous expenditure. Nor were these steps unusual. In many countries defacing of public or private property is not permitted. In some countries, electricity poles on earmarked roads may display uniform sized posters on payment of rent. No massive pictures, cut-outs and arches or other publicity extravaganza of the kind we often see in India are permitted in most countries.

Indeed, it is a moot point whether such media blitzkriegs are even effective. In some southern states, we have seen the vast competitive overspend on massive cutouts and arches, sometimes as tall as 60 feet (18 metres) erected on the roads of the main cities and towns. Yet in Tamil Nadu, voters have tended to return one of the two major Dravidian protagonists—the AIADMK and the DMK—so comprehensively that I wonder whether the millions spent on publicity gives the winner much advantage. Clearly, other more emotive issues drive the voter's preferences.

The need for reform also came up on the occasion of the diamond jubilee celebration of the Election Commission on 25 January 2010. It was noteworthy that among the galaxy of India's leadership that was present in New Delhi's Vigyan Bhawan were the three foremost constitutional authorities—President Pratibha Patil, Vice-President Hamid Ansari and Prime Minister Manmohan Singh. Vice President Ansari, in his thoughtful speech also called for introspection. 'Six decades [of the Commission] on, a fair verdict would be that the glass is neither empty nor full but well above the halfway mark. We have established and sustained procedural democracy. And yet, Dr Ambedkar's forebodings about the contradiction between political equality and social and economic inequality remains valid. The realization of "one person one vote and one vote one value" continues to be elusive.'[28]

He took the bull by the horns by adding that despite stringent efforts, unaccounted election expenses constitute the major expenditure of political parties and candidates. These related to the distribution of freebies, liquor and cash during elections, the phenomenon of surrogate advertisements and the extensive media-related malpractice of 'paid news' and 'coverage packages'. 'Each of these is a blot on the democratic process and on the objective of free and fair elections. Corrective action by the Commission and political parties is imperative.' On the enforcement by the Commission of procedural, inner-party democracy in political parties, Ansari added that the challenge for the parties now was to bring about substantive organizational democracy.[29]

Yet, over the passage of time, there have been quiet but significant changes in the rules of the game. I refer to three unrelated strands. The first strand I refer to is that in the face of increasing repugnance of political parties, civil protests erupted across the country in 2011. These were led by Anna Hazare, viewed by many as Jayaprakash Narayan's moral successor. An unexpected result was the emergence of the Aam Aadmi Party, a non-party experiment which entered the political arena in 2013, coalesced into a political formation which swept the assembly elections in Delhi in 2015, capturing an unprecedented sixty-seven out of seventy seats, without use of muscle power or significant sums of money.[30] The AAP today has its share of critics. However, for purposes of my argument, this is

---

28 'Address of the honourable Vice President of India, Shri M. Hamid Ansari at the Diamond Jubilee Celebrations of the Election Commission of India', 25 January 2010, eci.nic.in

29 Ibid.

30 'When the nice guys didn't finish last' by the author. See *The Hindu*, 9 January 2014.

beside the point. Its unexpected success at the hustings challenged the way politicians and parties did business. It also exposed the established norms of campaigning. This could be viewed in terms of a larger experimentation. It demonstrated that even in the heart of arguably India's wealthiest city, large funds were not needed to win an election. Money was collected more transparently than before and people-to-people contact was revived through neighbourhood meetings which replaced the need for large and more expensive public ones. They also complied very substantially with the rules laid down by the Commission.[31]

The second strand was quite different but no less significant. It lay in the propulsion of Mayawati and her Bahujan Samaj Party, which succeeded in bringing together the hitherto largely marginalized Scheduled Castes and its Dalit formations, into a formidable political instrument and a challenge to the existing polity. The creation of statues of Ambedkar, Kanshi Ram and of massive elephants (as well as the adornment of her person with expensive jewellery that appear to many as distasteful) could instead be viewed as symbols of empowerment—an announcement to the depressed classes that 'our time has come'. Within the space of two decades, the Dalit presence has been registered on the political landscape and increasingly in public discourse. The public disgust at the flogging of Dalit youth in Una, Gujarat, is a case in point. The Election Commission too became an active if unwitting participant in this ongoing empowerment of the 'invisible voters', through its policy of 'vulnerability mapping'. These invisible voters turned out to be mainly Dalits. This enfranchisement of the 'hidden voter' was to provide a distinct advantage to the BSP from the 2007 UP assembly election onwards, where the Commission proved to be a distinct force for empowerment.

My third strand takes me to the theory mooted by Bruce Ackerman, noted Yale law professor. He writes that separation of

31 Vasundhara Sirnate and Rahul Verma, 'Changing the Rules of the Game', *The Hindu*, 22 January 2014. Sirnate was a scholar at the prestigious Hindu Centre for Politics and Public Policy, Chennai.

powers in India has gone beyond the Montesquieu model to a *new* separation of powers as an antidote to the decline of virtues in our public life.[32] Rejecting both the Westminster and American models, he has proffered the model of '... constrained parliamentarianism as the most promising framework for future development of the separation of powers' where power is no longer divided between the three branches of government (the legislature, the executive and the judiciary), but are, in fact, dispersed between a number of other constitutional and administrative functionaries as well. Jeet H. Shroff developed Ackerman's thesis further when he wrote, 'For decades the Supreme Court has successfully crusaded against the growing clout and abuse of political power. ... From requiring asset disclosures by politicians, to automatically disqualifying convicted legislators and preventing them from contesting elections and now requiring political actors to record in writing their bureaucratic abuses of power, the Supreme Court justifiably lays claim to a large part of the glory in the increased political accountability we now witness.'[33] He also refers to the Election Commission's cutting to size two prime ministerial candidates in the course of the 2014 elections as one of the several instances when the 'new power brokers' have asserted themselves. He sees the recent actions of the Election Commission, therefore, as a part of this growing willingness in the 'new separation of powers' to do their constitutional duty by exposing political vice, as a 'potentially powerful realignment in our constitutional system, which pits all of these non-political constitutional actors against the political establishment'. 'Marshalled and protected' by the Supreme Court so far, the emergence of our other constitutional institutions may prove to be the most effective antidote yet to the steady decline of virtues in our public life.

---

32 'The New Separation of Powers', *Harvard Law Review*, Vol. 113, January 2000.

33 Jeet H. Shroff, 'Constitutional Limits of Political Virtue', *The Statesman*, 1 January 2014.

I would end this chapter as I began it, with some excerpts from Kofi Annan's thoughtful address at the National Electoral Institute of Mexico (INE) on 23 May 2018, on the eve of Mexico's largest single democratic election process on 1 July 2018. In his address titled 'Is Democracy under siege', he made an impassioned plea for supporting democracy and elections with integrity.

> As you know, dozens of politicians, electoral candidates, as well as the family members of political actors have been targeted and killed since the start of this [Mexico's] campaign. Unchecked, criminal violence can pose a serious threat to democratic institutions and indeed to democracy itself. Good elections are the best answer to the violence that aims to deprive the citizens of their right to choose their leaders—national and local—free of intimidation. Elections provide a moment for citizens to come together to debate and decide who will lead them, and for what purpose, and to renew their commitment to the democratic ideal. ... I remain a committed believer in the value of democracy as a catalyst for better governance, greater security and human development. The spread of democracy has been one of the most profound and positive developments that I have witnessed over my career. People around the world aspire to greater freedom and demand a greater say in politics. The transformative impact of democratic governance is evident even though it cannot always be measured during one electoral cycle. But the price of democracy and democratic governance is constant vigilance. ... Growing numbers of citizens in both mature and fledgling democracies either take democracy for granted, or doubt its merits. There is a perception that democracy is not delivering, reflected in lower levels of voter participation, falling membership of political parties and declining trust in politicians and institutions, all of which creates fertile ground for the rise of authoritarian leaders.[34]

34 'Is Democracy under siege?', Keynote address by Kofi Annan. Kofi Annan Foundation, 23 May 2018.

5

Paid News

I first heard of newspapers demanding money in exchange for favourable coverage during the elections to the UP assembly in 2007. At a meeting of the Election Commission with political parties in Agra, a candidate revealed that he had been approached by a journalist from a widely read vernacular newspaper who demanded money to write in his favour. He explained that this was distinct from buying advertisement space; since it would be carried as reportage, it would have more credibility. A large sum was demanded 'under the table'. We asked the candidate to give me a written complaint but he said that he was apprehensive that he would then be victimized by that paper.

A year later, when I was conducting a meeting in Gwalior of political parties during the 2008 Madhya Pradesh assembly elections, a candidate dressed in a crumpled kurta-pyjama walked into the room. His companion was carrying a large bundle of copies of a local newspaper. He placed these on the table and said, 'I am a candidate fighting the elections, yet you will not find my name anywhere. This newspaper demanded Rs 5 lakh from me to carry "positive" news reports about me. They said that this was a concessional amount because I belonged to a "poor" political party. I replied that I had no money to pay bribes. I have since been completely blanked out. See for yourself.'

I had, in the past, heard that sections of the press promoted celebrities, film stars, newly released films and new share issues offered by companies. But these stories were largely confined to Mumbai, India's film and commercial capital. Now the stench of corruption was much closer, for it had entered the very vitals of our election scene. What was previously condoned as corruption indulged in by fringe elements or the odd journalist who had become wayward had now become mainstream. In the Commission, we coined a name for this—paid news. With this began our campaign to devise measures to tackle a problem that threatened the very foundations of the world's largest democracy.

The Indian media comprises 70,000 registered newspapers, more than 1,000 television channels and more than 300 radio stations. The driving force behind the publication of paid news is obviously the fierce competition in the media, sharpened particularly during the past decade or so. With the entry of new players in the segment and the revenue pie having shrunk, media houses began to re-examine their business models. Several 'honourable' newspapers now chose to throw journalistic ethics to the winds and positioned themselves in the forefront of what they justified to be a legitimate commercial exercise.

They argued that since their profits were derived largely from advertising (the sale proceeds of newspapers amounted to less than 10 per cent of total income), paid news was a legitimate commercial activity. In so far as electoral coverage was concerned, the print media, in particular, began to publish the views of selected candidates or parties, not as advertisements but in news columns and even in editorials. In the process they were not at all concerned that they seriously confused innocent readers, who believed the items carried in newspapers to be the gospel truth. Do we all not say at one time or another, 'I read it in the paper'? Clearly the trust placed in our newspapers is now in peril.

As the exception began to become the rule, the Commission decided that however difficult the problem, this was a challenge that needed to be met headlong. We convened several internal meetings, calling in our CEOs from the states to obtain their feedback and listen to their suggestions. We took legal opinion. Our officers started to convene meetings with political parties and NGOs to assess what was going on behind closed walls. We soon realized that while this malaise was spreading, practically no one, not even the 'victims' who had been blanked out, derided or ignored were willing to complain formally. We found it surprising that even those politicians who were at the receiving end of 'negative publicity' chose not to raise the issue when they visited the Commission. They usually raised complaints about violations of the model code of conduct or other matters that concerned their parties or themselves. Gradually we stumbled on yet another disturbing trend—that of the paid news 'package'. What this meant was that some sections of the print and electronic media were offering a double deal that incorporated 'positive publicity' for the candidate who paid up while simultaneously ensuring 'negative' or no reportage for his or her principal opponent: it was the well-known marketing technique of 'pay for one, get the second free'.

From 2008 onwards, we began in right earnest to devise measures to fight this hydra-headed monster as another form of illicit expenditure that individual candidates were failing to declare in their expenditure reports to the Commission. On 8 June 2010, we issued detailed guidelines to our CEOs with measures to check paid news. Officials were dedicated to study the print media and analyse TV reportage. This was no easy task. Even the more suspicious reportage—for instance, stories that were wholly adulatory—were hard to establish, let alone conclusively prove. Black money, paid in exchange for favourable coverage was even more difficult to track, although we had enlisted the help of specialized agencies of the government to assist us.

Our officers already had their hands full with their day-to-day tasks of keeping the electoral machine ticking. That was a major reason to set up the Expenditure Monitoring Division, whose mandate was also to concentrate on fiduciary violations including this new and growing problem. Paranjoy Guha Thakurta wrote in

Firstpost as follows: 'It seems that the EC [Election Commission] is the only body in the country that is seriously trying to combat the pernicious practice of "paid news" ... advertisement masquerading as news.' He went on to say that '... much of mass media dominated by corporate conglomerates ... [are] primarily interested in maximization of profits ... the independence of the media and its ability to play an adversarial role against the establishment gets compromised.'[1]

Before the start of GE 2009, I decided to call on the chairman of the Press Council of India (PCI), the former Supreme Court judge G.N. Ray.[2] He received me at his house and I was with him for almost two hours. I urged that the Press Council of India, the body that regulates India's media, must take cognizance of this terrible phenomenon. He was already of this disposition and we discussed how the PCI and the Commission might work in tandem. I would like to believe that my visit strengthened the commonality of our views. He set up a subcommittee of the Press Council and appointed noted journalists Paranjoy Guha Thakurta and K. Sreenivasa Reddy to investigate and submit a report. Their findings were to be released on 26 April 2010 but internal schisms held those up until 30 July. Finally, what was released was a much watered-down version. What was ever more disturbing was that it was released not as a report but as a 'reference document'.

The reasons were not hard to find. The report had named some of the biggest media groups in the country, some of whom were themselves members of the Press Council. This resulted in 'heated discussions' within the Council; not unsurprisingly, there was 'lack of consensus' over the naming of names. The report made several valuable recommendations. It also called for the PCI to be given more powers that went beyond censures and warnings. It called for strengthening of the Working Journalists Act after the Delhi Union of Journalists who had complained that journalists who did not fall

---

1 Firstpost, 5 December 2013.

2 Ganendra Narayan Ray, judge of the Supreme Court, 1991–98, chairman, Press Council of India, 11 March 2005 to 4 October 2011.

in line with their managements' malpractices were either threatened with dismissal or their reportage was blacked out. Many prominent political and public figures gave evidence before the inquiry panel; some complained bitterly but privately admitted that they were afraid to antagonize the media.

The report also noted the payments for 'positive coverage', especially in the run-up to the elections, took various forms. While monetary benefits were preferred, non-monetary benefits included freebies like foreign junkets. The report recommended a number of guidelines to be framed so that news could be clearly differentiated from advertisements. Lamenting the Council's feeble powers, it suggested that the government arm the PCI with powers to fine, revoke licences and importantly, initiate criminal charges against errant papers. This, of course, would require legislative changes. It was only then that the regulator would become truly effective.

Quite the reverse happened. The report was internally suppressed by a powerful lobby within that pressed for a much watered-down version that was reduced to a mere footnote. Yet even this found its way into the public domain through a curiously circuitous route. It was leaked online. It would take another fourteen months before the Central Information Commission (CIC) would order the PCI to publish the report on its website.

The report[3] which makes for shocking reading has finally become available.[4] It provides a detailed account of instances of paid news in the national, regional and particularly the vernacular press during GE 2009.

In an article published in 2010, P. Sainath, the then rural affairs editor of the *Hindu* wrote:[5]

---

3 Paranjoy Guha Thakurta and K. Sreenivas Reddy, 'Paid News: The Buried Report', *Outlook*, 6 August 2010.

4 Press Council of India, 'Report on Paid News: How corruption on the Indian media undermines democracy' www.indiatogether.org.

5 P. Sainath, 'Paid News Undermining Democracy: Press Council Report', *The Hindu*, 21 April 2010.

The report explores several ways to curb the menace of 'paid news'. It seeks a far more proactive role from the Election Commission, for instance. It calls on the ECI [Election Commission of India] to set up a special cell to receive complaints about 'paid news' in the run-up to the polls. Where a prima facie case is established, it calls on the ECI to initiate action against offenders.

It asks that the ECI nominate independent journalists or public figures to help monitor the phenomenon during elections. It calls upon media organizations to desist from having their correspondents 'double up as agents collecting advertisements for their organizations and receiving a commission on that revenue', instead of regular salaries, retainers or stipends.

The report also calls for giving regulatory bodies like the Press Council more teeth. It further appeals to media organizations to adopt a number of principles that would curb 'paid news'. However, it recognizes that self-regulation and civil society oversight, while welcome and useful, can tackle the problem 'only to an extent'. There would have to be effective use of existing laws to 'apprehend those indulging in practices that are tantamount to committing a fraud on the public'.

This was not to say that the entire fourth estate had succumbed to the temptation. There were and are honorable exceptions who took up cudgels against a sickness spreading so rapidly that it would destroy the very credibility of electoral reportage.

The Hindu in its editorial of 31 October 2009 reflected, under the title 'Journalism for Sale' that 'the new shame' of paid news was the 'extensive and brazen participation of not insignificant sections of the news media, notably large circulation Indian language newspapers in two of India's largest states, Maharashtra and Andhra Pradesh. Candidates paid newspapers different rates for well-differentiated and streamlined packages of news coverage. Those who could not or would not pay for the packages tended to be blacked out.'

Perhaps the most influential voice to speak against paid news has been that of N. Ram, chairman of Kasturi and Sons Ltd that controls the Hindu Group of publications. Addressing IPS trainees at Sardar Vallabhbhai Patel National Police Academy in Hyderabad, he exhorted media organizations, both big and small, to observe 'self-regulation' adding that 'there will be public support for external regulation if we don't regulate corruption in the media'. He added that 'the delinquency of influential sections of the press was responsible for the emergence of the paid news phenomenon. The same article would appear under different names extolling a Chief Minister or an Opposition candidate who was willing to pay for the propaganda in the guise of news. ... It is not an ad, they cheat the election law. For the larger political parties, what it costs is minor compared with what they spend overall.'[6]

Another influential voice was that of the chairman, Centre for Media Studies (CMS), N. Bhaskara Rao, who, at a seminar held on 10 May 2010 in New Delhi observed that civil society and professional groups had so far been mostly passive. In part this was because they did not know to whom they should report such suspicious information. He advised the PCI to establish a 'helpline' during the poll process to receive complaints, holding that 'circumstantial evidence' should be good enough to seek an explanation where the writing was suspicious. He admitted that the media was concerned with maximization of revenue as an end in itself, while the PCI had been playing a somewhat 'reactive role'. The Commission was constrained by government's legal regime. He admitted that hard evidence was difficult to come by. He also wondered, when there was a model code of conduct for political parties, why there should not be one for the media. As others before him, he too urged the need for self-regulation. He even offered a compelling set of guidelines as a pointer to the way forward.

In its issue of 18 January 2010, the *Outlook* magazine lamented: 'It was April last year and the general elections had just been announced when marketing whiz-kids in the media saw a golden

---

6 'Self-regulation for media must to stop external regulation, says Ram. Corruption in the form of paid news is an awful phenomenon', *The Hindu*, 2 May 2010.

opportunity springing up. ... [W]hile it is generally believed that the malaise of publishing news in return for money had kicked in way back in General Election 2004, it was the scale of the phenomenon of paid news in 2009 that made many to wake up and take notice.' It went on to say that the Election Commission would put guidelines in place to rein in the practice. Justice G.N. Ray, the then chairman of the PCI was quoted as saying, 'The rot has set in in the system and, unfortunately, language papers emulated the leading papers, which had started the paid news trend ... this reached a peak during the recent elections. But the Press Council is trying to assert itself.' Paranjoy Guha Thakurta reflected on the opaque nature of these deals when he said, 'How does one prove that a monetary transaction has taken place? All such transactions are clandestine and one can only go by circumstantial evidence.'

Meanwhile the Commission, after legal examination, declared that paid news was an attempt to circumvent the provisions of Section 77 and Section 123(6) of the RoPA, 1951, which prescribes accounting and ceiling of election expenses, and makes exceeding the prescribed limits a corrupt practice. In other words, were any party or candidate found to have indulged in this electoral malpractice, the expenses, so calculated by Commission to be paid news, would be added to the expenditure ceiling.[7]

With a more clear-cut strategy in hand and with the GE 2009 looming on the horizon, we became increasingly proactive in the Commission. We set up special cells with dedicated officers to monitor news channels and the print media under the overall charge of our CEOs. This was a huge burden to place on our officials who were already stretched with their normal electoral duties. Despite this, they were able to detect, prima facie, hundreds of cases of paid news. In one of the most prominent cases that arose out of the November 2008 elections in Madhya Pradesh, Narottam Mishra, a cabinet minister, was linked to as many as forty-two such news items. Between 2009

---

7 Election Commission Order No. 491/Media/2010 dated 8 June 2010.

and 2014, the Commission identified more than 1,500 cases. Among them was that of the former chief minister of Maharashtra, Ashok Chavan. In this case, Kirit Somaiya, the Bharatiya Janata Party (BJP) leader, submitted to the Commission forty-nine identical news stories that praised Chavan and his government. Mr Chavan's defence was that these news items were published by the newspapers on their own volition. The Commission served notices to Chavan and the newspapers concerned.

Despite its limitations, the Commission notched up a few tangible successes. In October 2011, Umlesh Yadav became the first ever sitting MLA (from UP) to be disqualified for not declaring the expenditure incurred by her on advertising during her election campaign. She was banned from contesting elections for a period of three years.

Meanwhile, prominent sections of the international press too began to note these disturbing trends. The *New York Times* described the special arrangements between newspapers and politicians/ celebrities as 'private treaties'. The *New York Times* went on to say:[8]

> Paid news comes in various formats: opinion polls with results that are statistically dubious, extremely flattering or soft interviews of political candidates, and stories that are nothing more than candidates' press releases—sometimes published word for word from the press release, in multiple papers on the same day.
>
> 'Corruption implications of paid news has its impact on everyone—media, candidates and people—and it is one that causes maximum damage to the electoral process, V.S. Sampath, the chief election commissioner,' said at a conference on electoral reforms last December in Kerala.
>
> The Commission has consistently recommended to parliament that paid news be treated as a crime under the Representation of the People Act, on par with the rigging of ballots and the registration of fake voters. Without an amendment to the law, the Election

8 Malavika Vyawahare, 'Election Watchdog Fights Lonely Battle on Paid News Coverage', *The New York Times*, 25 April 2014.

Commission cannot prosecute candidates who pay for either favorable media coverage for themselves or for negative stories on their rivals.

Another influential voice, the *New Yorker* magazine, described a leading Indian newspaper 'dismantling the wall between the newsroom and the sales department'.[9] The *Wall Street Journal* noted that it '... was astonishing that a large section of the media is completely silent on this malpractice.'[10]

Some, but not nearly enough, influential Indian voices continued to speak out against obvious malpractices. T.N. Ninan, chairman and chief editor of *Business Standard* in a lecture termed it 'Indian media's Dickensian age'. He said:[11]

> We have never had such a vast audience or readership, but our credibility has never been so tested. We have never seen such a flowering of TV channels and such a spreading footprint for newspaper titles, but the market is more consolidated than ever around the top few players. The quality of what we offer to our public has never been better, but the same public can see that the ethical foundations of our actions have plumbed new depths. .... It is unquestionably the best of times, and it is also, unfortunately, the worst of times.

'It is not about corruption of individual rogue journalists', said P. Sainath, in his submission to the Standing Committee on Information and Technology. 'But it is a complex, highly-structured trade

9 Ken Auletta, 'Citizens Jain: Why India's Newspaper Industry is Thriving?' *The New Yorker*, 8 October 2012.

10 Tom Wright, 'India Media Buries Paid News Report', *The Wall Street Journal*, 1 June 2013.

11 T.N. Ninan, CASI Working Paper, Series No.11-03, 12/2011, A. Nand & Jeet Khemka Distinguished Lecture, 10 November 2011, Philadelphia: Center for the Advanced Study of India (CASI) 2011.

involving the media, corporations and ... the political class and there is not a single major state in the country without such instance.'[12]

Describing these as 'deeply worrying tendencies', N. Ram, summed up his worry list up in his usual forthright way when he said, in a lecture that he delivered in December 2011:[13]

> Increasing concentration of ownership in some sectors; higher levels of manipulation of news, analysis and comment to suit the owners' financial and political interests; the downgrading and devaluing of editorial functions and contents in some leading newspaper organizations; systematic dumping down, led by certain types of market research; the growing willingness within newspapers to tailor the editorial product to subserve advertising and marketing goals set by owners and senior management personnel; hyper-commercialization; price wars and aggressive practices in the home bases of other newspapers to overwhelm and kill competition, raising fears about media monopoly; private treaties with corporates that undermine the independence and value of news; rogue practices like paid news and bribe-taking for favourable coverage—these are deeply worrying tendencies.

In an age when battles are being increasingly fought on television, radio and the social media, it is imperative that 'paid news' should be treated as a cognizable offence and powers sought by the Election Commission to treat it as a criminal activity should be conceded by parliament. This will eventually be in the interest of every political party and candidate, because as politicians would realize, today's winners often end up being tomorrow's losers. 'Paid news' has become a double-edged weapon and only the establishments that own the newspapers or channels are the ones to benefit.

---

12 Standing Committee on Information Technology 2012–13, 47th Report, Lok Sabha Secretariat, 'Issues Related to Paid News'.

13 N. Ram, 'The Changing Role of the News Media in Contemporary India', Indian History Congress, Patiala, Punjab University, December 2011.

Prominent political leaders now began to speak out. In a piece published by the *Hindustan Times* on 6 March 2010, Prakash Karat, the then general secretary of Communist Party of India-Marxist (CPI-M) declared that publishing 'paid news' should be declared as an electoral malpractice under RoPA, 1951. Perhaps, nothing could be more telling than a statement made by Sushma Swaraj, then the leader of Opposition in Lok Sabha, who declared that she herself was offered a Rs 1 crore 'deal' during the elections, which she promptly refused. On another occasion, she succinctly said that paid news 'started out as an aberration, went on to become a disease and is now an epidemic'. Ambika Soni, when she was minister of information and broadcasting (2009–12) declared that paid news was '... eating into the vitals of a free and fair media; it was undermining the media's claim to be upholding democracy'. Prakash Javadekar, presently Union minister for human resources development, was even more explicit when he said: 'They have rate cards and approach you with different kinds of packages—exclusive stories, front page, negative coverage for opponent and so on. The candidates are forced, no one can risk a black out during an election.' More tellingly he added, 'In thirty years of my political career, campaigning for the BJP... the commercial question was not there. In the past ten years, things have changed drastically.'[14]

The most important constitutional voice raised was that of Vice-President Hamid Ansari. At the diamond jubilee of the Election Commission of India, held on 25 January 2010 to which the Commission had invited him, he warned against the commercialization of news content for revenue generation. On another occasion, he went on to say, 'The recent practice of leveraging political and economic content in our media for overt and covert revenue generation have the malevolent potential to tarnish our polity and even destabilize the economy.' He added that

---

14 Quoted in Anuradha Sharma, 'In Need of a Leveson? Journalism in India in Times of Paid News and "Private Treaties"', Reuters Institute Fellowship Paper, University of Oxford.

deception, opaque flow of political information, or slanted economic data prevented political and economic actors from exercising rational and well-considered choices.[15]

On 8 June 2010, after consulting several political parties, media groups and other stakeholders, the Commission decided to take necessary steps to halt these malpractices. It was agreed that these were attempts to circumvent the provisions of Section 77 and Section 123(6) of the RoPA, 1951 which prescribed accounting and ceiling of election expenses, the exceeding of which is a corrupt electoral malpractice. The legal provisions under Section 127A of the RoPA, 1951, make it mandatory for the publisher of an election advertisement, pamphlet, etc., to print the name and address of the publisher as well as printer, and failure to do so attracts penalty of imprisonment up to two years and/or a fine of Rs 2,000. For the purpose of Section 127A (1) of the RoPA, 1951, 'election pamphlet or poster' means any printed pamphlet, handbills or other document distributed for the purpose of promoting or prejudicing the election of a candidate or group of candidates. ...' Thus, paid news would also fall in the category of 'other document' liable to be included in 'election pamphlet and poster' and action taken accordingly. Hence, an obvious case of news reporting in the print media dedicated to, or giving advantage to, a particular candidate or party while ignoring/causing prejudice to other candidates and parties would require investigation.

Taking note of this phenomenon that was now beginning to directly affect parliamentarians and political players across the board, a parliamentary standing committee on information and technology of the Ministry of Information and Broadcasting was mandated to inquire into 'issues related to paid news'. Their comprehensive report was presented in parliament in May 2013.[16] The first such

---

15 'Commercialisation of news content is a dangerous trend: Hamid Ansari', *The Hindu*, 29 January 2010.

16 http://164.100.47.134/Isscommittee/information%20technology/15Information technology47.pdf.

work by a parliamentary body on media corruption, its report detailed how sections of the Indian media accepted large sums of money from politicians in exchange for favourable coverage during elections. Indeed, it gave several examples of confirmed cases of paid news. The standing committee—made up of parliamentarians drawn from across the political spectrum, was set up under the chairmanship of Rao Inderjit Singh, (then chairperson of the standing committee on information technology)—took evidence from the Ministry of Information and Broadcasting, the Prasar Bharati, the Commission, the PCI, the Editors Guild of India, CMS as well as two former chief election commissioners among a host of others. The committee acknowledged and endorsed some of the principal recommendations that had been made by the PCI's subcommittee, namely, that the Representation of the People Act, 1951, be amended to make incidence of paid news a punishable electoral malpractice. The Press Council Act, 1978, should also be amended to make its recommendation binding on the electronic media as also that Section 15(4) of the Press Council Act be amended to make the directions of the Press Council binding on all government agencies. Indeed, they went so far as to suggest that the PCI either be wound up or recast with powers to 'take care' of the print media. A similar statutory body be created to handle the electronic media, which hitherto was not covered under the Press Council Act. In an array of other wide-ranging conclusions and recommendations, the committee held that the election laws needed to be reinforced to empower the Commission to not only deal with defaulting candidates but also against the media entities concerned. The report also recognized that apart from newspapers, TV channels and radio, the phenomenal growth of the Internet as well as mobile telephony had come to play a very important role in recent years, with mobile telephones having crossed the one-billion mark.

The committee deplored the phenomenon of 'private treaties' drawn up between some media houses and corporate entities, wherein non-media houses transferred certain shares to the media companies in lieu of advertisements, space and favourable coverage.

(This covered a very wide gamut of corporate advertising, including the advent of new products and films, but it did worryingly also include election coverage.) Among its important recommendations related to cross-media holdings, which promoted monopolies in media the committee proposed a restriction similar to what was in place in many countries in Europe and the USA.

Taking on board the experience of many of those who gave evidence, the committee wryly noted that paid news was hardly ever highlighted by the media themselves. Indeed, large sections of the media were 'completely silent' on the issue. Importantly, the committee prodded the government to take lessons from the Levenson Inquiry in the UK.

The Levenson Committee in the UK was set up not because of paid news, but to investigate the broader question of ethics in the media. The cry for 'self-regulation' made by several respected media voices had found reflection in the UK, following a phone-hacking scandal in 2011 and the public revulsion that followed. This was reinforced when a judicial public inquiry was set up under Lord Justice Levenson. Its proceedings were widely covered and followed by people in the country. 'Many newspapers shockingly hide their lack of accountability behind the mantra of "press freedom",' Levenson concluded. After a number of public hearings Lord Justice Levenson held that the main press regulator, the Press Complaints Committee, stood discredited. He recommended that a new independent body with powers to investigate and sanction serious breaches be set up and that it should be backed statutorily by parliament. This body would both protect the freedom of the press as well as provide protection to those who saw themselves as victims of the press, not through expensive litigation but by arbitration.

Corroborating the findings of the PCI and other agencies, the parliamentary standing committee on information and technology in the Ministry of Information and Broadcasting submitted a report to parliament in May 2013 on the subject titled, 'Issues related to paid news'. The tell-all report—the first such work by a parliamentary body on the subject of media corruption—detailed how sections of the Indian media accepted large sums of money from politicians in exchange for favourable coverage during elections. According to the report, there were 126 confirmed cases of paid news, with sixty-one candidates admitting to buying positive coverage in the 2012 Gujarat elections. Prodding the government to take lessons from the Leveson Inquiry in the UK, the committee proposed a slew of measures, kicking off a fresh regulation debate in the country. All this took place at a time when the media in India was 'booming'.[17]

Interestingly, David Cameron, the prime minister who appointed the Levenson Committee, while endorsing most of its recommendations chose not to give the new body proposed by Levenson any statutory backing. He was promptly accused by his critics of backing off in the face of 'press power', especially as both the Labour and Liberal parties had endorsed legislative reform. What resulted, (and is still being assessed) was allowing one or more independent self-regulatory bodies to be established. A significant section of the press in the UK established their own regulator on 12 September 2014, called significantly the Independent Press Standards Organization (IPSO). This followed the winding up of the PCC. There remain vocal critics who allege that this body is not 'Levenson compliant' and remains in close proximity with powerful press barons as well as their financial backers. That said, the establishment of the IPSO is an important step forward towards self-regulation within the media. The Indian media would do well to emulate this model in the continued absence of real powers, statutorily derived, for the Press Council of India.

The Cobrapost Sting

The most recent and perhaps the most indefensible and pernicious role of important sections of the Indian media was revealed in a sting operation conducted by Cobrapost which reported on how some

17 Anuradha Sharma, 'In Need of a Levenson? Journalism in India in Times of Paid News and "Private Treaties"', Reuters Institute Fellowship Paper, University of Oxford, 2013.

media houses 'were prepared to strike business deals to promote the Hindutva agenda and help polarize voters in the run up to the 2019 election'.[18] Cobrapost reported that as many as two dozen news organizations were willing not only to cause communal disharmony among the citizens but also tilt the electoral outcome in favour of a particular party for a price. Only two media houses did not succumb to this blatant temptation. The list of the who's who of Indian publishing has sadly exposed the fact that the barring a handful, the rest were willing to go along with deals that would help ring their cash registers by up to 20 per cent of their annual profits. The results of this sting were predictably blacked out by the media, leaving it to a few newspapers and websites such as the Wire, Scroll and The Print to report on a scandal that BBC referred to as 'The story barely reported by Indian media'.[19]

The Influence of Social Media

One of the most remarkable indeed almost revolutionary happenings in the last decade has been the spread of mobile telephony and the Internet. In 2008, there were an estimated 1.03 billion mobile handsets in the country with approximately 85 per cent of households owning one or multiple sets. With the widespread ownership of mobiles has come the extensive usage of SMS (short message service). The Internet has brought about its own revolution—having spawned social media, encompassing Twitter, Facebook and others which have spread like wildfire. For the Commission this has come to present both an opportunity and a host of problems. It is now able to spread its own messages such as urging the youth to vote as well as to answer frequently asked questions. This capability was demonstrated during GE 2014 which

18 'Cobrapost Sting: Big media houses say yes to Hindutva, Black Money, Paid News', The Wire, 26 May 2018.

19 Justin Rowlatt, South Asia Correspondent, BBC, 28 May 2018.

was a testimony to the success of the Commission's youth outreach campaign through the SMS, among other methods.

The negatives are harder to grapple with. As political parties and candidates begin to realize the power and the reach of social media, three things have occurred. First, the cost of the bulk SMS messages was not being added to the total candidate expenditure. The second, some of these anonymous messages also violate MCC guidelines. Because they travel under the radar, it is difficult for the Commission to proceed against them. Some of these messages violate both the Constitution and statute, especially when it comes to issues causing communal disharmony and are directed against particular communities or religions. All these are difficult to trace especially within the short electoral time available. In the process, the 'name and shame' power of the MCC can be given the go-by. Violations may strike at the root of existing legislation that seek to protect the Scheduled Castes and Scheduled Tribes, for instance, or may in other ways contravene the penal code. As the Commission has tried to play the role of a fair and far-seeing umpire, it has in the past been accused of overreach, encroaching into political space or individual freedoms. However, if there are going to be fundamental breaches, the Commission would perhaps see this as a 'reasonable restriction' not dissimilar to the Union government sometimes suspending Internet services to prevent troubles in particular states limited to short spans at certain junctures.

This will be a formidable challenge for the Commission in the years to come as both social media and mobile telephony continue to proliferate in size and space. The Commission has no instant answer, and policies necessarily have to be shaped as the situation and circumstances warrant.

The Way Forward

This chapter has examined, without labouring the point unduly, that paid news has not just compromised the media but that it has also reflected the political establishment in poor light for entering into a compact with the underbelly of the media. In many cases that amounts to bribery and corruption under existing laws. How would the framers of our Constitution, whom we frequently quote to uphold what is still sacrosanct, have reacted to such a situation?

Enough has been written above to demonstrate what has gone and is going wrong. Many constructive suggestions are already on offer. Another committee would, in my view, not add substantially to the recommendations of the parliamentary committee. What is required is the implementation of these as also the specific recommendations made by the Commission.

Foremost among these is to amend the Representation of the People Act, 1951, making paid news a cognizable offence. This would see many errant contestants disqualified. Equally overdue is to replace (or strengthen) the creaky Press Commission with substantive powers that go well beyond censure. The I&B ministry, the nodal ministry concerned, which was chastised by the parliamentary committee needs to take action. The electronic media continues to be governed by the now archaic Cable Television Networks Regulation Act, 1995, that I had a role in drafting when I was joint secretary in that ministry. It is outdated now. Fresh legislation is required to create a new regulator to comprehensively bring the electronic media under its ambit.

The Press Council and the Broadcasting Council of India must strive to protect press freedom for which they have been constituted and which is essential if the press is to retain its status as the fourth pillar of democracy. Contrary to trends in the West, newspaper readership in India is far from declining even in this digital age. It is growing, arguably between 9 and 10 per cent. Since its leading lights have already reflected on what has gone wrong, it must equally enjoin on them to press for a Levenson-type of structure from within, knowing that the existing regulatory edifice has proved ineffective.

The political establishment is often at the mercy of these recalcitrant elements in the media. It needs to take a unified stand against them. Many of its members admit, sotto voce, that those who might benefit in one election may well be at the receiving end of another. Money ensures no long-term loyalties. The political establishment needs to close ranks to ensure that parliament passes the requisite legislation, which makes paid news a cognizable offence and in the process, strengthen the Commission whose impartiality continues to be recognized.

I hold that the Election Commission will have to forge fresh initiatives. Article 324 gives the Commission wide powers that need to be and can be shaped to meet the challenges that it now faces, not just to protect the election process but indeed to uphold the very keystone of the democratic arch that it has striven so hard to create over the last seven decades. The Commission does rely on the government of the day to steer through parliament various recommendations regarding paid news. However, it can also initiate the process by convening frequent meetings with all the various stakeholders—the recognized political parties (Central and state), the Ministry of Information and Broadcasting, the Press Council, the Editors Guild and the Broadcasting Council. Fresh ideas and initiatives will emerge and these may well result in cohesive strategies. I do believe there is no alternative to dialogue. I am also confident that if such meetings are held regularly, important new ground will be broken.

6

Post-Truth:[1] The Influence of Social Media on Elections

SINCE its inception in 1950, the Election Commission of India has engaged with an array of electoral practices on the ground, and gained many insights, in the process, to curb any undue influence that might distort the electoral outcomes. The Commission's objective—to ensure a level playing field for all contestants—has remained unchanged. Having witnessed manifold extraneous influences on the elections—from the use of 'money and muscle power' to entice or coerce voters, attempts to dodge the MCC, all in order to influence voter behaviour and skew the people's mandate—the Commission has engaged with various democratic institutions of the nation to strengthen the electoral processes. But this process has not always been smooth, especially when the reforms required have been outside the Commission's jurisdiction.

As I have highlighted through various instances in this chapter, the use of money power to create biased media content for any

1 The expression 'post-truth politics' was coined by blogger David Roberts defining it as 'a political culture in which politics (public opinion and media narratives) have become almost entirely disconnected from policy (the substance of legislation)'. It was widely used during the campaigns for the 2016 US presidential election.

candidate has already become an epidemic. Since the time I served as the CEC until the recent elections—both for the Lok Sabha and state assemblies—the influence of media on electoral outcomes has exploded to an unfathomable extent, ranging from paid news to often vitriolic social media campaigns. Today, the spread of social media and its role in political campaigning is questioning the very relevance of the MCC. There is very limited regulatory control, especially given the wide ambit of available platforms to share content. It is this very aspect that makes social media a tool for furthering political, social and cultural expression. But it also allows for spreading of misinformation[2] that often enough choose to reinforce already prevalent biases. This can adversely affect voter judgement and can help aggravate discord. In retrospect, I believe that the use of paid political advertisements during the 2009 general election ushered in what William Davies of the *New York Times* identifies as the Age of Post-Truth Politics,[3] a period when social media allows for 'individuals having growing opportunities to shape their media consumption around their own opinions and prejudices, and populist leaders are ready to encourage them'.[4]

'Social Media' covers various platforms through which a user can create, share and curate content. This extensive universe of social media platforms is a labyrinth that will be very difficult, if not near impossible to curtail, often setting up a stage for legitimization of personal biases and prejudices. 'Not long ago, social media held out the promise of a more enlightened politics, as accurate information and effortless communication helped good people drive out corruption, bigotry and lies. Yet, Facebook acknowledged that before and after last year's American election, between January 2015 and August this year, 146 million users may have seen Russian misinformation on its platform. Google's YouTube admitted to 1,108

2 Misinformation (noun): false or inaccurate information, especially that which is deliberately intended to deceive, Oxford English Dictionary.

3 Without any factual evidence nor citation of its sources.

4 William Davies, 'The Age of Post-Truth Politics', *The New York Times*, 24 August 2016.

Russian-linked videos and Twitter to 36,746 accounts. Far from bringing enlightenment, social media have been spreading poison.'[5] A total clamp down on social media by the state would certainly be viewed as authoritarian and would go against democratic practices. In India, social media is proving to be a powerful tool for politicians, media and civil society to engage with the polity and increase awareness of political developments among people in remote areas. Elsewhere, as witnessed during the Arab Spring, it created a space for people to unite and to secure a stable democratic political system, and in the process to revolt against what they viewed as oppressive and authoritarian regimes.

Social media with its capability to network and share information with each other in a free manner has become the mightiest weapon of the present era. But this very aspect has also led to the spread of misinformation, which can be used by populist leaders to validate biases and distract the polity with rhetoric, instead of creating a healthy discourse on policies. The 'click-bait' phenomenon we see on social media ensures that online content is curated which is based on individual preferences. Moreover, social media platforms rely on the sharing of these information to maximize profits. The controversy around Russia's use of social media to disrupt the recent US presidential election has cautioned other democracies to become wary. An article in the *Conversation* notes: 'As the US election scandal shows, big social media platforms not only have few safeguards to prevent the deliberate manipulation of information, but they also have financial interests in maintaining the status quo. Unfettered flows of information and unconstrained advertising revenue are key to their business models. And this model is tremendously profitable.'[6] Under the guise of free sharing of information, social media platforms have become a source to gauge and manipulate user behaviour.

---

5 'Do Social media threaten democracy?', *The Economist*, 4 November 2017.

6 'Regulate Social Media Platforms before it's too late', *The Conversation*, 7 November 2017.

In the Indian electoral context, apart from disturbing the MCC, social media has thrown up another challenge. The no-campaign period of forty-eight hours prior to voting must now include any form of campaigning on social media too. But given the difficulties in identifying the original source of content generation, let alone its being shared through the multitude of social media platforms, the challenge just might become a paradox even as the Commission uses the social media to create an informed polity and maintain fairness in our electoral process. Taking stock of these developments, the Commission has set up a fourteen-member panel under its senior deputy election commissioner, Umesh Sinha, to examine this challenge. The committee's recommendations on the influence of social media on electoral conduct would help us gauge the relevance of MCC in the age of post-truth.

The reforms are by no means confined to India. In navigating through these difficulties, the Commission could learn from measures taken by other democracies. Foreseeing the intangible influence social media can have on the smooth running of elections, Canada has set up the Canadian Election Integrity Initiative to counter the spread of misinformation. In the United States, members of Congress have proposed the Honest Ads Act, which would require social media platforms to publish information about the advertisers and maintain a public archive of political advertisements. Though I have highlighted a few of the controversies surrounding social media's role in domestic politics, the subject requires a deeper study of the ramifications of social media on each democracy's political landscape, particularly in the conduct of elections in the age of post-truth.

In April 2018, Facebook CEO Mark Zuckerberg was summoned before the United States Congress in the light of the Cambridge Analytica controversy. Although the two-day congressional testimony of Zuckerberg ended without any specific accusations directed at the social media giant nor its CEO, a statement made by Zuckerberg perhaps highlights the idea that has led to the development of this chapter. When asked by David Loebsack—a US representative from Iowa—whether it would be possible for Facebook to exist if it did not collect and sell data, Zuckerberg quibbled over this statement, but concluded that 'we (Facebook) wouldn't exist if we weren't collecting information that people share with us. There is no doubt that Facebook is armed with personal information of its users, a valuable resource which', according to various allegations, is being used by politicians, businesses and foreign agents to influence user (and electoral) behaviour. It is no wonder Mukesh Ambani, the chairman of Reliance Jio—the telecom giant that captured 128 million users within a year of its launch—has called data the new oil.[7] But with personal information of its users made available, the question about its misuse is reignited in every controversy. Considering the many controversies that have erupted, such as Cambridge Analytica Information Operations,[8] and the Aadhaar data leak, etc., Zuckerberg's statement is a matter of concern.

Cambridge Analytica, a British political consulting firm, which uses data mining, data brokerage and data analysis for electoral process, involved famously with Donald J. Trump's presidential campaign and the Leave EU campaign in 2016, was accused by media outlets of unlawfully acquiring personal information of Facebook users for campaign purposes. Its purpose in electoral campaigning was in micro-targeting potential voters to influence their voter behaviour. In today's world, when most of the world's population is constantly connected to the Internet of Things (IoT), we have learned that the applications (Apps) and platforms we use through our smartphones and computers gather user information and behaviour to micro-target advertisements. It is from the advertisements that most of these Apps earn their revenue. But Cambridge Analytica was not subject to criminal investigations because of its role in influencing voters through targeted campaigning, but instead was subject to an

7 *The Economic Times*, 27 September 2017.

8 'Information Operations' is code for fake news and Russian propaganda aimed at hurting public discourse. See also 'Data breach: Government again sends notices to Cambridge Analytica, Facebook', *The Times of India*, 25 April 2018.

investigation for the 'illegal acquisition of user-data' from Facebook, in other words for the breach of privacy rights of Facebook users.

In a different case, the Federal Bureau of Investigation (FBI) investigated and charged thirteen Russians, overseeing the Russian operation named Translator Project, to 'incite political discord in the United States, damage Hillary Clinton's presidential campaign (along with those of Bernie Sanders and Jill Stein) and later bolster the candidacy of Donald J. Trump'[9] by spreading distrust towards the candidates and the political system. By assuming fictitious identities through fraudulent documentation or stolen identities, Russian trolls (allegedly under the directions of Russian government) used social media to spread misinformation and create distrust among Americans towards a particular candidate. The concern for the American intelligence in this case was the unwarranted influence in its electoral processes by foreign or third-party agents. According to a US congressional study, the social media propaganda generated by Russian operatives in key swing states during the 2016 presidential election generated 30 to 40 per cent of election-related tweets, a situation made effortless by social media's already existing avenues to create and spread duplicitous, inflammatory or false information through advertisements. Politics is getting uglier, because social media has played its part in spreading misinformation or outright untruth, thereby clouding voter judgement and spreading mistrust and even hate.

Misinformation and the Age of Post-Truth

These are but a few instances where either internal or third-party actors unlawfully acquire personal information and analyse the

---

9 Scott Shane and Mark Mazzetti, 'Inside a three-year Russian campaign to influence US voters', *The New York Times*, 16 February 2018. Mazzetti is a Pulitzer Prize–winning American journalist for *The New York Times* and currently serves as its Washington Investigations editor. Scott Shane is a reporter in the Washington bureau of *The New York Times*.

data to create targeted advertisements to influence the user. The controversy is so big that its impact is felt in India too. Cambridge Analytica's alleged involvement with both the Indian National Congress and Bharatiya Janata Party in the 2014 general elections and the upcoming general elections in 2019, should become a matter of concern for our lawmakers. Are we sufficiently equipped to ensure the integrity of our elections? In this clutter of controversies breaking out about breaches in data privacy, the issue of utmost concern for governments is surely providing security to personal online data of their citizens and users.

The European Union has passed the General Data Protection Regulation (GDPR) on data protection and privacy for all individuals under the EU. It was approved by the European Union parliament in the April of 2016, came into force in May 2018. The GDPR seeks to penalize organizations not in compliance with the new regulations replacing the Data Protection Directives 95/46/EC.[10] The regulation is expected to set a precedent for similar moves to be made by other democracies. It also sets a precedent in extending the protection of fundamental rights and freedom of natural persons to the protection of personal data.[11] In his questioning on the Cambridge Analytica controversy before the United States Congress in March 2018, Facebook CEO Mark Zuckerberg informed them that it (Facebook) plans to apply the key aspects of GDPR to its users, though it is not identical in each country. Legislation regarding protection (and misuse) of personal information varies across countries, most of which are more diluted versions, if not completely stripped-down version, of GDPR. With Facebook seemingly willing to comply and replicate GDPR, India should follow suit and replicate its objectives in India. It would go hand in hand with Information Technology

10 European Union General Data Protection Regulation (EUGDPR), official website [www.eugdpr.org]

11 Subject matter and objectives, Article 1, General Data Protection Regulation, 2016.

CEC Navin Chawla, accompanied by election commissioners V.S. Sampath and S.Y. Quraishi submitting the list of elected candidates to President Pratibha Patil on 18 May 2009

ukumar Sen, the first CEC, inspecting ballot oxes in 1951

Election materials being carried across river Spiti in HP in October 1951

otos in this section, courtesy of the Election Commission of India

Campaigning in Jaipur, 1952

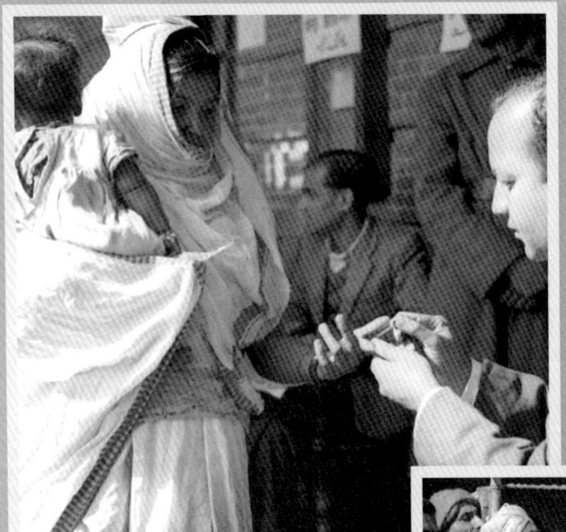

Polling in Delhi in the first general election, January 1952

A disabled voter being carried to the polling booth in the first general election in 1952

A sealed steel ballot box being taken to the counting centre in 1952

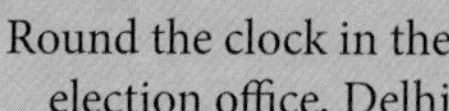

Round the clock in the election office, Delhi

Campaigning in Delhi, 1952

Different boxes for different parties, 1952

Burqa-clad ladies voting in the walled city of Delhi, January 1952

Voters on their way to polling station, West Rajasthan, 1957

Display of election results, Red Fort, Delhi, 1971

A young mother from the north-east casting her vote, 1971

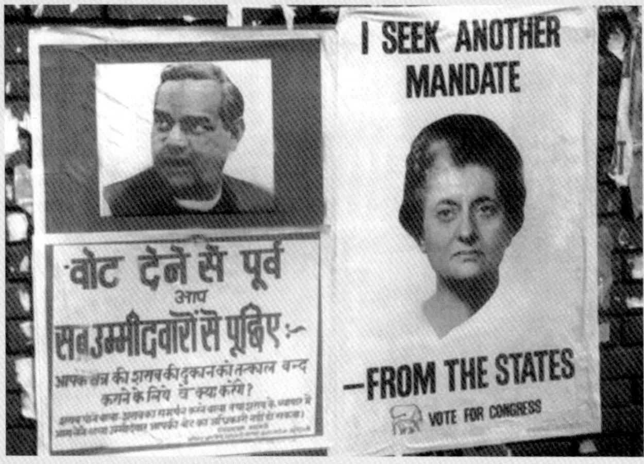

Posters of Atal Bihari Vajpayee and Indira Gandhi seeking votes

Mixing ballot papers before counting in the pre-EVM days, New Delhi 1998

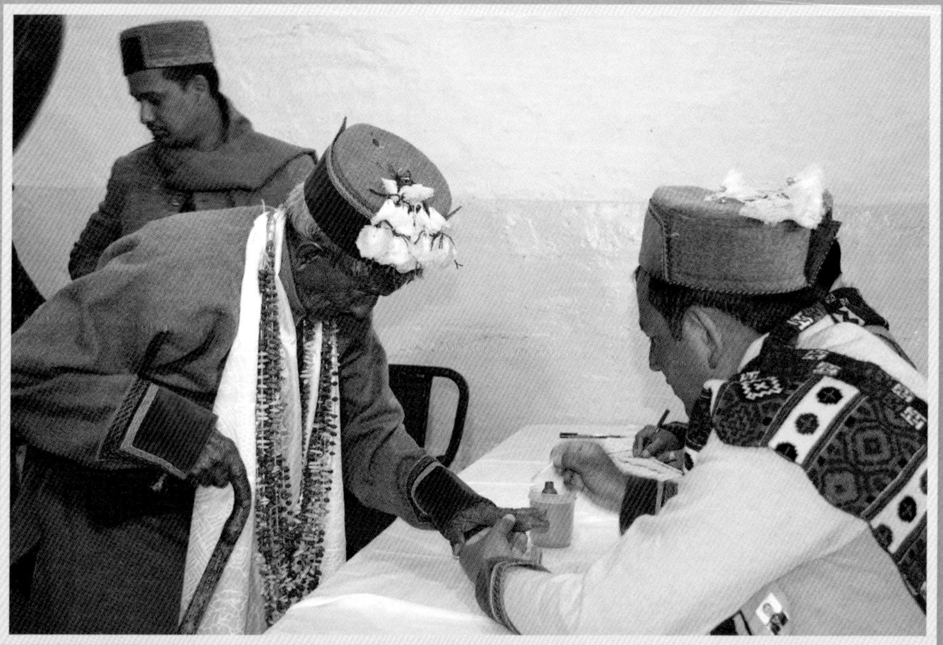

India's oldest voter Shyam Saran Negi votes in Kalpa, Himachal Pradesh

Women voters in Rajasthan, 2009

The highest polling station in Himachal Pradesh

Creating voter awareness in Punjab

Creating voter awareness

iver rafting for voter awareness

Happy voters

The lone voter of Banej village within the Gir lion sanctuary, Gujarat

VMs being carried to a polling station in snow-bound Himachal Pradesh

EVMs being carried by mule in a remote area

Lady presiding officer and other polling staff use a country boat to reach a polling station with EVMs

EVMs carried across a bridge in a remote corner of Arunachal Pradesh

EVM training being given in a field in Bihar

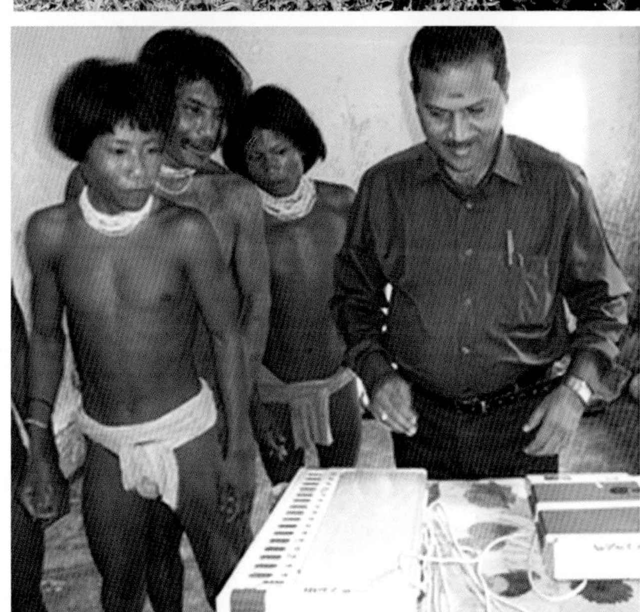

EVM being demonstrated to voters from the Shompen tribe in Andaman and Nicobar Islands

Missionaries of Charity sisters after casting their votes, Meghalaya, 2014

Bridegrooms also vote!

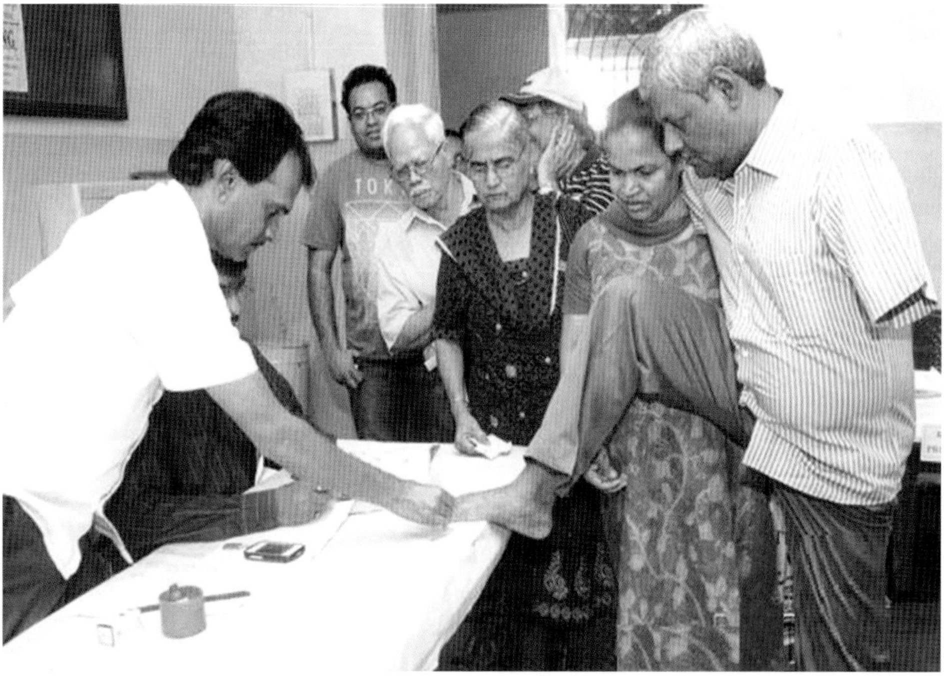

Man without hands getting ready to vote

n elderly couple being carried to the polling booth

A job well done

Well begun and very well done

The EC has pulled off a magnificent job. But we need to shorten the long election period

The Hindu

Hindustan Times, New Delhi
Date 14 MAY 2009

All set for counting of votes to...

Election Commission reviews arrangement; 60,000 people will be...

EC did great job; can it be better?

For poll panel, it's a job well done

Chetan Chauhan
New Delhi, May 13

Election Commission to take action against erring officers

For failing to note down type of identity card voters carried

Special Correspondent

- Only candidate, four others can enter chamber of Returning Officer to collect election certificate
- Results to be late as Observers have to check EVMs at end of each round of counting

POLL BY NUMBERS
- 70 lakh officials on duty
- 2400 central election observers deployed
- 12 lakh EVMs used
- 71.4 crore people voted
- 8,070 candidates contested

News Clippings - Lok Sabha Election - 2009

The Election Commission in the news

In Bhutan (left to right): Dasho Kunzang Wangdi, CEC Bhutan; Navin Chawla, CEC India; H.M. Jigme Singye Wangchuck, the fourth king of Bhutan; and Mrs Rupika Chawla

(From the author's collection

Minister Ravi Shankar Prasad's assertion on 22 March 2018 to keep a check on social media platforms.[12]

Another brewing concern during these controversies was the need to curb the spread of misinformation—as was the situation during the Russian hacking of the 2016 US presidential election, and a series of 'fake news' that hit news channels like a storm in the US and India. In the last two years alone, almost all major national news channels in India have inadvertently or otherwise helped in spreading fake news, which has included the use of doctored images and footage and spreading of malice to shape public opinion. A recent sting operation has exposed several powerful media outlets—both print and electronic—who agreed to participate, in varying measures, in the spread of doctored information to impact Indian elections.

In the previous chapter we saw the full-blown emergence of paid news and its undesirable influence on the sanctity of Indian electoral democracy. The increase in readership and viewership, fuelled by the exponential increase in the number of media and newspaper outlets, soon led to paid news becoming part of the popular discourse that influenced voter behaviour in the midst of election fever. In these years, paid and fake news have emerged as wholly destructive elements to our democratic process. With almost every actor in India's political discourse—including government, political parties, news outlets—having been accused, at least once, of spreading fake and malicious information, social media has become virtually a hornet's nest. Possibly to curb this practice, the government issued an order in April 2018 to suspend or cancel the accreditation of a journalist if found to be generating or propagating fake news. The move was in line with similar measures taken by Malaysia and the European Union, especially Germany, Italy and France. But amidst concerns of it being a Machiavellian plot to control the freedom of the press, the government withdrew the order. Similar criticism has arisen in Malaysia against a bill that seeks to penalize spreading of

12 'Govt will not tolerate data abuse by firms to influence elections: Prasad', *Business Standard*, 1 August 2018.

fake news, as being aimed at curbing dissent and free speech ahead of a general election. In Myanmar, it is widely recognized that Facebook is the main source of news for many. This may well have deepened the hatred for the Rohingya, victims of ethnic cleansing. The third concern, therefore, would be to regulate online content without it being perceived as an attack on the right to free speech.

The age of post-truth is, therefore, a worrying period for a democracy. As Barrack Obama rightfully warned us, 'If we are not serious about facts and what's true and what's not, if we can't discriminate between serious arguments and propaganda, then we have problems.'[13] But dealing with this problem is not easy: while taking steps to curb the spread of misinformation on the social media, authorities must uphold freedom of speech and expression. If this is not done with finesse it can tarnish the sanctity of a democracy and its apparatuses. While governments across the world are experimenting with diverse sets of actions to control this menace, the Election Commission of India must make its model code of conduct relevant to the age of post-truth and social media, thus ensuring fairness and integrity in the electoral process.

Other democracies too are taking precautionary measures, and collaborating with social media platforms to stop any unwarranted influences in the electoral processes. Facebook Canada had launched the Canadian Election Integrity Initiative in the last quarter of 2017 in time for the Canadian federal election. Its website states its main objective is to 'protect and safeguard the integrity of the electoral process in Canada.'[14] This initiative was in response to the instances of Cambridge Analytica and Russia–US election controversy, and necessitated further by the Cyber Threats to Canada's Democratic

13 'Barack Obama on fake news: "We have problems" if we can't tell the difference', *The Guardian*, 18 November 2016.

14 facebookcanadianelectionintegrityinitiative.com.

Process Report,[15] commissioned by the minister of democratic institutions, Government of Canada.

Considering the many controversies regarding social media being used to influence elections, I find there are three major instances that the Commission will have to look into. First, as seen in the US–Russia election controversy, the Commission must take cognizance of the unwarranted interference in political affairs by third parties or foreign governments. Second, it needs to secure its apparatuses and information against breach, given the burst of fake news or misinformation that can spread like wildfire. Third, the Commission also must look at curbing social media's role in influencing voter behaviour using fake or malicious news about rival candidates. Additionally, the Commission must ensure that the forty-eight-hour restriction on campaigning prior to voting should apply to the social media also, notwithstanding the difficulties in applying the code to social media, given the multitude of available platforms and media outlets to create, share and curate campaign content.

In the US, the Honest Ads Bill is pending approval in the Senate which will regulate campaign advertisements online by Internet-based companies, extending the regulation on paid campaigns from television, print news and radio to include Internet activity. A similar move in India would go a long way to help the Commission curb campaigning on the Internet during the crucial forty-eight hours before the voting starts on the polling day. More importantly, it would help regulate fake and malicious news from upsetting the electoral processes.

The Election Commission is right to be deeply concerned. The Commission and Facebook did work actively together to boost voter registration amongst youth and first-time voters but, unfortunately, it has now felt the need to review this relationship. For the data that Facebook has already harnessed could help mould public opinion.

---

15 Communications Security Establishments, report on Cyber Threats to Canada's Democratic Process, June 2017.

Under fire in the Cambridge Analytica controversy, Mark Zuckerberg announced that Facebook is strengthening the security features ahead of general elections in India and Brazil. But is this a question of too little too late, a case of closing the stable doors after the horses have bolted? For Facebook, which sees India as a key market with over 217 million users every month, the Election Commission would need to exercise diligence and caution.

7

The EVM: A Controversy That Refuses to Die

THE use of electronic voting machines (EVMs)—comprehensively used throughout the country from the 2004 general election onwards—has become something of a controversial issue. Quite unnecessarily so. For the last two decades, I have observed that when some political parties or candidates have lost elections, they have been quick to blame the EVMs. Yet, when they win at the hustings where the same machines were being used, they celebrate their victories with gusto! In fact, they are at pains to defend the machines and praise the Commission.

The EVMs in India have had a long and rather chequered history. Its introduction was very gradual, in part because of the number of legal challenges it had faced over the years. When Chief Election Commissioner T.S. Krishnamurthy[1] decided to take the plunge and use the EVMs instead of ballot boxes, he had satisfied himself that the introduction of this little machine had successfully faced many trials and tribulations. Nonetheless, its countrywide application twenty-two years after its first usage in 1982 continues to be met with considerable reservation by some political parties who cite prevailing illiteracy levels as well as the socio-economic backwardness in parts of the

1 He was the CEC from 8 February 2004 to 15 May 2005.

country. Apprehensions were expressed by many that many voters, particularly in rural India, might not get to vote by not understanding how to use the machine properly—perhaps by pressing the wrong button or simply being intimidated by a new-fangled gadget.

The history of the EVM, and its convulsions, is worth narrating. In 1977, the then CEC S.L. Shakdhar[2] asked the Electronics Corporation of India Limited (ECIL), a Government of India undertaking, to devise a prototype of an electronic voting machine, which would meet the requirements of Indian conditions and also be compatible with the basic features of the marking system of voting which was already in practice. The first prototype was ready by 1979, which the Commission demonstrated to the representatives of political parties. Two years later, in 1981, Bharat Electronics Limited (BEL) also came out with its version of the EVM and made a demonstration to the Commission.

The initial prototype was 15 inches (38 cm) long but in order to give each political party the same breadth on the ballot paper, the EVM size was increased to a length of 20 inches (50.8 cm). A sturdy design was agreed to incorporating features of both the designs, and approved. In 1982, EVMs were used for the first time, on an experimental basis, at fifty polling booths in Parur assembly constituency in Kerala. A.C. Jose of the Congress party lost to Sivan Pillai of the CPI by over 2,000 votes. The use of EVMs in Parur was challenged in the Supreme Court on the technical ground that there was no enabling legal provision for the use of EVM. In 1982–83, EVMs were used in ten other constituencies in seven states and UTs. These ten elections were not questioned. In 1984, however, the Supreme Court ruled in the election appeal *(A.C. Jose vs Sivan Pillai and others,* AIR 1984 SC921*)* a that specific provision in the law was an essential prerequisite to provide legal sanction for their use, and a repoll was ordered in Parur using ballot paper. (Jose won the elections by a margin of more than 2,000 votes.) It took another four years before the law was amended by parliament in December 1988 and a new Section 61A was inserted in the RoPA, 1951.

2 He was the Chief Election Commissioner from 18 June 1977 to 17 June 1982.

However, EVMs could not be used immediately, for just before the 1989 general elections, some important leaders of the opposition parties raised doubts about the reliability of EVMs. The Commission decided not to rush through their usage till all doubts were cleared.

The government meanwhile referred this matter to the Electoral Reforms Committee appointed in February 1990. The committee witnessed the demonstrations and was convinced but, nonetheless, set up a Committee of Experts in April 1990 headed by the late Professor S. Sampath.[3] The committee unanimously accepted that the machines could not be tampered with. Upon receiving their recommendations, the government notified amendments to the Conduct of Elections Rules, 1961, on 24 March 1992.

After nationwide debates and deliberations in different forums for over a decade, in 1998, EVMs were (still selectively) used in sixteen assembly constituencies in Madhya Pradesh, Rajasthan and Delhi. Following these elections, the Commission decided to ask the Centre for Study of Developing Societies (CSDS)[4] to conduct a feedback study. The study concluded that the trust level in the EVMs was high. Most voters now perceived EVMs to be tamper-proof. Finally, in 2004, the EVMs were used in 687,402 polling stations throughout the country. In a nationwide independent study again done by CSDS after the 2004 general election on the question of 'EVM vs Ballot Paper', the overwhelming majority (82 per cent) favoured the EVM.

Legal Challenges

The EVM's advent had faced legal challenges galore. An early objection had come in 2001 from the late J. Jayalalithaa[5] who

---

3 The committee consisted of Prof. S. Sampath (chairman), Dr C. Rao Kasarbada and Prof. P.V. Indiresan (members).

4 An Indian research institute for social sciences and humanities based in Delhi.

5 Politician and former actress, she was the chief minister of Tamil Nadu five times.

questioned their use in a petition before the Madras High Court.[6] The PMK[7] and the CPI[8] were co-petitioners. In its judgment of 10 April 2001, the Madras High Court observed that the Commission had taken every precaution as a 'prudent normal person' might take in this matter and the 'margin of error was negligible'. The court held that it embodied a simple and perfectly sound technology, 'without defect'. The court also observed that the advantage of using EVMs outweighed those of conventional ballot boxes. The contention of the petitioner about failure of EVM usage in Japan and United States was held to be inapplicable to the Indian situation. The petitioners appealed to the Supreme Court but their plea was summarily dismissed and the order of the high court was upheld.[9]

A second challenge emerged in the Kerala High Court[10] which, after lengthy hearings, rejected a petition that the EVMs were subject to 'piracy'. Its verdict was upheld by the Supreme Court in Civil Appeal (AIR 2003 SC 2271). A third objection was raised in the Karnataka High Court[11] by the candidate who lost the election to the Yelahanka parliamentary constituency held on 6 October 1999. The issues rested on his complaint that the EVMs that had been used were vulnerable to 'mischief'. The high court in its order of 5 February 2004 rejected the plaint and instead held the invention of the EVM to be a great achievement in electronic and computer technology, a 'secure and safe' device, indeed a 'national pride'.

---

6 High Court of Madras, *AIADMK and Others vs Chief Election Commissioner and Others*, CSDS writ Petition No. 3346 of 2001.

7 Pattali Makkal Katchi.

8 Communist Party of India.

9 *All India Dravida Munnetra Kazhagam vs the Chief Election Commissioner and Ors,* 2002/UJ (1) 387, Madras High Court.

10 *T.A. Ahammed Kabeer vs A.A. Azeez*, Kerala High Court, Election Petition 4 of 2001. Order of 9 January 2002.

11 *Michael Fernandes vs C.K. Jaffar Sharif*, Election Petition No. 29 of 1999, Karnataka High Court, 2004.

In spite of these accolades, there were other roadblocks ahead. In 2004, well-known advocate P.N. Lekhi filed a petition in the Delhi High Court.[12] He alleged that EVMs had been tampered with to benefit a UPA win in the general election of that year. The Delhi High Court found no merit in the arguments. A major issue came up before the Nagpur bench of the Bombay High Court[13] in the same year. Here, the petitioner alleged that the machine could be rigged by using 'remotely operated devices', even without actual access to either strongrooms (where machines were stored between and after elections) or to the actual EVM. The high court, in its order of 21 October 2005, dismissed the petition on grounds that the witnesses were not able to aver a single instance to show that the EVMs could actually be so tampered with.

~

During this long and tortuous journey, there was even an occasion when the Comptroller and Auditor General (CAG) lost patience with the Commission for 'wastage of money' spent on developing the machines. However, the then CEC, M.S. Gill[14] decided to forge ahead and deployed EVMs in selected constituencies in Rajasthan, Madhya Pradesh and Delhi. This could, in hindsight, have looked like a somewhat cautious beginning. Limited though it was, it nonetheless proved to be a game changer, for the constituencies were in two major states, while elections in Delhi, being the capital, invariably received disproportionate media attention. Once its efficacy had been demonstrated to the political players, the manifest advantages of using machines over ballot papers became a great deal more attractive. Unlike ballot boxes which had in the past

---

12 Writ Petition No. 8790, Delhi High Court, 2004.

13 *Banwarilal Purohit vs Vilas Muttemwar*, Election Petition No. 1 of 2004. Decision on 21 October 2005.

14 Dr M.S. Gill was the chief election commissioner from 12 December 1996 to 13 June 2001.

been 'stuffed', damaged and even occasionally stolen by delinquent elements, the EVMs were electronically sealed and therefore their data remained secure. No longer could angry voters tear up ballot papers or 'stuff' ballot boxes with illegal ballots, nor pour ink into boxes as miscreants had done from time to time in the past. This system also avoided 'spoilt' or invalid votes, which occurred when voters sometimes marked their preferences inaccurately or between two sets of names.[15] Very often, where winning margins were narrow and 'spoilt votes' could tilt the balance, the losing candidates would demand a recount. Finally, the EVMs would save an estimated 200,000 trees from being cut, to produce over 10,000 tonnes of paper required for general elections. With assembly elections added, millions of trees would be saved over time.

~

In this context, I recollect my own quite harrowing experience very early in my career as a civil servant. A year or so after my appointment as the subdivisional magistrate in Delhi, elections were announced in 1973 to the Delhi Metropolitan Council. I was appointed the returning officer for two north Delhi constituencies of which the Kamla Nagar constituency was the more highly populated. Because it also included a significant chunk of Delhi University's North Campus, it had seen a fierce campaign in the run-up to the poll day. Predictably, voting had been heavy. By the time I started the counting of votes at about 8 a.m., there were crowds of supporters and party officials from both sides thronging the roads outside the polling station. While paper ballots were first removed from ballot boxes, made into bundles of hundred each and divided amongst scores of officials who had to do the actual counting, the crowd of supporters swelled, shouting slogans in favour of their respective candidates or parties. It was not unusual for counting to go on for up to twelve hours. However, by the time I declared the result it was almost 1 a.m. the next morning. The margin

15 Very often, in cases of narrow wins these 'spoilt' votes were the reasons why losing candidates often asked the returning officer for a recount.

of victory was narrow. This was in part because many ballot papers were 'spoiled' on account of wrong or incorrect markings, which resulted in the winning margin being nail-bitingly thin. The defeated candidate appealed to me for a recount. As per the instructions of the Election Commission, recounts in all cases where margins were small were recommended. What might have taken just a few minutes had EVMs been in use, took another couple of hours. By the time I declared the final result, dawn had broken. The candidate who had won after the first count was eventually declared the winner. I sometimes run into him and he never fails to recall the day of his triumph. For me on the other hand, it had been a tension-ridden night, which I too am unlikely to forget.

EVMs in GE 2009

It was also a valuable lesson learned early in my career that in elections every vote matters. Decades later, the advent of the EVM ensured that electronic counting enabled the results to be declared effortlessly and on the very day of counting itself, sometimes within just a few hours. In a country where as many as seven hundred million votes needed to be counted, the use of this little gadget proved nothing short of a miracle, not the least because it also ensured that no vote was lost. Yet, in spite of legal victories and their use in three general elections and over 110 elections to state assemblies over three decades and more, the EVM continues to be buffeted in stormy seas. A concerted attack would emerge in 2009. Since I was at the helm of affairs at that time, I am well placed to discuss the 2009 challenge.

It was in July of that year, just a few weeks after the completion of the general elections, that my erstwhile colleague Omesh Saigal telephoned and asked to see me immediately. I was about to chair a scheduled Commission meeting before I left on an official visit to France that night, but he was adamant and said the matter could brook no delay. Indeed, he said he was on the way to my office even as we spoke. When he arrived, he had brought with him a written complaint that the EVMs used in the recently concluded elections in May 2009 had been tampered with, or at the very least, were in theory vulnerable to mischief. My sixth sense told me that this was likely to blow into a major political issue as Saigal was known for his proximity to L.K. Advani. While he spoke, I concluded that he might have already briefed Advani before he came to see me. In any event, I lost no time in placing his allegation before the full Commission, although it was not a scheduled agenda item.

In the meeting we concluded that while the issues that had been raised were not new, they should be examined anew by one of our senior-most officers. Thereafter, the matter would be placed before our Expert Committee.[16] That evening I left to fulfil my engagements in Paris. When I was halfway through my four-day visit, the story of the EVMs being 'rigged' broke out prominently on the front pages of the national press. A number of political figures including (predictably) L.K. Advani as well as Subramanian Swamy, alleged widespread tampering. I decided not to waste any time in tackling the issue. Our ambassador in France, Ranjan Mathai (later foreign secretary), was quite surprised that I wished to cut short my visit midway, for the Indian embassy had taken great pains to set up back-to-back meetings for me. I asked my hosts in Paris to forgive me for my precipitate departure and returned forthwith to Delhi to meet the challenge head-on.

Upon my return, the Commission decided to put the questions raised and doubts expressed through the grinder afresh. The second Technical Expert Committee (TEC) that had been set up in 2005 comprised three eminent experts, headed by Prof. Indiresan. We had continued to meet them at regular intervals, especially whenever a new issue was raised or any advice was needed. We now invited them to re-examine these allegations, notwithstanding the fact that these had been answered quite comprehensively in the past and some even settled in the courts.

---

16 The second Technical Expert Committee was set up in December 2005 consisting of Prof. P.V. Indiresan (chairman), Prof. D.T. Sahani and Prof. A.K. Agarwala.

These included, inter alia, whether old EVMs were less tamper-proof than the new ones. Was there any danger in using the older variant of EVMs and was it possible to reverse engineer either EVMs or chips or to replace its hardware or to read back the programme code in any manner? Was it possible to change the chip? Even as EVMs were being used in other countries, were ours the only EVMs that were 'stand-alone', which could not be connected to a computer and the only ones which were non-operating-system EVMs? Was this what made our EVMs unique, safety-wise? We also asked whether it was possible to verify that the chips in our EVMs had not been replaced. In other words, could every chip used in our EVMs be identified individually and verified, making sure that the chip could not be changed? Was it even possible for any private manufacturer to make a lookalike EVM that could be used to impersonate the machines that were manufactured for the Commission? (This question would arise quite dramatically in May 2017 when the Aam Aadmi Party [AAP], that presently rules the city of Delhi, demonstrated 'tamperability' on a lookalike machine on the floor of the Delhi Assembly.)

The manufacturers of the electronic voting machines were two highly reputed companies whose ownership rested with the government, and were, in common parlance, known as public-sector companies. These were Bharat Electronics Limited (BEL), which was under the administrative charge of the Ministry of Defence, and the Electronics Corporation of India (ECIL), a company under the administrative control of the Department of Atomic Energy. (Intermittently, over the years, the Commission had received requests from private manufacturers to produce the machines but these requests had always been turned down). We now mounted the most in-depth examination of every issue that had been raised. After weeks of intense deliberations with our Experts Committee and the companies' technical experts, the Commission satisfied itself that there could not have been a single credible case in the whole country where a result had been altered as a result of tampering in the manner that had been alleged as either possible or probable.

Over the years, the Commission had always kept political parties abreast of the number of steps that have been taken to secure the machines at all stages, in the weeks leading up to elections and in the post-election periods. Procedures had been put in place to enhance transparency and provide every opportunity for political parties and candidates to participate in testing the reliability of the machines at several levels. There were regular audits. There is a first level of testing, much before the machines are allotted to various constituencies from storage points, when party representatives are invited to participate in these tests. They are then permitted to select 5 per cent of the machines at random, in which up to 1,000 votes can be polled, to verify their reliability.

The EVMs are then sent out to constituencies but, once again, little is left to chance. A computer programme allocates, again at random, machines to various constituencies. Here, a second level of testing is conducted at the constituency headquarters. From constituency headquarters, the EVMs must travel to all the polling stations therein. Yet again nothing is left to chance. For a third time, the machines are randomly allocated by using a computer programme to the actual polling stations. Here too the candidates are allowed to test the machines of their choice. The serial number of each machine sent to each polling station within each constituency is always shared with the candidates who would need to provide these numbers to their own representatives at the respective polling stations. Altogether almost four million personnel were trained over several months prior to elections.

Randomization all the way down the line lies at the heart of the Commission's EVM delivery system. Parties and candidates are encouraged to inspect any machine when these reach the constituencies and check their unique numbers. This includes all machines held in reserve. These are then grouped and lots drawn at random to assign the groups of EVMs to the assembly segments. Each candidate or party can accompany these lots to the assembly segment strongrooms for storage till the polling day. The entire process was videographed. The parties or candidates are free to post their representatives to 'guard' the machines while they were stored. Each candidate would have his or her unique machine numbers duly signed by the DEO, which could be cross-checked at the time of the mock poll that preceds the D-day, and anytime till the process of counting of votes actually began.

It was only after we were satisfied that all the questions raised had been cleared by our experts that we invited those who had expressed any doubts, (political parties and individuals alike), to actually demonstrate tamperability on any of a hundred machines that we had assembled at random in the Commission headquarters. For the first time ever, it was 'open house' for any stakeholder to come forth to challenge the machine's reliability. A wag called it 'State-sanctioned hacking'.

We announced the working week between 3 and 7 August 2009 for this purpose. This was preceded with the Commission publicly announcing its position through a detailed press note that ours were stand-alone machines which could in no way be networked with any computer or other external source. The chip contained in the EVM had a one-time-only programme, not dissimilar to a pocket calculator programmed to follow only a few commands and which was not capable of being manipulated from, or by, any outside source. The source code for our EVMs was not known to anyone but a clutch of experts in the manufacturing companies. It was certainly not known to us in the Commission. The conditions that we created were not dissimilar to that of an average polling booth. All 'naysayers' were free to 'tamper' with any of the machines, in front of our officials, members of the expert committee and our legal team.

This was also an opportunity for that crop of persons who invariably popped up before every election with 'fixing' solutions. Some candidates, having heard of techies who could 'fix' the machines for a fee, made efforts to locate such 'technical advice'. A few prominent dissenters brought out papers on EVM vulnerabilities tested by them on lookalike machines. We now invited any one who wished to challenge the EVM to do so. Since transparency was vital, it was made clear that video cameras have been installed to record the proceedings, which would be submitted to any court of law that asked for the result of such trials.

Meanwhile, Subramanian Swamy had moved the Delhi High Court[17] questioning the expertise of the Commission's Expert Committee. He alleged that the chip in the EVM could be injected with a 'trojan' which could be 'triggered' after a pre-designated event or sequence of events had been put into motion. For example, the programmed 'trojan' could be 'triggered' if a certain predetermined pattern were activated. In such an eventuality, the EVM would continue to function normally until such time as the 'trojan' was operated by one or a few designated 'conspirators' who cast their votes in the prearranged pattern. Thereafter, as per the 'trojan's' design, the EVM would record extra votes in favour of the conspirator's choice. For instance, that might mean that every other vote or second vote or third vote or fourth vote or fifth vote (depending on the 'programme') would automatically go to that candidate in whose favour the machine had been rigged, irrespective of the button pressed.

Our 'demonstration week' proved rather tumultuous. Some of those who came were not satisfied with the way the demonstrations were conducted. Most of them wanted to examine the chip more closely. Some wanted to photograph the chip; others wanted to take the machine away to examine it more closely. The representatives of the manufacturers, who were present and whose companies held the Intellectual Property Rights (IPR) refused permission for what they believed were attempts at reverse engineering through attempts to copy the internal design and measurements. They wanted the demonstrations to be conducted in the manner that a voter might attempt in an election booth. We, in the Commission, did not have the right to overrule the manufacturers and their engineers. An impasse occurred. Neither side was willing to cede ground. Our

---

17 *Dr Subramanian Swamy vs the Election Commission of India,* Civil Writ Petition No.11879 of 2009 in High Court of Delhi.

manufacturers firmly held that any attempt at reverse engineering would compromise the machine for all time.[18]

Meanwhile, the court hearings continued on schedule. It was during these hearings that the petitioner proposed that if a 'verifiable paper trail' were created, that would assuage his doubts. The voter would then have the opportunity of verifying the name and party of the candidate for whom he or she had pressed the button. Swamy, in his rejoinder added: 'It is once again emphasized that the petitioner, at no stage, has made the averment that there has actually been any fraud through the EVMs of the respondent; only that any electronic machine can be hacked or rigged and hence adequate safeguards are essential to meet the constitutional obligation for conducting free and fair elections.'

This was an idea well worth pursuing, for although the Commission was (and I believe still remains) convinced about the machine's integrity, as a fair umpire of the game it was necessary to travel the last mile to convince political players that the entire process was not only fair but transparently so. This is how the idea of a paper trail was born.

A Paper Trail

This led to yet another round of consultations with our Expert Committee and the manufacturers of our EVMs—BEL and ECIL. It soon became clear from my first meeting that it was no easy task to create a complementary machine that would create a 'paper trail'. Certainly, it was not something that could be readied overnight. Both manufacturers, though conscious of the priority now attached to the issue by the court and the Commission, wanted to proceed with due caution. I chaired several meetings between them and our Experts Committee. We requested them to demonstrate their prototype as

18 In 2010, in what the Commission considered a serious crime, an EVM was stolen during the transportation of EVMs from the jurisdiction of the CEO, Maharashtra, where they were to be used in the assembly elections. An FIR was immediately registered in Maharashtra.

soon as they could develop one. It was clear that they needed several months for research and development.

Even before I demitted office in 2010, at least three demonstrations of early models of the machine were conducted before the full Commission and our Expert Committee. The initial prototypes did not inspire confidence. The margin of error could be as high as 15 per cent, as compared to the EVM's tested error rate of a less than 1 per cent. But these were still early days and the manufacturers needed more time, especially as they received our feedback. What was required was a printer attached to the EVM which would enable the voter to verify her or his vote—that is, the candidate's name and election symbol—through a glass case. It would remain on view for a few seconds before being dropped into a drop box. A beep would announce closure. Under no circumstance could the paper be allowed into the hands of the voters for fear of misuse. Candidates who bribed voters—and voters open to bribery—would otherwise benefit by the display of the paper trail in the hands of a voter, as he or she exited from the booth.

There was also the matter of additional expense which the government would have to bear. While an EVM cost as little as Rs 15,000 (as compared to almost US $15,000 for machines used in most other Western countries as well as in Mexico and Venezuela), this new machine christened the Voter Verifiable Paper Audit Trail (VVPAT) would cost very much more. Under the guidance of the expert committee (TEC) more sophisticated models were developed and are being developed well after I demitted office in mid-2010.

The legal process took its own course. The matter also came up before the Supreme Court, which ruled that in order to make EVMs completely tamper-proof and the process transparent, a voter verifiable paper audit trail had become essential.[19] The Election Commission duly informed the Supreme Court that it was already working on the concept and its Technical Advisory Committee had already approved a design. The VVPAT was put through field trials

19 *Subramanian Swamy vs ECI,* SC 2013.

in July 2011. These field trials had been conducted in five different climatic zones (Leh in Ladakh, Thiruvananthapuram in Kerala, Sohra in Meghalaya, Jaisalmer in Rajasthan and Delhi). A second set of trials were conducted a year later. On 19 February 2013 the final model was approved by the TEC. The court appreciated this 'pragmatic and reasonable approach' of the Commission and permitted it to introduce the machines in phases. This was a prudent decision, for where electoral fortunes could be decided by a single vote, a high degree of error would create many more problems than it might solve.

The final design was appraised by political parties on 10 May 2013. So that there should be no legal hitch on their usage, the Conduct of Election Rules 1961 were suitably amended. In September 2013, VVPATs were put to the test in a bye-election in Nagaland. Although the apex court had sought their introduction in a phased manner in time for GE 2014, the technology was still at a nascent stage. However, when it came to the 2017 assembly elections in Punjab, Manipur, Uttarakhand, UP and Goa, the Commission felt more confident of VVPAT's wider use. As many as 53,500 VVPAT machines were selectively employed in a little over a hundred constituencies.

Finding the money to foot the bill became a hurdle. The Commission addressed the Central government several times asking for release of funds for deploying VVPATs in the Gujarat and Himachal Pradesh elections. Finally, prodded by the Supreme Court, government cleared the allocation of the funds required, enabling the Commission to issue a letter of intent to buy 16.15 lakh VVPAT machines at an estimated cost of Rs 3,173.47 crore. As with EVMs, this order was divided between Bharat Electronics Ltd and Electronics Corporation of India Ltd. The Commission now stood committed to deploying VVPATs in all forthcoming elections including GE 2019.

~

Away from public scrutiny, the holding of any general election throws up a crisis a minute, especially when the actual process gets going. As preparations for the 2009 general election, the EVMs were a source of another wholly unexpected problem. The crisis I unexpectedly had to face was one that former CEC T.S. Krishnamurthy would not have anticipated in 2004 when he universalized the use of EVMs. It fell in my lot to face this particular crisis, which I now reveal for the first time. What triggered it was an all-time high number of candidates who had thrown their hats into the ring.[20] I was aware that in every election there were always 'dummy' or 'cover' candidates put up by all political parties. The reason was perfectly justified. Parties were careful that if their main candidates were incapacitated in some manner or withdrew from the fray at the eleventh hour, they would need a standby candidate, who would eventually withdraw after the main candidate filed his or her nomination. We also knew that there were almost always some frivolous and non-serious players. Then there were 'spoilers' or blackmailers, out for short-term gains. However, as each day passed, we became seriously worried that this time we could be left with more contestants than we had machines.

As it is well known, a single EVM can accommodate up to sixteen candidates and no more. As the number of potential candidates rose, we made detailed calculations of every last machine (including those that we kept in our reserves). I realized to my growing dismay that with each passing day demand began to outpace supply. EVMs were not available to be bought off the shelf. The manufacture of EVMs by our two public sector utilities took months. It involved an arduous process for which there were rigorous protocols in place, all of which were rightly time-consuming. Nonetheless, we called in our manufacturers for urgent confabulations to explore whether they might have held any reserves with them. I was not surprised to learn that they did not have a single spare machine. A crisis loomed. It threatened an enterprise as mammoth as our general election. I have now lost count of the many tension-ridden internal emergency meetings that ensued, some of which were even held at my official residence at 9, Motilal Nehru Marg, New Delhi, which often went

20 See Chapter 1: 'The Great Indian Election'.

well into the night. As we brainstormed, our discussions were fortified by endless cups of tea and coffee which my family prepared in our kitchen. Did this *have* to happen in my time, I asked myself.

To be sure, we were (and remain) a three-member Commission, but as the adage goes, it is the head that wears the 'uneasy crown'. I knew that I would receive the plaudits for an election well done, but equally be held to be the 'villain' (or at the very least incompetent) if things went wrong. It needs to be clarified at this point that I was not yet the head of the Commission. N. Gopalaswami[21] would continue to be CEC till April 16, retiring after the first phase of elections on 20 April 2010 on attaining the mandatory retirement age of sixty-five. As it happened, he took no particular interest in this crisis. Having recently failed to get me removed from office, he lost interest in the day-to-day work of the Commission, although we were just a few weeks away from D-Day.

Clearly, what was needed was an acute mobilization of any surpluses we could manage if necessary by scraping the bottom of the barrel. This meant that the small percentage of surplus machines that we kept in each state for emergencies would now shrink, and shrink drastically. It would barely leave us any cushion. What were the alternatives? We considered the possibility of staggering the elections into more than the five phases that we had envisaged so that the problem of transporting the spare machines might become easier. We debated whether we should conduct the elections in two distinct halves, but that posed a number of logistical difficulties. I was praying that the final picture of 'real candidates' (which would emerge only after the last date of withdrawals was over) would afford us much needed breathing space. But as an administrator, I had learned over long years to never plan for 'best case' scenarios, but always to factor in the 'worst case' ones. So, we began a detailed and meticulous plan for a contingency that involved moving unused machines from first-phase states to second-phase states, and from the second to the third

21 N. Gopalaswami was the Chief Election Commissioner from 30 June 2006 to 20 April 2009.

and so on. Fortunately, the Commission had already hired special planes from the national carrier to help facilitate the movement of men and materials. I had also called on the chief of the air force, Air Chief Marshall Fali H. Major, to loan the Commission as many helicopters as the Indian Air Force might spare. We decided to divert some of these to meet our unexpected challenge.

What a relief, then, that by each of the 'last date of withdrawals' (this was a multi-phased election, so each of the phases had its own last date), a large number of candidates gradually withdrew from the race for their own reasons. Clearly, some were 'dummy' candidates while others were of the 'frivolous' variety. In the end, the final numbers of contestants dropped from a gargantuan 11,252 (almost twice the number of contestants in 2004) to 8,070. This was still dramatically higher than the 5,435 contesting candidates of 2004, up by 2,635 or 48.4 per cent. It is true that there had been more contestants in at least two previous general elections but those were times when ballot papers were used and not EVMs. Whatever their reasons, these withdrawals enabled us to just about manage, although we were stretched far beyond normal limits. Hard pressed as we were, we set up a 'war room' to implement the movement of thousands of unused machines from one state to another upon the completion of each phase of polling. These detailed exercises to move unused machines by planes, trains, helicopters and road transport by the safest possible means were conducted by our deputy election commissioners (DECs) at headquarters in conjunction with our CEOs in the states and they, in turn, with their respective DEOs (district magistrates), adding enormously to their already heavy burden. In the end, they acquitted themselves ably without anyone getting wind of how difficult this exercise had been.

~

In hindsight, some advantage did accrue. We had always practised the randomization of EVMs in the past but on a somewhat smaller scale. Now in having to move such large numbers of reserves from one state of the country to another, this squarely quashed the suspicion that if EVMs remained forever in the same state or even the same constituency, they could be tampered with whilst in storage before an election was announced. Now, with these pan-India movements, these accusations, however muted, were squarely met. For instance, state-level political parties registered in, say, West Bengal did not necessarily exist in Gujarat or Rajasthan and vice versa. Similarly, names of candidates necessarily differ from state to state. It would finally give the lie to the accusation of rigging of machines and put an end to all suspicions. Or so I had hoped.

This was not to be. Despite years of technical scrutiny by experts, long-drawn-out consultations, judicial endorsement and years of successful conduct of elections throughout the country, another storm would break just nine years later. This occurred in March 2017, immediately after the results of the elections to five assembly elections in UP, Uttarakhand, Goa, Punjab and Manipur were declared. The results for UP and Punjab, in particular, caused the loudest outcry of 'rigging'. It was alleged that the EVMs had been manipulated by the parties that had won the elections. On 10 April, thirteen political parties submitted a joint representation to the then CEC Nasim Zaidi[22] that they suspected that the EVMs used in these elections were 'conclusively' tampered with.

The loudest share of the protest was directed against the UP assembly results, which gave the BJP an overwhelming victory. The outcry was from all those political parties that had lost. In one voice, they blamed the EVM for their respective debacles. The most strident voices belonged to the BSP, SP, INC and the AAP. Delhi chief minister Arvind Kejriwal's ire was also directed towards the VVPAT machines which he alleged had been 'selectively' used in UP. He voiced his fear that these machines were now being brought to Delhi to 'manipulate' the forthcoming local body elections, where his party had a major stake. Voices within these parties stridently demanded that the Election Commission abandon the EVMs altogether and

22 The twentieth chief election commissioner, he was in office from 19 April 2015 to 6 July 2017.

revert, once again, to the ballot paper system for all future elections. This demand was rejected by the Commission. and now the Supreme Court has on 22 November 2018 rejected a plea to order the use of ballot papers in place of EVMs.[23]

To assuage some of these fears, I went on record in an article[24] that the EVMs of 2006 manufacture had been used in at least three elections held in UP between 2006 and 2014, prior to their being deployed once again in 2017. Each election provided different outcomes. The Bahujan Samaj Party won in 2007, the Samajwadi Party (SP) won in 2012, while the BJP emerged victorious in 2017 *on the same machines*. In the Parliamentary elections of 2009, the Congress and the SP had done well. In 2014 it was the BJP that triumphed. It beguiles imagination to suggest that an EVM manufactured in 2006 could have been programmed to suit particular outcomes. In any event, in its rejoinder, the Commission officially announced that it is fully satisfied with the tamper-proof working of EVMs.[25]

An excerpt from the *Indian Express* editorial best summed up the furore with these words:[26]

> Faced with the scale of the BJP win in UP and Uttarakhand, some of its rivals are behaving like bad losers. Reluctant to admit that their tactic and their strategy could not withstand the Modi wave, and that the drubbing they have received at the hands of the voters may require them to reassess their politics in deeper ways, some leaders are questioning the credibility of the electoral process itself. BSP supremo Mayawati, Uttar Pradesh Congress chief Kishore Upadhyaya and the outgoing Chief Minister Harish Rawat, have claimed that the electronic voting machines (EVMs) were tampered

---

23 'Supreme Court rejects pleas calling for ballot papers to replace EVMs', *The Indian Express*, 23 November 2018.

24 See N. Chawla, 'When the nice guys did not finish last', *The Hindu*, 9 January 2014.

25 'Don't blame EVMs for poll defeats, says CEC', *Sunday Hindustan Times*, 2 June 2018.

26 *The Indian Express*, 13 May 2017.

with. Mayawati has formally complained about the EVMs to the Election Commission and has demanded fresh polls with ballot papers. She has also claimed—with no evidence whatsoever—that if the EVMs continue to be used till 2019, 'there will be no democracy left in the country'.

This is nothing but petulance and a lack of grace in defeat. India's democracy is far from flawless, but voters trust the polling process as free and fair. Over the years, the EC has deservedly emerged as one of the country's most trusted institutions, a fair and independent monitor of the poll process. Courts, too, have backed the EC's efforts to weed out the flaws and distortions. Political parties across the spectrum reorganise the sanctity of the polling process, and instances of the loser blaming it on the EVM, the EC or polling officials are rare. There have been times when candidates have been defeated by a narrow margin—Congress leader C.P. Joshi lost an assembly election from Nathdwara, Rajasthan, in 2008 by a single vote—and they have challenged the verdict in court, but such cases have been few and far between.

~

There was yet another twist to the tale. On 9 May 2017, the AAP arranged a dramatic demonstration on how the EVMs had been manipulated to suit a particular party on a lookalike EVM, on the floor of the Delhi Legislative Assembly in the presence of all seventy legislators. The national and local press too were present in the media gallery in large numbers. One of the AAP legislators proceeded to conduct a blow-by-blow account of how a 'trojan' could be introduced into the chip prior to an election which would inexorably produce the result that had been programmed. It was a slow and deliberate performance, conducted graphically under full media glare. No sooner was it over than it led, predictably, to an immediate storm. I found myself inundated by telephone calls from the press and TV channels. As it happened, I was at that time not only away from Delhi but far removed from a TV set, so I was unable to witness the 'live' demonstration. However, those who called me obligingly described its details to obtain a sound byte.

From their description, it was clear to me that the demonstration had been conducted on a specially manufactured lookalike. It was not possible for anyone to have obtained an EVM that belonged to the Election Commission, for all our machines lay in the safe custody of DEOs/ DMs. When I did see the playback on TV channels later that day, the lookalike was, of course, quite different from the Commission's own machines. Nor could I glean any information on where the lookalike had come from. Nonetheless, I had no hesitation in dismissing claims of tamperability, especially having subjected our EVMs to the most rigorous scrutiny in 2009 and 2010. We had made it known widely at the time that the software used by Commission was burnt into a one-time programmable/masked chip, which could not be altered in any way. Nor could the EVMs be networked either by wire or through wireless technology with any other system or machine or the Internet. The Commission responded by organizing a 'hackathon' challenge in the following month on the lines the Commission had taken in my time. However, despite these efforts, allegations did not stop being levelled by the AAP and the BSP, although I believe, they were more muted.

An Impenetrable Administrative Structurc

I was also at pains to point out to the press that the Commission has an almost impenetrable administrative system in place which is unique amongst countries that use EVMs. Unlike some other countries which rely on a mix of government officials and volunteers, including university students, to lend a hand on polling day, the Indian election machinery is made up of government officials belonging to either the Union or state government. As government servants, they bring to their duties the accountability that they carry throughout their careers. They are bound by a rigorous code of conduct which carries an in-built penalty system that would accrue on the slightest signs of dereliction of duty. The use of EVMs in India cannot, therefore, be divorced from the context of our supervision exclusively by and accountable to the government's and Commission's administrative mechanism.

It needs to be said that this system of control, devised carefully over the years by the Commission, is shaped like a pyramid headed by the CEO in each state to whom all the DMs/ collectors/ ROs and SPs report in so far as election-related work is concerned. Hence, the DM is also responsible for the safe storage of EVMs during non-election periods, and every aspect of usage during elections, right up to the counting of votes and declaration of results. Were an election petition to be filed, it is he or she that is responsible to the court for any orders that they may issue relating to the election. During polling, the collector/RO assigns his subordinate staff to booth and other election-related duties. To suggest that EVMs are open to being manipulated at any stage of their usage, transportation or storage is not possible, unless the machines are snatched away in some dramatic robbery during polling or stolen during their transportation thereafter. In such an eventuality the election would be annulled by the DM/ RO.

Yet, it is difficult to deny that the 'live demonstration' by the AAP on the floor of the Delhi assembly did succeed in casting doubts in many minds and to that extent it succeeded in its endeavour. It also led to a petition being filed in the Delhi High Court, seeking to declare the proceedings of 9 May both unconstitutional and illegal. The petitioner claimed that the proceedings were violative of the Constitution and the principles of separation of powers, as a result of which the legislature did not have the power to discuss any issue which lay in the exclusive domain of the Election Commission.

To address these fears, the Commission convened a meeting of all the recognized parties. Seven national and thirty-five recognized state parties attended. Most of them agreed to support EVM usage if this was now accompanied by a paper trail. They demanded that a percentage of the slips would be counter-verified. Not everyone was convinced. The AAP, BSP, PMK and Trinamool Congress (TMC) announced that they had lost faith in EVMs. They wanted the ballot paper system to be reintroduced. Others said they would be satisfied if some minor changes were made and the display time increased beyond seven seconds.

More recently, the EVMs were once again used in conjunction with VVPAT machines in all polling booths in the elections held to the assemblies of Gujarat and Himachal Pradesh in December 2017. One polling station across each constituency was cross-checked at random to see if the results tallied. It was a rather small sample. The representatives of political parties were present during these checks. The tally matched in these cases. The first hurdle in the use of the VVPAT had been successfully crossed.

The Commission has taken several additional steps to help assuage doubts. It announced that VVPAT machines will now be comprehensively used in GE 2019—each EVM hooked to a dedicated VVPAT machine. During the course of counting of votes, the Commission will tally a percentage of EVMs with the paper slip generated by the VVPAT bearing the candidate's name and party symbol. If the Commission were to tally every single vote cast with each corresponding VVPAT, it may as well revert to the ballot paper system. Recently, a new generation of EVMs has lately been developed. These were used in 1,800 polling stations in the Karnataka assembly elections held in May 2018. Developed by ECIL and BEL, the 'EVM Mark 3' has a host of new features. Any attempt to prise open the machine, or to alter any component, (even a screw), will cause the machine to automatically shut down. The Mark 3 Control Unit too has taken a quantum leap forward. The earlier generation of control units could accommodate only four balloting units, with sixteen candidates per EVM. The Mark 3 Control Unit can accommodate as many as twenty-four ballot units and as many as 384 candidates.

I continue to hold the view that the generation of EVMs used in the 2009 general election under my watch were beyond tampering. With the introduction of the new generation of EVMs that have been developed, the machines are even more foolproof. I can, therefore, only advise aggrieved parties or candidates that in future they should look inwards rather than blame a machine, whose use has greatly enhanced the capabilities and esteem of India's election process in the democratic world.

8

The Maoist Factor in Elections

MADHUMITA Karmakar tried to dissuade her husband Sougata, twenty-eight, from reporting for Lok Sabha poll duty in Jhargram, West Bengal. She was worried. '"Not this time, please, I told him", she recalled, fighting back tears. "Being seven months pregnant, I tried to stop him, saying our baby is about to come into the world."'[1] This was Sougata's third poll assignment in as many years. 'I was always jittery, I always tried to stop him because of reports that Maoists targeted polling officials but he never listened to me. ... This time, it was different with our first baby expected soon.' She was relieved when he called her on his mobile phone after the polling was over. He reassured her that he would be home in a few hours. After a few hours, when Madhumita tried to call him up again, all she got was a recorded reply: 'This number is not reachable'. Half an hour later, his death was reported on TV.

The Maoists had blown up the jeep in which he was travelling near the Jharkhand border on the completion of poll. A remote-controlled mine shattered the vehicle and killed all its three passengers. Besides Sougata, the Jhargram sector-in-charge Prasad Banerjee, thirty-three, and driver Sanjoy Das, forty-three, were also killed. This tragedy

1 *The Indian Express*, New Delhi edition, 1 May 2009.

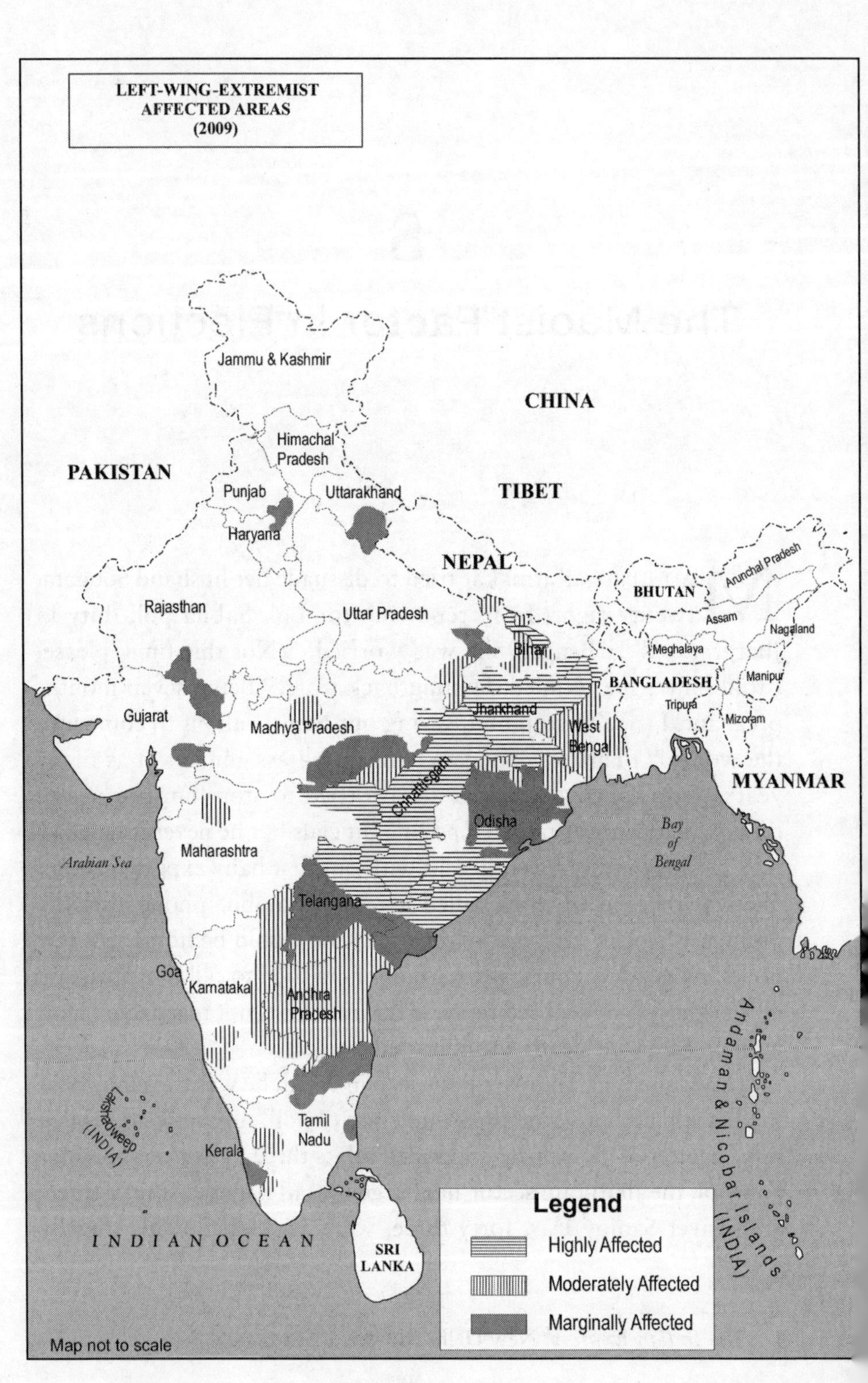
LEFT-WING-EXTREMIST
AFFECTED AREAS
(2009)
Jammu & Kashmir
CHINA
Himachal
Pradesh
PAKISTAN
Punjab
Uttarakhand
TIBET
Haryana
NEPAL
Arunchal Pradesh
BHUTAN
Rajasthan
Uttar Pradesh
Assam
Nagaland
Bihar
Meghalaya
Manipur
BANGLADESH
Gujarat
Jharkhand
Tripura
Mizoram
Madhya Pradesh
West
Bengal
MYANMAR
Chhattisgarh
Odisha
Bay
of
Bengal
Maharashtra
Arabian Sea
Telangana
Goa
Karnataka
Andhra
Pradesh
Andaman & Nicobar Islands
(INDIA)
Lakshadweep
(INDIA)
Tamil
Nadu
Kerala
Legend
Highly Affected
Moderately Affected
Marginally Affected
INDIAN OCEAN
SRI
LANKA
Map not to scale

summed up my fears and apprehensions of conducting elections in Maoist-dominated areas of the country.

I do not intend to go into the reasons that have caused the growth of this armed insurgency—a protracted war of sorts that has been waged against the state since the 1960s. Its history is complex and arguments, for and against, continue to be made. Underlying the Maoist philosophy has been their opposition to the very concept of the democratic state. They have reaffirmed, time and again, their belief that the Indian State in its current form is a collaboration of 'imperialists, the bourgeoisie and the feudal lords'. Their objective is 'annihilation of class enemies and establishment of a new democratic state under the leadership of the proletariat.'[2] Their view was (and remains) that it is a people's war against an unjust government. Hence, the conduct of elections must be opposed by all means, marking a shift in their struggle, from seizure of lands and resources to undermining the state and seizing power,[3] which justified the use of extreme violence. Towards this end, anyone opposed to their boycott call remains a potential target. That includes political parties and candidates, election staff and ordinary voters.

Because of the Commission's determination to conduct polls in all districts, whether Maoist-affected or not, and since I conducted the reviews in the Maoist-affected states as well—which were widely reported in the local press—it was inevitable that I would be the target of the Maoist leadership's ire. I was soon placed under security cover, which was periodically reviewed in the Ministry of Home Affairs, and was constantly 'upped'. I simply asked no questions and accepted the security restrictions imposed on me, although my regret is that I would have wished to travel much more extensively in these areas.

---

2 Central Committee (P) CPI (Maoist), 'Strategy and Tactics of the Indian Revolution', Maoist Documents, 21 September 2004.

3 Naxalism (the earliest Maoist movement in India) was born out of people's struggle against the feudal class in Naxalbari, West Bengal, in 1967.

It was as early as 2006, when the then prime minister, Manmohan Singh, described Maoist threat as the greatest internal security problem that India faced. Between 2006 and 2010 there were an estimated 9,000 incidents in Maoist-dominated states. In 2008 alone, there were 721 deaths in 1,591 incidents of Maoist violence.[4] Despite these incidents of violence, the Commission was determined to ensure that elections be conducted on schedule, but by avoiding the risk of loss of life or limb by all means. By 2008–09, Maoist influence was estimated to have spread in varying degrees up to 180 administrative districts[5] (out of a total of 610 districts in the country), spread over nine states, namely, Jharkhand, Chhattisgarh, Bihar, Odisha, Maharashtra, Karnataka, West Bengal, Uttar Pradesh and Andhra Pradesh.[6]

Our problems were by no means confined to remote areas; there were many urban pockets which provided the Maoists shelter and weapons, and where they were indistinguishable from the population at large. Hence our canvas was very wide indeed. It was well recognized that in the 'red corridor' of heavily forested central India, their threat was all too real. Much of the infrastructure that was needed to set up polling stations, such as schools and other government buildings, had been badly damaged; several roads, bridges and mobile towers had been blown up. Movement, communication and safety were, therefore, major issues. It was conjectured that there were up to 20,000 armed Maoist cadres at the time.

Their modus operandi of disrupting the electoral process was well known from earlier elections. To prevent vehicular movement on arterial roads, they were known to have planted explosive devices, often deep under road surfaces. Some of these were the result of

---

4 See Table: Extent of LWE violence during 2008–17 on page 227.

5 The figures of affected districts vary. The Institute of Conflict Management placed it at 195 in April 2009. See map on page 208.

6 The Institute of Conflict Management; South India Terrorism Portal placed the number of left-wing-extremist-affected districts at 195. (see map on page 208.)

advance planning, which also meant Maoist penetration within the civil administrative structure. They had targeted practically all the arterial roads in their strongholds much in advance. At the time of road repairs or the tarring of roads, landmines were buried at strategic points, especially on or near culverts. Many of these were so powerful that even 'mine-proof' vehicles could not withstand the blasts.[7] Aimed against any and all security forces, these lethal implants were evidently done in connivance with (or by threatening) road contractors. Gelatine sticks and explosives, frequently looted from mining sites, were strategically hidden under bridges and culverts. This enabled them to choose their timing to blow up passing vehicles, as they did in Sougata's case.

Compounding our problems were the large number of landmines that had been buried under foot tracks in the jungle. Their principal targets remained the security forces, but election officials and candidates were also fair game. Their methods were often quite cruel; in the past they had terrorized voters by chopping off the fingers of voters who defied their diktats. If political parties and candidates employed posters, banners and flags for their campaigns, the Maoists too used wall writings, pamphlets and posters to threaten voters, political leaders and poll officials alike against participation in elections. Political leaders were often chased away if they entered to campaign in villages under Maoist control. Police parties were all too frequently attacked. All of this made political activity, the very life blood of elections, very difficult. However, their special targets remained the security forces, for by killing them they could also loot their weaponry to augment their own armouries.

Voter insecurity had also to be constantly addressed, for if voters did not feel confident enough to come out to vote, the Maoists would have achieved their aim. Equally importantly, candidates needed to move around for electioneering. The constantly fluid situation

---

7 A poignant reminder would come in the form of a deadly blast that blew up a 'mine-protected vehicle (MPV) on 13 March 2018 bringing to the fore the heart of the problem, the construction of new roads to usher development projects.

in 2009 did not make for easy movement, but nevertheless, basic precautions that candidates needed to take were being regularly spelt out to them by the district authorities. This was vital, as timely information and putting into place alternative plans, helped save many lives. Witness the carnage in Bastar four years later, on 25 May 2013, which wiped out almost the entire state leadership of the Congress party. Twenty-four top leaders and five security personnel were killed in the deadliest attack on the political establishment in recent years by Moist extremists in India. Therefore, to ensure the safety of the entire election machinery, including the Central police forces, no detail was too small and no travel too inconvenient to enforce strict compliance with our instructions.

To understand the extent of the problems that we faced, I visited most of the critical areas. Police and civilian officials briefed the Commission in detail. It was as a result of successive visits to the affected areas that we gained some understanding of what we were up against. Sometimes, the press would get wind and report these meetings. In any event, these briefings became known to the Maoist leadership for they reacted in their newsletters, and on other occasions they ominously stepped up their attacks to signal their strength.

Gaining some first-hand knowledge, I soon became aware that the effort that went into the setting up of polling stations in these troubled areas, which held a great deal of potential risk, necessitated micro planning. The actual planning was carried out at ground level by the district magistrates/collectors and SPs working under the overall supervision of the senior-most police and civil officers of the state in conjunction with the officers of the Commission. These were difficult duties for our poll officials. Mainly teachers and revenue officials, they had often to walk extremely long distances over dangerous terrain, all the while carrying EVMs, in order to set up their stations. Walking became necessary because transporting our staff by road had become dangerous. Sometimes, where they had been unable to bury explosives under roads, the Maoists simply blocked them by felling trees and laying them across the roads to slow down movement, providing them the opportunity to attack the security forces from their vantage points, as they did to brutal effect in the Gadchiroli district of Maharashtra on 22 May 2009 when sixteen policement were slain. In all these cases, security and civilian officials alike put duty before life, and in my mind, remain the true heroes of that election.

I also came to realize that it was a vital requirement to press into duty as many helicopters as the Commission could obtain from the air force. These would compress the need for long and dangerous jungle treks. They would also help paradrop security officials where needed, or rescue electoral staff in case of danger. I had a number of detailed meetings with the senior-most officers in these problematic areas. At my request, some young district magistrates and SPs who were serving in what were termed 'highly affected' districts at cutting-edge levels, and knew the terrain better than most, were invited to brief the Commission. Their eyes and ears were closest to the ground, and I was glad to hear their accounts first-hand.

Each of these meetings made me realize even more deeply that it was incumbent on us to do everything possible to safeguard our officials. Our staff were not, after all, military men or security personnel trained for combat. Ours was a 'civilian force' that was being led into a conflict zone for which they were not prepared. Helicopters were the answer if we wanted to carry out our electoral mission safely and efficiently.

We requested the defence secretary to meet the Commission. We spelt out our needs. The initial response was not very encouraging. The air force could only spare a much smaller number than I had envisaged. Although I was disappointed, I decided to speak to the defence secretary once again, this time on the phone. He was the 'proper channel' to the air force high command. I asked him to request the air chief once again to accede to the Commission's request for more helicopters. He reverted to me a day later. He regretted that the air force found it difficult to agree.

I then embarked on an unusual step. The lives of our 'boys' were vital to me. I was about to become the CEC in a few days.

Under Article 324 of the Constitution, I had the responsibility for the conduct of elections and had the power to requisition help. So I decided to call on the air chief to explain our problems in these sensitive areas and pursue the Commission's earlier request.

Air Chief Marshal Fali Major graciously received me at his home. Over cups of tea—our meeting went on for over an hour and a half—I explained my predicament, fears and apprehensions, hopes and strategy. I believe I was able to convey my views adequately. By the time I had finished explaining the predicament of the Commission, the air chief marshal, who listened with care and sympathy, responded most positively. He offered me everything I asked for and more. He even approved my proposal to convert two helicopters into air ambulances equipped with a doctor, paramedic staff and life-saving medicines and equipment that could fly to nearby designated hospitals. The deployment of these saved many lives and lessened the hardship of our officials to a very considerable extent, thanks to Air Chief Marshal Major.

Maoist Violence during Elections

The election year of 2009 would witness several violent election-related incidents perpetrated by the Maoists. Despite all our precautionary arrangements, which certainly saved lives, there were many violent incidents that took place in the different Maoist-affected states. The early signs were ominous. Three days before the first day of poll (13 April 2009), ten paramilitary troops were killed in Koraput in Odisha when Maoists attacked a bauxite mine and seized explosives, which was invariably their intent when they attacked mining operations that necessitated the use of explosives. On the opening day of elections (16 April 2009), when most of the Maoist-affected parliamentary constituencies went to polls simultaneously, six BSF personnel were killed in a landmine blast in Latehar district of Jharkhand. The BSF personnel were on their way for poll duty when their bus was attacked. Altogether seventeen deaths took place from 101 incidents on the opening day. Four days later, on 22 April, six police personnel were killed in as many as twenty different incidents. We also faced many tension-filled hours in the Commission, when the Maoists hijacked a train with at least 300 passengers on board in Jharkhand, forcing it to travel to Latehar district. The train was released later that day. By some miracle, there was no loss of life.

On 30 April, when the three Maoist-affected constituencies of West Bengal went to polls, Sougata and his companions were killed. The mechanics of Maoist violence on the poll day varied: they included attacks on polling parties, landmine blasts, firing on polling stations and snatching of EVMs after polling was completed and poll parties were on their return journeys. The Maoists also gave poll boycott calls in many places and threatened voters with dire consequence if they violated Maoist diktat.

While I had been conscious of the difficulties of our election staff, I gradually began to understand the many hardships that the jawans faced when on election duty. They were constantly on the move with barely any respite. After each phase of polling they would be transported by train to another station where they would have to become operational as soon as they arrived at their new destinations. When I learned that their housing conditions, albeit temporary, were usually large dormitories or barracks often without basic amenities, the Commission laid down instructions that became standard operating procedures, providing for adequate rest and food and other amenities during their difficult assignments. Most of them were young men who had no experience of tackling insurgencies amidst thick jungles and difficult terrain. I twice went to visit those injured in hospital, and was glad that we had made arrangements for their rapid evacuation.

An incident that took place on the Kaimur Hill range in Rohtas district of Bihar just a day prior to the elections on 16 April, pointed to the new realities of Maoist violence marked by increased fire power and unprecedented audacity. Normally, Maoists fired on security forces when the latter were on the move, or when they enjoyed the advantage of being on elevated ground or hidden behind forest cover. They also tended to resort to direct attacks when security forces were in small formations. The Kaimur Hill incident saw a much larger force of about 300 Maoists who launched a synchronized attack on a full company of the Border Security Force (BSF) consisting of more than seventy-five men. It was close to midnight when they surrounded a government school where the BSF jawans were pitched to provide security to several polling stations in thc vicinity. The Maoists used rocket launchers and other sophisticated weapons in this daring attack. The BSF jawans retaliated. About seventeen Maoists were reportedly killed while one BSF jawan was injured. That the Maoists were prepared to take on a full company of a professional force would also shape future strategies of handling Maoist encounters.

Another aspect of the Maoist violence that confronted the Commission were attacks on school buildings. Since schools are most often used as polling stations and teachers as polling officers, they became special targets of attacks intended to disrupt the electoral process. A 2011 study by the Human Rights Watch shows that at least thirty-six schools in Jharkhand and twenty-three in Bihar were attacked by Maoist insurgents in 2009. While Maoists have frequently cited use of school buildings by security forces as their reason for attacking schools, Human Rights Watch has found that Maoists had also damaged or destroyed numerous schools that were *not* actually occupied by security forces. In any event, this adversely affected education in these regions resulting in poor attendance and increasing dropout rates.[8] Taking this into account the Supreme Court in 2016 ordered the security forces not to use schools as military bases.

~

8 See 'Education under Attack', Global Coalition to Protect Education from Attack, 2014, http://www.protectingeducation.org/education-under-attack-2014. Also see UN Convention on Rights of the Child, 'Concluding Observations on the Report submitted by India under Article 8 para 1 of the Operational protocol', para 28; and UN General Assembly, 64th Session, 'Promotion and Protection of the Rights of Children', para 135.

On 22 May 2009, the police forces would suffer some of their worst setbacks in the Gadchiroli district on the Maharashtra–Chhattisgarh border where at least sixteen police persons including, for the first time, five policewomen, were gunned down by Maoist forces just as soon as the election ended. The incident occurred after a contingent of police personnel had been rushed to clear some trees that had deliberately been felled by Maoists to block the busy state highway leading to Chhattisgarh. The unsuspecting personnel were killed in an ambush laid by a group of seventy to 100 Maoists.

The Maoist attacks on police patrols in the Gadchiroli district continued throughout the year. On 8 October, just prior to the Maharashtra assembly elections in November 2009, they killed seventeen policemen belonging to an elite police team conducting routine exercises near the Chhattisgarh border. This ambush coincided with the grisly beheading of a suspected police informer and setting a panchayat office on fire. The renewed burst of Maoist attacks appeared to be designed as much to mock the Commission and me,[9] as to mock the Union home minister's 'offer' for talks before 'annihilation' and claims by Maharashtra police that Maoists would not be able to enforce their poll-boycott call in the district. Coming barely five days before the Maharashtra assembly elections, the ambush cast its shadow on polling in the three constituencies in the district. The Maoists' poll boycott call had already impacted campaigning. Political parties and candidates

---

9 Azad, the spokesperson of the Central Committee of the Communist Party of India (Maoist), pooh-poohed the media claims that the successful completion of the first phase of the elections showed 'how democracy had won against anarchy, how ballot proved to be superior to bullet, how people defied the Maoists and came forth to exercise their franchise braving the bullet, and such endless rhetoric'. He went on to target the Commission: 'The Chief Election Commissioner-designate Navin Chawla howled that "democracy triumphed over Maoist extremism on 16 April".' See Sumanta Banerjee, 'On the Election Boycott Tactic of the Maoists', *Economic and Political Weekly*, 19 September 2009.

had long since abandoned the area despite the considerable security provided to them.

From hijacking trains, bombing railways stations and torching oil tankers to ambushing policemen and gunning down civilians, Maoists spread their terror across a 'red corridor' along what was once estimated at almost 40 per cent of the country's geographical area. The ease (and seeming laxity) with which the police personnel walked into some of these traps in one of Maharashtra's most affected districts reflected the inadequacies of the police force and its lack of specialized training. The police forces were often ill-equipped and poorly trained to fight this particular type of guerilla combat. Police strength in critical states like Chhattisgarh, Orissa and Jharkhand in 2009 was well below the national average of forty-four policemen per 100 sq. km. For example, that year Orissa spent just one-third of the planned outlay while in Jharkhand up to 60 per cent of the funds spent had been improperly utilized. At the same time, the Central and state governments need to address the root causes of the problem that lie mainly in socio-economic inequalities and deficiencies in basic infrastructure and services.

Despite all these obstacles, elections *were* held on time. There was 55 per cent polling in the first phase and 65 per cent in the second. This was quite a good turnout considering the circumstances, and the press commented on the triumph of the ballot over the bullet. Despite the violence and threats to disrupt the elections in 2009, the Commission's campaign featuring cricketing idol M.S. Dhoni successfully helped to ensure a higher turnout of voters in the Jharkhand assembly elections later in the year in November 2009 when 52 per cent defied the Maoists' boycott call to come out to vote. This was accompanied by stricter vigil and stronger security measures, and an election spread over five phases. It is interesting to note that in the sixteenth general election in 2014, when the option for NOTA was first introduced, as many as 1.1 per cent of voters chose this option, interestingly in predominantly Maoist strongholds. I would see this as yet another validation for the electoral process.

Salwa Judum

In Chhattisgarh, a growing discontent with Maoist strikes and their opposition to developmental works, led people from villages affected by violence to mobilize against Maoists. '*Salwa Judum*' meaning 'purification hunt' in the Gondi language received support from the government. They were armed cadres and deployed as part of anti-insurgency operations in Chhattisgarh. Since its inception in 2005 till the beginning of 2007, the government under the Chhattisgarh Police Regulations appointed 4,048 'Special Police Officers' (SPOs). The SPOs named Koya Commandos, after a tribe in Dantewada, were paid Rs 1,500 a month and were trained to handle arms. Salwa Judum was active mainly in the Bastar and Dantewada districts of Chhattisgarh. It is alleged that Salwa Judum consisted of local youths; they were accused of burning to ground 644 villages, resulting in large-scale displacement of villagers caught in the conflict between Maoists and Salwa Judum activists. In 2007, against the backdrop of controversies surrounding the militia's activities and state sponsoring of violence, a writ petition (*Nandini Sundar vs State of Chhattisgarh*, WP (Civil) 250 of 2007) was filed seeking to disband Salwa Judum. On 5 July 2011, the Supreme Court disbanded the militia declaring it illegal and unconstitutional and directed the state to retrieve all arms, ammunition and accessories. The apex court further asked the state to investigate all instances of alleged criminal activities of the group.

A commentary by the Institute of Peace and Conflict Studies, titled 'Elections in Maoist Heartland' had noted in the run-up to GE 2009 that 'elections were unlikely to have any impact on the Maoist violence raging in the state'. The author further observed that national parties like the BJP and INC had not addressed the major issues that attracted and sustained the Maoists in these regions, such as marginalization of tribals and the controversial anti-Maoist Salwa Judum campaign.[10] While one cannot argue with the need for political parties and the state to address the deep-seated malaise, the very holding of elections in areas affected by Maoist extremism has demonstrated the power of the vote as a tool in democratic change.

~

This internal conflict has deeply affected India's governance, security, economy and rule of law. In February 2009, the government initiated an Integrated Action Plan which involved more coordinated operations side by side with economic development projects at the grass-roots level. However, the government's track record in understanding this very complex problem has been spasmodic at best. A much more comprehensive, holistic and sustained policy involving across-the-board views, particularly within the severely affected states, was long overdue. Conducting future elections as an important index of successful democracy would depend on the ability of the government to find solutions to this growing cancer within.

I have no doubt that the conduct of elections in Maoist-affected areas has emerged as the foremost challenge to democratic elections. As has been said in many forums, Maoist extremism by its nature and ideology is against democracy and averse to elections. Hence, disrupting every election has become a fundamental pillar of Maoist behaviour, which they believe will lend them advantage to seize power from the state. In the specific context of GE 2009, a statement issued by the Communist Party of India (Marxist-Leninist) (CPI-ML), in Naxalbari, West Bengal, in April 2009 and an interview given by the spokesperson for the Central Committee of the Communist Party of India (Maoist), conducted by the Maoist Information Bulletin on 10 April 2009, bear witness to the extreme views that the Maoists hold, regarding the democratic election process. The CPI-ML called for the complete destruction of the system to attain 'real freedom'

10 On 5 July 2011, the Supreme Court disbanded the militia declaring it illegal and unconstitutional.

while the CPI(Maoist) Central Committee spokesperson described the 2009 elections as 'the most complex, most crisis-ridden and most fragmented in the annals of the so-called Indian Parliamentary democracy'. The spokesperson had provided details of how Maoists enforced poll boycott and helpfully explained the difference between 'poll boycott' and 'active boycott' justifying 'active boycott' which included 'some counter-offensive' actions aimed at 'destroying the enemy forces'.[11]

Changes in the Commission's Strategy

In the past and in accordance with local diktats, Maoists used to target only the security forces sparing the polling staff and other civilians. But preceding GE 2009, attacks on civilian officials and polling stations were stepped up to deter the voters. This was particularly evident in some hard-core Maoist areas where communication was limited and Maoists were strongly entrenched. As the poll schedule was known well in advance, so too were the routes and timings of travel by candidates and polling parties. There was danger too for the safety of polling staff, not to mention ordinary voters who dared to defy the boycott call, even in some of the so-called liberated zones, although the normal functions of day-to-day governance were largely marked by their absence or were, at best, spasmodic. (The 'hard-core Maoist' areas, however, had not been visited by any senior government official for years together and so they had not been recipients of any government services or any special schemes.)

Because of this evident danger, poll officials had in the past contrived to conduct 'bogus' polls instead of real ones. On the appointed poll dates, fictitious reports would be filed that poll parties had reached their designated stations, polls had 'started' and 'been completed on time'. While fully understanding the reasons for their apprehension, we decided against any form of 'stage-managing'. Faced

11 Maoist Information Bulletin, 10 April 2009.

as we were with the dichotomy of interests between the need to ensure security of our personnel and the need to maintain the integrity of elections, we addressed ourselves to finding some pragmatic solutions. The first was to shift the polling stations to areas that we could secure better. For this it was necessary to consult the political parties and candidates concerned, which was done. In some of the most dangerous areas, we also changed poll timings. Since it was mandatory to conduct the polls for eight hours, we began at 7 a.m. instead of 8 a.m. and ended the poll at 3 p.m. This helped the escorting police forces to ensure the safe return of polling personnel (with polled EVMs) under proper security cover, both on ground and from the air. These two initiatives were kept secret and implemented at the eleventh hour, which helped reduce incidents of violence and eventual casualties, because the Maoists preferred to attack our election teams on their return journeys to snatch the EVMs and destroy them.

Perhaps nowhere did I read a more succinct and comprehensive summing up of the dangers and difficulties we faced than in the *Hindu*, in its editorial 'The Maoist threat'. The editorial had noted that far fewer Central police forces had been made available for GE 2009 than we had hoped for.[12]

> Media commentators are calling Lok Sabha election of 2009 the most violent election ever. Bombings of police officers and paramilitary personnel, claiming dozens of lives; attacks on poll staff and party workers; the hijacking of a train in Jharkhand—is India's democracy at risk of being undermined by the growing Maoist insurgency in its heartland? The answer is no, there is no need to panic. Actually, insurgents succeeded in targeting the election process in merely 71 of the 76,000 polling stations identified as vulnerable to attack during Phase I, a minuscule 0.09 per cent. Their success was, moreover, the result not of the Maoists' enhanced capabilities but of poor security management. In November 2008, 300 companies of central police forces were committed to securing the elections to the Chhattisgarh Legislative Assembly. For the Lok Sabha elections, only 160

12 *The Hindu*, 14 April 2009.

companies were made available. In Jharkhand, 96 companies were provided against an estimated requirement of 220. What is more, multiple clusters of Maoist-hit constituencies went to the polls on the same day, a decision which did not allow for the saturation of troubled areas by the available forces. What the violence ought to do is provoke some introspection on India's responses to the Maoist insurgency. Last year, 638 people—210 of them civilians and 214 police personnel—died in Maoist violence. In 2007, the death toll was similar in pattern: 650 fatalities, 240 of civilians and 218 of police personnel. Maoist violence now claims more lives than the fighting in Jammu and Kashmir.

The Road Ahead

In 2010, before demitting office at the Election Commission, I prepared a road map that I believe is valid even today. It rests on five major premises:

1. Unless very strategic gains are achieved in containing the Maoist problem in the country, the conduct of elections in Maoist areas is likely to become increasingly difficult in future.
2. The classification of districts and parliamentary constituencies as Maoist-affected requires further fine-tuning, and a professional approach guided by empirical data needs to be adopted in this regard. Mere labelling on broad terms may not suffice. To get priorities right, categorization needs accuracy.
3. There should be a conscious realization that in 'hard-core' Maoist areas the writ of the local administration does not run in the normal course. The task of conducting elections and its limitations should be seen in the overall context of ground realities prevailing in the area and not in isolation.
4. The requirements of ensuring free and fair elections at any cost and the need to minimize the loss of human lives must

be finely balanced. Pragmatic solutions need to be constantly evolved to address these needs and requirements.

5. Management of elections in Maoist-affected areas should be considered an area of specialization. Continuing research, planning, documentation, training and identification of managerial talents in specific areas of responsibilities should become part of future strategies.

Recent History

In early 2014, the *Hindu* carried an article that would indicate a change in direction:[13]

> The districts of Chhattisgarh partially controlled by Maoists—with 12 Assembly constituencies—voted overwhelmingly in 2013. Compared to 2008, voter turnout in 2013 increased by 9.67 percentage points in 12 constituencies, while the overall polling was 6.81 percentage points higher than in the previous election. The record rise in polling illustrates that rebel-dominated constituencies embraced the democratic process more avidly than the rest of Chhattisgarh. The rise in polling in south Chhattisgarh, where nearly 600 companies of additional paramilitaries (almost double of 2008) were posted for election, was attributed to force escalation and reduction in Maoist strength. 'We requested the civil society—individuals and organizations—including a few Gandhians to ask the Maoists to exercise restraint during elections,' said the DGP. So, clearly, a record deployment of force was not the only reason for non-violent polling. Several examples illustrate how Maoists allowed calibrated polling in 12 constituencies, partly in areas controlled by them. ... There is enough evidence to suggest that Maoists put up their preferred candidates in the Assembly elections. While the names of such candidates are withheld for security reasons, a scrutiny of booth-wise results in Maoist strongholds underscores the presence of

13 Suvojit Bagchi, 'Different strategies for different booths', *The Hindu*, 6 January 2014.

> strong support for a few candidates. … [T]he rebels adopted different policies for separate booths, rather than fanatically nurturing one overarching official policy to boycott the elections. While it could be argued that many of these booths were shifted out of the respective villages, thus reducing the poll percentage, what is puzzling is that the Maoists are adopting contradictory approaches. It is now evident that the Maoists asked the villagers to walk 15 to 20 kilometers in some of the relocated booths to exercise their franchise, like in Elengnar, while resisting polling in some other areas. From a preliminary survey of 90 per cent of south Chhattisgarh's booths, it seems that the rebels have encouraged calibrated polling in some areas for the first time in several decades, while refusing to expose the villagers from robust base areas. So, in the final count, it could well be premature to suggest that the rebels were forced to allow polling uniformly across Bastar.

On 13 March 2018 would come another chilling reminder that this conflict is far from over. In Chhattisgarh's particularly troubled Sukma district, Maoists used heavy explosives that ripped through a 'mine-protected vehicle' (MPV) killing nine CRPF personnel. This also reflected the head-on collision between the government's strategy to create roads (that would eventually bring development and wean village folk away from Maoist domination) and the Maoist riposte to prevent this from happening. The CRPF has been deployed to protect the not unsurprisingly reluctant contractors engaged in road building. A former DGP of the CRPF, K. Durga Prasad, reiterated what the Commission knew only too well: 'The best way to travel in Maoist areas is by foot.'[14]

There is no clear beginning or end to this internecine conflict amongst our own people. The deep divide has been captured rather poignantly in a bunch of letters recently recovered by the police from a Maoist hideout in Dantewada district of Chhattisgarh. They carried no names or addresses. Perhaps, they were being dispatched through a hand-to-hand postal system, which is the means of communication

---

14 'Maoists kill 9 CRPF men in Sukma', *Hindustan Times*, 14 March 2018.

for Maoists in the jungles of Bastar. The letters tell their stories 'of increasing police and government influence in some areas; promises to intensify Maoist military and political schooling; of consolation, solace and loneliness.'[15]. A letter, recovered from a Maoist leader Situ's bag says, 'It is happening such that the enemy is targeting our RPC (Revolutionary People's Committee) and sangham, and their target is to finish them off. We have given responsibilities to the sangham of the villages where they reside. Whatever they know, they are doing. Therefore, you should also think that you left behind your parents, sister, brother and everyone else in the village for the people, to solve the problem of the poor people, and to fight against the thieves. Think comrade. There are illnesses, but the party is responsible. Whatever subjects the commander raises, don't think of them as criticism. Don't get angry and don't think about going home. Heat, rain, cold—these are all problems that will always come. We are working for the people.'

At the end of 2017, the government would adopt a four-pronged strategy to fight internal insurgencies. Termed Samadhan, this includes security-related interventions, development-related interventions, ensuring rights and entitlements of forest dwellers and better public-perception management. In recent years, a concerted attempt has been made to block their sources of funding.

In sharp contrast to the attacks on security forces in 2009 in Gadchiroli district, a police operation conducted on 22 April 2018 as one of a series of anti-Maoist operations witnessed signs of Maoist retreat. Thirty-seven Maoists were killed, which for the first time included some of their senior commanders and cadre members. The police commandos, who took part in the operation, belonged to an elite anti-Maoist squad called C-60, raised by the Maharashtra police. No fatalities were reported among the security forces. Significantly, this attack was conducted in an area where the Maoists had felt

15 'In Chhattisgarh, letters seized from Maoist camp tell story of govt push, dire situation', *The Indian Express*, 26 March 2018.

secure for decades. The success of the security forces was ascribed to improved intelligence and strengthened outreach.

The Maoists concede they have lost ground in their heartland and are under increasing threat in their remaining safe havens.[16] As security forces are making significantly more pin-pointed attacks as part of a larger strategy, Maoists have suffered potentially devastating reverses in the past few years, not just in Gadchiroli but across the wider theatre of their dominance—the so-called Red Corridor. Within the logic of the war that is being waged, it is expected that there will be retaliation for their losses in Gadchiroli. Revenge attacks may come wherever and whenever the opportunity presents itself. It remains to be seen what the impact of this seemingly prolonged warfare will be during the forthcoming assembly elections in Chhattisgarh in November 2018, and in the general elections that follow in 2019.

Table showing the extent of LWE violence during 2008–17

Year	Incidents	Deaths
2008	1591	721
2009	2258	508
2010	2213	1005
2011	1760	611
2012	1412	415
2013	1136	397
2014	1091	319
2015	1089	230
2016	1048	278
2017	908	263

Source: Ministry of Home Affairs

16 Ajay Sahni, 'Devastating impact on Maoists, but be prepared for revenge attacks', *Hindustan Times*, 24 April 2018.

MAJOR MAOIST ATTACKS DURING 2008 to 2017

Year	Date	Deaths	Total Death Toll (*for the year*)	Incident Information	Where
2008	16 February	12	71	Police personnel killed in a Maoist raid on police training school, police station and an armoury	Odisha
	29 June	38		Four police personnel and 60 greyhound commandoes attacked on a boat	Balimela reservoir, Odisha
	16 July	21		Police van blown up with landmine	Malkangiri district, Odisha
2009	13 April	10	81	Paramilitary troop attacked near bauxite mine	Koraput district, Odisha
	22 April	-		Hijacked a train with 300 people on board	Latehar district, Jharkhand
	22 May	16		Police personnel attacked in forest area	Gadchiroli district, Maharashtra
	10 June	-		Nine police officers and CRPF personnel ambushed during routine patrol	Saranda forest area, Jharkhand

MAJOR MAOIST ATTACKS DURING 2008 to 2017					
Year	Date	Deaths	Total Death Toll (*for the year*)	Incident Information	Where
2009	13 June	10		Police personnel attacked with two landmines and a bomb blast	Bokaro district, Jharkhand
	16 June	11		Police personnel attacked with landmines, followed by armed assault	Jharkhand
	16 June	4		Police personnel ambushed	Palamau district, Jharkhand
	23 June	-		Attacked Lakhisarai district court, Bihar and freed four Maoists	Lakhisarai district, Bihar
	18 July	1		Villager killed	Bastar district, Chhattisgarh
	18 July	-		Road construction vehicle burnt down	Bijapur district, Chhattisgarh
	27 July	6		Landmine blast	Dantewada district, Chhattisgarh
	4 September	4		Villagers killed in forest area	Dantewada, Chhattisgarh
	26 September	2		BJP MP Baliram Kashyap's sons killed	Jagdalpur, Chhattisgarh

MAJOR MAOIST ATTACKS DURING 2008 to 2017

Year	Date	Deaths	Total Death Toll (*for the year*)	Incident Information	Where
2009	8 October	17		Police personnel killed in an attack on police station	Gadchiroli district, Maharashtra
2010	15 February	24	145	Eastern Frontier Rifles (EFR) attacked at their camp	Medinipur West district, West Bengal
	4 April	11		Anti-Maoist force Special Operations Group attacked with landmine blast	Koraput district, Odisha
	6 April	76		A Chhattisgarh police official and 75 CRPF personnel killed in ambush	Dantewada district, Chhattisgarh
	8 May	8		CRPF personnel killed when a bullet-proof vehicle was blown up	Bijapur district, Chhattisgarh
	29 June	26		CRPF personnel killed in an ambush	Narayanpur district, Chhattisgarh
2012	18 October	6	6	CRPF personnel killed and many injured in an ambush	Gaya district, Bihar

MAJOR MAOIST ATTACKS DURING 2008 to 2017

Year	Date	Deaths	Total Death Toll (*for the year*)	Incident Information	Where
2013	25 May	28	33	Congress leaders including state Congress chief Nand Kumar Patel, former Union minister V.C. Shukla and former state minister Mahendra Kumar among others were killed	Sukma district, Chhattisgarh
	2 July	5		Police personnel including superintendent of police for Pakur were killed	Dumka area, Jharkhand
2014	28 February	6	32	Police personnel including an SHO killed	Dantewada district, Chhattisgarh
	11 March	15		Security personnel killed	Sukma district, Chhattisgarh
	10 April	8		Six commandoes and two others killed in an attack on CRPF jeep	Jamui district, Bihar
	14 June	3		Three passengers killed and six injured in hijack of Dhanbad–Patna express train	Jamui district, Bihar
2015	11 April	7	7	Police personnel killed	Sukma district, Chhattisgarh

MAJOR MAOIST ATTACKS DURING 2008 to 2017					
Year	Date	Deaths	Total Death Toll (*for the year*)	Incident Information	Where
2016	19 July	10	10	CRPF commandoes killed in forest area	Aurangabad district, Bihar
2017	12 March	12	36	Personnel of 219 CRPF battalion killed and weapons were seized	Sukma district, Chhattisgarh
	24 April	24		CRPF personnel killed	Sukma district, Chhattisgarh

Source: 'Naxal attacks: A chronology of major incidents since 2008'[17]

17 India TV, New Delhi, 25 April 2017.

9

Jammu and Kashmir 2008: A Historic Election

Background

IF I was asked to pinpoint the most challenging assembly election during my tenure, it would be the Jammu and Kashmir (J&K) legislative assembly election, which we held over a five-week period between November and December 2008. It was also the precursor to the general election held in April–May 2009—a dress rehearsal for the Big One—for the enormous logistical difficulties that we faced in Jammu and Kashmir would prove to be a valuable learning experience for what was to follow a few months later.

Elections in J&K have invariably involved a number of factors that are inherent in the very nature of the region. There are three disparate regions in this state: Jammu, Kashmir Valley and Ladakh. Each of the regions is different from the others in terms of religion, ethnicity, language, food habits, dress, local traditions and customs.

Geographically large but sparsely populated Ladakh, which comprises Buddhist-dominated Leh and Shia-Muslim-dominated Kargil remains cut off from the plains during its long and cruel winter. Jammu with its Hindu-majority population straddles both mountain districts as well as the plains. The Kashmir Valley comprises a

Muslim-majority population that has little in common with either of the other two regions. Historically, they coalesced into the kingdom carved out by the Dogra rulers; the last ruler was Maharaja Hari Singh[1] who entered uneasily into the new Indian Union when he signed the Instrument of Accession on 26 October 1947. At that time, a part of his territory was annexed by Pakistan following an armed conflict. Since then, the armies of India and Pakistan have faced one another across an international border and they have fought three wars: in 1947, 1965 and 1971. While the regions of Jammu and Ladakh faced no problems after their merger with India, Kashmir has faced all kinds of problems from the start, with varying degrees of hostility from across the border, which continue till this day. Even in the presence of the most sublime beauty, a visitor to the Valley is often conscious of underlying tensions.

J&K is the only state in India which enjoys special autonomy under Article 370 of the Indian Constitution. It also remains the only state to fly its own flag alongside the national flag. It has its own Constitution. At the time of the merger, the maharaja of Kashmir's special status was recognized by the viceroy who agreed to certain special terms and concessions to ensure the feasibility of the merger of a Muslim-majority state into the Indian Union. For while the ruler was Hindu, his subjects were largely Muslim. Moreover, this was a border state bearing immediate proximity to Pakistan. Technically, as a border state it was free to choose between the new dominions of India and Pakistan. The maharaja, after his initial prevarication of wanting to remain independent, finally opted to merge with India. Viceroy Lord Mountbatten, hammered out a special status for Jammu and Kashmir wherein the Indian parliament's jurisdiction was limited to defence, communication and foreign affairs. The Supreme Court was accorded only appellate jurisdiction. The Indian Union had no administrative control over Jammu and Kashmir; indeed, laws enacted by parliament would not apply to Jammu and Kashmir. Even

1 The father of statesman and parliamentarian Dr Karan Singh.

the Election Commission's jurisdiction applied only to the elections of the president and vice-president of India.

This would change dramatically in 1954 with the implementation of the Constitution (Applicable to Jammu and Kashmir) Order, 1954. It extended the jurisdiction of the Union parliament to almost all subjects in the Union List. There were some important exclusions—the holding of elections according to the provisions of the J&K Representation of the People Act, for instance. The jurisdiction the Election Commission of India was extended to J&K by a special amendment as late as 1959. Even here, there were notable exceptions. Elections to the state assembly would occur every six years, not five. Only permanent residents of the state were eligible to vote or stand for elections to the state assembly. Stricter rules would apply, e.g., Section 24F of the J&K Representation of the People Act would automatically debar a member who was disqualified for corrupt practices for a period of ten years.

Into this complex scenario must be added the large-scale exodus of the Hindu Pandit population on or after 20 January 1990, when almost 300,000 Hindus were forced by terrorists to flee the Valley, leaving behind homes, property and domicile status. It was genocide of a kind—many fled to neighbouring Jammu and others to Delhi and beyond. A majority of Pandits are still apprehensive of returning to their original homes.

Conducting elections in J&K, and more particularly in the Valley, have always been difficult for a whole host of reasons. The people of the state have had serious misgivings about the Commission, which many viewed as a mere tool of the Central government, which was always available to do the bidding of the government in power. This fear was not altogether without basis. The 1983 election saw Farooq Abdullah's National Conference win a majority. However, his government was dismissed within a year in the most questionable of circumstances. The Central government appointed Farooq Abdullah's own brother-in-law, G.M. Shah, in his place. Shah was seen as a puppet and had no credibility as a result.

The election that followed in 1987 was, sadly, the 'nadir' of all elections. A compliant Commission conducted an election that was widely seen as a travesty; the results it declared did not find acceptance, neither nationally nor internationally and least of all in the state concerned. Much has already been written about the political problems and constitutional issues peculiar to the state; suffice it for me to point out that it would still take time before a degree of credibility was restored to the reputation of the Election Commission, particularly in the Valley.

~

My own exposure to J&K and the Valley in particular had started sixteen years earlier. At the end of 1992, I had been appointed to the post of joint secretary in the Ministry of Information and Broadcasting with special responsibilities for the 'electronic media'. 'Electronic media' was a rather grand description for the government-run TV channel (Doordarshan) although All India Radio's (AIR) reach was vast and comprehensive.

My taking over as joint secretary in the ministry coincided with heightened militancy, particularly in the districts bordering Pakistan. This period of intense militant activity and terrorism lasted from the late 1980s to the mid-1990s. By 1993–94, militancy had already extracted a heavy toll on both AIR and Doordarshan's transmissions from Srinagar and elsewhere in the Valley. Our only television studio in Srinagar was shut down, the target of rocket attacks. Our staff were too terrified to come to the studios, while those who used to travel from Delhi for short spells on deputation, simply opted out. So dangerous was the situation that if the voice of an AIR announcer was recognized in a broadcast, this often meant a militant's bullet in his knee.

When I made my first official visit to Srinagar as joint secretary at the end of 1992, I found a melancholic state of affairs—shuttered studios, cobwebbed equipment and a handful of staff that braved the odds to open the studio doors for me that morning. With so much violence about, it was not surprising that transmissions from Srinagar had come to an abrupt halt. The officials and staff fled the studios in the face of violence. The studios also became targets of occasional rocket attacks. When broadcasts did resume, they were not from Srinagar but from the iconic AIR building in Parliament Street in the heart of New Delhi.

After obtaining the political mandate from the government, I set about trying to set things right. With the assistance of our redoubtable broadcaster, poet Farooq Nazki, who was then station director of All India Radio and Doordarshan in Srinagar, I travelled to J&K including its border areas at least two dozen times over three years. I often camped in Srinagar for days at a time and with Farooq Nazki's help we began to revive the morale of local staff and artistes.

We needed safe housing. Since the state was under governor's rule, I approached the tough-talking governor of Jammu and Kashmir, Gen. K.V. Krishna Rao (Retd).[2] With not a little help from his able secretary, IAS officer Parvez Dewan, I was able to persuade him that if we were to restart broadcasts from the Srinagar studios, it was essential for me to provide our staff with the safest housing then available in Srinagar. The governor agreed but said with a smile that he did not think that we would ever give up this accommodation. With that in hand, I slowly persuaded our Delhi-based staff to take the risk of travelling to Srinagar, even for a week at a time. Without this offer, my efforts would have been a non-starter. Gradually, confidence began to return. A cautious beginning was made. In the absence of artistes, I persuaded college students to 'take over' the studio of the newly minted second TV channel, christened Kashir. Sitting on the sidelines, Nazki and I would watch them enact their college plays interspersed with songs and dances.

Meanwhile, Prime Minister Narasimha Rao's principal secretary, arguably the most powerful bureaucrat, A.N. Varma, supported my endeavours. Even as a middle-level joint secretary, I drafted

---

2 General K.V. Krishna Rao (Retd) was governor of Jammu and Kashmir from 11 July 1989 to 19 January 1990 and a second time from 13 March 1993 till 2 May 1998.

a cabinet note that gave the AIR and Doordarshan staff a special compensation package of Rs 10 lakh to the family of any staffer killed by militants. To further bolster confidence, I often travelled with our 'boys' on the same flight. It was important that they felt that they enjoyed the confidence of the government, without which no one was willing to takc any risk. When local staffers were shot or hurt, I flew to Srinagar to visit them in the hospital or sit with them in their rooms as they recovered.

Meanwhile, our engineers and technical staff at AIR and Doordarshan were equally magnificent. Under the charge of then superintending engineer (AIR) N.S. Ganesan,[3] they reinstalled or repaired the transmission towers that the militants had destroyed. Many of these were on the Indo-Pak border itself—not an easy place in those days to work in. Yet within the space of two years, broadcasts were beginning to be heard and seen on the TV channels across the border districts of Rajouri, Poonch, Baramulla, Kupwara and Bandipore, where earlier Pakistan's radio and TV channels had reigned supreme.

While these endeavours were on, it was inevitable that I would encounter the might of the Hurriyat Conference leadership. I soon learned that I was viewed as one of the hated faces of 'Delhi', largcly, I suppose, because I was there so frequently, and that too at a time when not too many officers ventured there. On at least two occasions, I was accorded the 'honour' of being met with a 'bandh' at my arrival in Srinagar. Partly because of this, the local police refused to take chances with my security.

I was housed in a barricaded room in one of the two elegant and identical guest houses along the Jhelum that had been built in the art deco style by the late maharaja of Kashmir. I always requested if I could occupy one of the two guest rooms on the first floor, so as to enjoy the view of river and the colours of the chinar trees that lined it. But the security forces viewed the upper floor as susceptible to rocket attacks. These were then fired from shoulder-held rocket

---

3 Ganesan retired as engineer-in-chief of Doordarshan.

launchers, which were a favoured weapon in those times. In fact, even the secretariat building, the symbol of the state government, had not been spared, having been damaged by rockets on at least two occasions that I can remember, both times leading to casualties.

The account of my three-year endeavour to restart broadcasting from the Valley might well deserve a separate book. For purposes of this chapter, however, suffice it to say that my experiences of the Hurriyat Conference leadership and the separatist forces over those three tumultuous years (1992–95) indisputably shaped my thinking. Even though I was a mid-level officer, I had made it my mission that transmission of radio and, by now, two TV channels must resume from Srinagar. The blatant propaganda that came over the airways and satellites from Pakistan were now countered from J&K. Towards this end, each transmission tower that we set up or re-established in the border districts felt like my own little victory and that of our dedicated engineers and staff.

The 2002 Election

To bring the narrative back to the elections, it is important to unequivocally state that the elections prior to 2002 had been viewed by many people in J&K with utmost suspicion. The widely held belief was that they had been 'rigged'.

It was in 2002 that CEC J.M. Lyngdoh[4] decided to rectify the damage. It is useful to recount the steps that he took. When we prepared for elections six years later I studied his detailed account of the difficulties that the Commission had encountered.[5] Lyngdoh was determined to demonstrate to the people of the state, and indeed to the country at large, that the legislative assembly election under his

---

4 He was the chief election commissioner from 14 June 2001 to 7 February 2004.

5 J.M. Lyngdoh, *Chronicle of an Impossible Election: The Election Commission and the 2002 Jammu and Kashmir Elections*, New Delhi: Penguin Viking, 2004.

watch would be free and fair. His first step was to set the electoral rolls in order, for they were in a complete mess and, therefore, open to misuse. A drive was undertaken to cleanse the rolls by removing all bogus names—the names of the dead and those who had shifted out of their constituencies. A determined effort was made to computerize the rolls. This was easier said than done, because this task involved printing the rolls not only in Hindi and English but also in the Nastalik script of Urdu, a script derived from the Persian and used in Kashmir. Lyngdoh also decided to create photo electoral cards. The Kashmiri Pandits, as a special case, were allowed to retain their original domicile on the rolls. Further, citizens who had turned eighteen were encouraged to come forward to be enrolled. A 'clean' and up-to-date roll had to be a prerequisite for the conduct of a fair election.

The Commission took another major step by introducing EVMs in the state for the first time. But EVMs could not replace the ballot paper without the requisite amendment to the law. The CEC took this up with the then chief minister Farooq Abdullah. A legislative amendment was also required to allow computerization of the rolls and use of photo identity cards. Lyngdoh writes as follows in his book:[6]

> In the maharaja's stately guest house, we had the first meeting with Chief Secretary, Tony Jaitly. As usual, preparations for the elections were discussed. Then there was just that suggestion of arrogance in Jaitly's comment that the time allowed for preparation depended on when the chief minister would like the elections to be held—on which point he was immediately disabused. It was the Election Commission and not the chief minister who decided the election schedule. Later, I emphasized to the political parties and the media that the Election Commission's visit had nothing to do with early elections, that in fact the elections were far away, that a lot of preliminary work had to be done by us, that free and fair elections were the objective—not

6 J.M. Lyngdoh, *Chronicle of an Impossible Election*, New Delhi: Penguin Viking, 2004, pp. 145–46.

any old elections—and that the Election Commission would decide when they would be.

The Commission's next step was to invite all the political players to a meeting. At this meeting, the political parties criticized the inaccuracies in the electoral rolls and demanded more accurate ones. They wanted them to be supplied free of charge to recognized political parties, not at the last minute, but well in time. However, they endorsed all three innovations introduced by the Commission: the use of EVMs, identity cards and special facilities to enable the Pandit migrants to vote outside the Valley, be it Jammu, Udhampur or Delhi or elsewhere—a first-ever case.

Yet, rising expectations in the Valley were not easy to fulfil in view of increased militancy. House-to-house intensive surveys were essential but they posed a challenge. They were often dangerous to conduct and the staff were quite naturally apprehensive. Generating accurate identity cards was an even more difficult exercise because womenfolk were often reluctant to share details with the enumerators. Printing of the electoral rolls in Urdu for the first time was also a daunting task.

Fortunately, Uttar Pradesh had an Urdu Academy. The experienced CEO of UP at the time, Noor Mohammad, took up this formidable task and managed to deliver on time. What helped enormously were that death registers were maintained in each district, which were found to be quite accurate. These proved very helpful in deleting the names of dead voters that still lurked on the rolls. In fact, in the earlier elections it was against such names that fraudulent votes had often been cast, not only in Jammu and Kashmir but all over the country. It was when the Commission began to systematically focus on weeding out such names did this pernicious practice come to an end.

The creation of photo identity cards was another essential step taken to reduce fraudulent voting. The prototype of credible voter photo identity cards was devised in consultation with the India Security Press at Nasik. This task was undertaken when the

Commission became aware that militant organizations could easily forge identity cards printed in local presses. Security measures were devised to keep these away from the hands of impersonators. This necessitated a great deal of work which proved well worth the while, because this demonstrated to all political players and equally to those who wished to subvert the election, that the Commission meant business.

There were other blips on the horizon, some of which again emanated from the state government itself. Again, in Lyngdoh's words:

> The state government had played passive partner in the matter of identity cards, and the reason became clear when the chief minister visited the Commission with Tony Jaitely on one side and director general of police A.K. Suri on the other on 16 May. Farooq began by lightly disclaiming any intention to rig the elections. He said, however, that it was not the right time to launch the EPIC programme. The identity cards might very well be resisted by militant organizations. Alternatively, the cards could be forged, creating further complications for the state government. Also, women, particularly in the rural areas, would not cooperate. One swiftly reminded him that more than six months earlier he had welcomed having identity cards but had since retreated apparently on the advice of the officers by his side. ... Finally, the chief minister was told that if conditions for issuing the cards were not right, the elections could bide till such conditions obtained. Farooq graciously took the view that if the commission felt so strongly about it, he would go along with it. He wryly wished the programme good luck and facetiously asked us to send him his photograph so that he could get his card made.[7]

Meanwhile, many polling stations, especially high in the mountains, were difficult for candidates and voters to reach. These needed to be rationalized (as was being done elsewhere in the country), so that people did not have to walk more than 2–3 kilometres to cast their votes. This rationalization process meant that

7 Ibid., pp. 154–55.

about 9,000 EVMs were required. Importantly, security personnel had to be detailed for each of the candidates. In the face of a barrage of threats by militants, they had to campaign in safety. Security was also provided to the observers from the Government of India, who were sent to supervise the process and ensure its fidelity.

The measures that the Commission undertook in 2002 remained relevant six years later. In fact, many of the problems were uncannily the same. While the ground rules remained largely unchanged, there was one critical difference. The steadfastness of purpose and unanimity of views that existed in 2002 between J.M. Lyngdoh and his colleagues T.S. Krishnamurthy and B.B. Tandon in the face of arguably their most challenging election, was instead marked by acrimony, mistrust and bitterness in 2008. It is important to shed light on this, for without doing so, the problems of conducting this particular election can never be fully understood.

Discordant Voices in the Commission

While, in 2002, the Commission wanted to conduct the elections on time, in 2008 CEC N. Gopalaswami was against conducting the election at all, preferring that it be clubbed with the general election slated for April/ May 2009. It was on this issue that we entered onto a collision course: I was determined that this election should be held on time so that the new assembly was in place before the mandated deadline of 10 January 2009. S.Y. Quraishi would crucially veer around to my way of thinking, but Gopalaswami remained adamant to the end. His stated view was that there was a risk of people boycotting the poll. He did not want to risk a low turnout. As he did not often share his real reasons, I would sometimes have to glean his thinking through the writing of his favoured columnists to whom he shared his thinking daily.[8] With them he not only divulged his thoughts, but often enough the proceedings of the Commission. This

8 Gopalaswamy would blame me in his letter to President Pratibha Patil in January 2009 of leaking information to a political party, even as his leaks to a select section of the press continued throughout his tenure as CEC.

was especially so to a favoured correspondent of a business paper. (It goes without saying that this traffic ended after he retired from the Commission.)

The summer of 2008 had not augured well for the state. The decision of the then governor S.K. Sinha to hand over 39.88 hectares of forest land to the Amarnath Shrine Board proved to be a much more emotive issue than the governor had perhaps been led to believe. It snowballed into a major political controversy. The decision to transfer land to the Board provided the separatist movement, more particularly the Hurriyat Conference which was always ready to fish in troubled waters, a stick to beat the government with. While Jammu simmered, the Valley erupted in anger. As passions were aroused, communal flashpoints occurred with alarming frequency.

The evolving situation offered the various political players in J&K their own reasons to support or to oppose the coming elections. It has almost always been the case that emotive issues are exacerbated by political parties to suit their immediate electoral prospects. Had elections not been due that year, it is possible that the forest land issue may have died a natural death before the autumn set in. In any event, so troubled were the waters of the Dal Lake that summer that the shikaras—those beautiful houseboats unique to these otherwise serene waters—were parked forlornly to one side of the lake, as tourists fled from the daily rash of stone pelting and burst of tear gas shells.

There were other more sinister factors at work. The Valley and the border districts of Jammu had for a very long time been the principal focus of Pakistan's ISI-supported infiltration of militants and funds. Their lines to various separatist leaders and dissidents were an open secret. Gen. Ashfaq P. Kayani who had headed the ISI for three years had, in 2007, been appointed to the even more critically important post of the chief of the army staff. Cross-border firing, stoked by the ISI, continued almost uninterrupted.

Political clamouring soon reached a fever pitch. The peacemakers advocated the need to reach out to the Hurriyat Conference leaders and separatists (of various hues), without whose cooperation, they argued, the elections in the Valley would be a washout. Other voices including those in the press expressed alarm that militants and infiltrators would cross the Line of Control (LOC) to create turmoil aimed at disrupting the election process. There were accusatory voices in some sections about the Raj Bhavan's alleged anti-Kashmiri bias.

While keeping myself abreast of these concerns, I continued to make quiet inquiries. As we approached winter, it was common knowledge that the passes would be impenetrable after the first few days of snowfall. While some infiltrators could sneak in, terrorism from across the border tended to diminish in the cold months. The routes that the militants used to cross into India were well mapped. Some years ago, I had occasion to survey these, as well as the fences that had been erected on our side of the border. I had seen first-hand some of the measures that the security forces had undertaken. I was aware too that since 2004–05 illicit border crossings had diminished to about four on a scale of ten.

Moreover, the Central police forces sent to quell the summer disturbances were still in the Valley which I viewed as a plus point from our narrow focus of electoral management. I believed we were in a strong position to request the Ministry of Home Affairs to retain these forces till the end of the year. I was quite emphatic about my views which I expressed in every meeting of the Commission. (Outside of Commission meetings there was practically no communication between Gopalaswami and me). I continued to constantly factor in the ever-changing field realities.

Meanwhile, the All Parties Hurriyat Conference had, as usual, set its own agenda and constantly upped their political demands. Many of these demands did not concern the Commission. They were directed at the Manmohan Singh government. What concerned us in the Commission was the Hurriyat Conference demand that government officials should boycott the poll process. The Commission was all too well aware that in 1996, militants had placed coffins near several polling stations (and posters of coffins at others) to send an unmissable message to candidates and voters alike. This made me all the more determined that the electoral space could not be ceded to them or left unfilled. It was far preferable that a political party, or any combination thereof, fill that space.

It was also clear that the dangers of such a call being heeded would make it even more difficult to conduct the general election a few months later. In any event, the preparations for these would begin almost immediately after the assembly polls got over. I realized too that if we did not hold elections now, that burden would fall on me because from 20 April 2009 I expected to assume charge of CEC. I would then have to conduct the elections both to the J&K assembly and parliament simultaneously. As I weighed the pros and cons of the situation, it became clearer to me with each passing day that the assembly election must be held on time, the semi-final before the final round, as it were.

There were other subterranean currents in flow. Gopalaswami and I were by now so seriously at odds that anything I said, or any position I took, was viewed by him with utmost suspicion. I think he was wary too because at the height of the summer agitation I had expressed reservations against holding the elections amidst the turmoil and police firings caused by the Amarnath agitation, which was seemingly out of hand. However, as the weeks passed and things began to improve with the confidence-building measures taken by the government, I veered towards a more positive frame of mind.

When S.Y. Quraishi decided to go with me on the holding of the J&K election on time, the CEC threatened us with a note of dissent. I had no quarrel with that approach, for I had myself offered notes of dissent in the past. I firmly believed that in a three-man Commission, it was not necessary for each of us to hold similar views in all cases; a majority of two to one was as acceptable as it was in the Supreme Court, where judges often pronounced dissenting orders or recused themselves. Within the Commission, Gopalaswami was holding to his stand that the elections were an unnecessary risk and that the Valley, in particular, would see very low polling.

Both Quraishi and I were aware of both these eventualities. Once the risks were identified, as the Commission invariably did in every election as a part of our standard operating procedures, we would begin to address them. As to low polling, we were not unduly concerned. In 2002, the poll percentage in Srinagar had been a mere 4 per cent. There had also been over forty election-related deaths. What was vital was that the election as a whole should be free, fair and peaceful and perceived to be so by everyone locally, nationally and internationally.

The schisms within the Commission were not resolved even when we travelled to the state to consult the stakeholders for a second time in October. We were accompanied by a clutch of officials, who had already made several preparatory visits to do the groundwork. The term of the assembly, which had been dissolved following the break-up of the Congress–PDP coalition on 11 July 2008 in the wake of the Amarnath land transfer agitation, was due to end on 20 November 2008. Because the state had been placed under governor's rule, which could last for up to six months, the election would need to be completed no later than 10 January 2009.

Reviewing Electoral Preparedness

During our two-day visit (7–8 October 2008), the Commission began its business by formally calling on the then governor N.N. Vohra. The state was under governor's rule, since the time the last elected government had resigned in July 2008. The governor gave us his perception of the events as they were building up, and an overview of the law and order situation. It is pertinent to note that we did not stay at the Raj Bhawan (which in any case was perhaps too small to accommodate all of us). We stayed then, as later, at the Nehru Guest House, some distance away. Had we stayed at the Raj Bhawan, the local press would surely have tried to play up issues of proximity between the governor and the Commission when there were none. The beauty of the serene Dal Lake and the mountains beyond is magical at any point of time and October is always the best month. However, we did not have any leisure to take in the beauty of the landscape, as our days were full and our minds preoccupied with the matters at hand.

After our courtesy call on the governor, we began as was customary our meetings with the political party delegations in the magnificent sitting room of the Nehru Guest House. Those meetings were held with the recognized national and state parties, and conducted in alphabetical order, so as not to ruffle any feathers. There were enough local sensitivities in Srinagar at play already.

The Commission had already held one set of interactions with the political parties in September. The BJP had then favoured an early poll; the CPI-M too was ready for elections. The INC was unsure but said it would go along with any decision that the Commission took. The regional parties, however, were distinctly nervous and both the National Conference (NC) and People's Democratic Party(PDP) said the situation was still not conducive for polls that winter.

This time around ten recognized parties met us. These included the national parties (BJP, BSP, CPI-M, INC and Janata Dal [JD]) and state parties like (NC, Panthers Party, PDP, JJD). Many of the leaders cautioned us against taking any hasty decision in view of the recent troubles and the polarization that had set in, especially between the Jammu and the Kashmir regions. However, the NC delegation, while stating that the people of the state had lost confidence in the democratic process, was even unhappier with governor's rule, which they deemed as a most unrepresentative form of government. '... [A] government made up of a group of retired bureaucrats is hardly likely to be able to reach out to the people of Jammu and Kashmir', scoffed Omar Abdullah, the president of the National Conference.[9]

On the other hand, Mehbooba Mufti, the PDP president, welcomed the confidence-building measures (CBM) that had been recently taken, including the opening of the LOC for trade, but felt much more needed to be done before the atmosphere became conducive for elections. The CPI-M's lone candidate M.Y. Tarigami wanted more time to enable political activities to gather steam before announcement of elections. However, he declared that his party

9 'On the eve of EC meeting, Omar Abdullah backs elections', *The Hindu*, 17 October 2008.

was prepared for elections. The J&K Pradesh Congress Committee reiterated that it was ready to abide by the Commission's decision. Bhim Singh, the articulate voice of the Panthers Party, was ready for elections whenever they were announced. He told the Commission team that 'installing a popular government without any delay was not only in the national interest but also the primary responsibility of the Commission.[10]

The Commission also met Chief Secretary S.S. Kapur[11] and the Director General of Police Kuldeep Khoda on Tuesday 6 October, to ascertain their views on the holding of elections, and the problems as they saw them against the backdrop of the four-month-old agitation. Both were seasoned officers with their ears close to the ground. Kuldeep Khoda,[12] a Kashmiri Pandit, till recently a resident of downtown Srinagar, was the third Kashmiri officer to be appointed to head the state police force as DGP. It was important to know what he thought of the situation, because law and order was crucial.

I was all too conscious that in 2002, as many as forty-eight people had been killed in election violence. There was a string of incidents for which local militants as well as terror outfits from across the border would claim credit. These occurred all over the Valley and in the border districts of Jammu. Even the heart of Srinagar was not spared. What had rocked the country was the assassination, on 11 September 2002, of the state's law minister, Mushtaq Ahmed Lone, while he was addressing an election rally in Kupwara. This was followed by indiscriminate firing that killed five security guards. A civilian and at least four others were seriously wounded. Pakistan's Lashkar-e-Taiba (LeT), was amongst the militant outfits that claimed responsibility. A week earlier an independent candidate, Abdul Rehman Sheikh, had been gunned down. On 9 September, violence again claimed fourteen lives in various parts of the Valley, while twenty-six people were hurt in grenade attacks in Srinagar itself.

---

10 *Daily Exelsior*, Srinagar, 8 October 2008.

11 IAS officer of the 1974 batch.

12 IPS officer of the 1974 batch.

On 16 September, Salahuddin, the chief of the Hizbul Mujahideen, brazenly announced a reward of Rs 4 million 'to bump off' J&K chief minister Farooq Abdullah and his son Omar.

There was more violence to follow. On 17 September, the editor of the Urdu daily *Srinagar Times*, S.G. Mohammad, and his security officer were both shot at by unidentified gunmen. The attack followed a warning by the 'United Jehad Council' demanding the local press to 'mend their ways or face the consequences'. On 18 September, two NC workers were killed in downtown Srinagar while sixteen others were killed in sporadic attacks across the Valley.

Just prior to the second phase of elections, militants attacked a government school in Udhampur killing a teacher and a class X student. The following day, 19 September the state's tourism minister narrowly escaped an assassination bid when a grenade was lobbed at her motorcade. Just a few days earlier, her house had been attacked. Militants also abducted a grandson of an NC leader from his residence in Poonch and thereafter set his house on fire.

It was, therefore, the issue of security, rather than a low voter turnout, that dominated my mind. Since the state was under governor's rule, we had as a matter of course requested the three advisers to the governor, Messrs H.H. Tyabji, S.S. Bloeria and C. Phunsog to meet us to discuss the security environment, among other subjects. I had known Sudhir Bloeria since the time he had been chief secretary of the state and I had interacted in the past with C. Phunsog. I had a high opinion of both these gentlemen. I had not known H.H. Tyabji personally, but he had an equally impeccable reputation. All three advisers gave us a detailed appreciation of the political landscape; they made their presentation of the pros and cons in a strictly professional manner. However, they were careful not to advise definitively on whether the Commission should go ahead with elections or not.

What was also invaluable were the several hours of detailed interactions with CEO B.R. Sharma and DGP Kuldeep Khoda, both of whom knew the pulse of the people of the state. We went into all the aspects of electoral and security management in detail: the updating of the rolls, the physical verification of polling stations, the distance voters would need to travel, the state of readiness of our EPICs and the extent of disturbances we would face if the clerical staff of the government went on indefinite strike (as reports suggested) to stymie the whole election before it could even begin.

During the Commission's visit to J&K, I asked Sharma if the possibility of the Urdu-knowing staff going on strike had receded. Was he confident about conducting the election, I inquired. His answer was an unequivocal yes. I received the same confident reply from DGP Khoda. Now with both our CEO and the DGP expressing confidence, I was convinced that we could go ahead. For several weeks, B.R. Sharma had, with quiet purpose, been implementing the mandate of the Commission. It was interesting that a Srinagar newspaper, *Daily Excelsior*, reported on 7 October that the CEO had physically verified 8,109 polling stations; that the rolls had been updated; and that the names of 340,000 bogus voters had been deleted through the efforts of our BLOs. 'For the first time after 1988,' it commented, 'an intensive revision and "super" checks of the roll had been conducted'.[13] This was in stark contrast to the previous seventeen years when only supplementary lists of names were added, leading to many incorrect entries.

The revision of electoral rolls became all the more important after the police had stumbled upon what they termed as a terrorist–official nexus that threatened to become another major headache. This was when an EPIC, the accepted proof of identity in the state, was recovered from the body of a Lashkar-e-Taiba terrorist. He was obviously using a fictitious name. It therefore became incumbent upon us to ascertain the extent of this misuse in the hands of militants and terrorists. If this was as widespread as some election sceptics would have us believe, it could compromise the election. This led to another round of discussions with both the Union home ministry and the security officials of the state. We considered the possibility

---

13 'Full EC on 2-day visit to J & K from today – Assessment of situation before polls', *Daily Excelsior*, 7 October 2008.

of issuing new means of identification or allowing alternative identity proof. This was no easy task as the electorate of 650,000 voters was widely dispersed. Moreover, 60 per cent of the voting population had already been issued their cards. Of them, 448,000 were enrolled as recently in 2008. These included 368,000 lakh young voters who were enfranchised with cards for the first time.

While these uncertainties were being examined, I was surprised to find a report in a well-known national newspaper on 5 October 2008. The report said that the *Centre* was planning to hold the elections in J&K in the last week of November. It went on to state that any further delay in holding elections in the Valley 'would not leave a good impression on the international community'. The report added that, 'The Centre has been sounded by security agencies not to overlap elections in the Valley with five other states slated to go to the polls around the same time.'[14]

After so many years of making it clear that the Commission was not playing to the Centre's directions, and even more conscious of the need to remain distanced from the Centre in the eyes of the people of J&K, this report, (and some similar ones) were completely misleading. All aspects of election management, including security arrangements, lay in the domain of the Commission. It was, therefore, surprising that such a well-respected paper could carry such an erroneous report.

By now the law and order situation in the Valley had worsened ahead of a 'pro-independence' rally planned to the famous Lal Chowk in Srinagar by the separatists. At this rally, they proposed to exhort the people to boycott the elections. Sensing violence and possible police action, the law and order agencies decided to clamp down on the separatists. All ten districts of Kashmir were brought under indefinite curfew. Most of the separatist leaders were placed under house arrest. Jammu and Kashmir Liberation Front (JKLF) chairman Yasin Malik was taken into custody. When the senior Hurriyat Conference leader Syed Ali Shah Geelani, also under house arrest,

14 Report by Namrata Biji Ahuja, *The Asian Age*, New Delhi, 4 October 2008.

complained of chest pain, he was rushed to a hospital in Srinagar. The city began to resemble an army garrison as thousands of local policemen and military personnel were on the streets to enforce this indefinite curfew.

Amidst all this confusion, Geelani did a volte face and urged the people to resume their normal duties with effect from 7 October. He postponed the Lal Chowk march to a future date. It was against this difficult and confusing backdrop that the Commission reached Srinagar on 7 October 2008 to meet and ascertain the views of the political parties and others, on the feasibility of holding elections.

From my own fairly long experience, there was often a hiatus between the statements of the Hurriyat Conference leaders and their action. I turned to A.S. Dulat, who had arguably a formidable understanding of the state, having served there for long years as the Intelligence Bureau chief. He later distinguished himself as head of the Research and Analysis Wing (RAW).[15] Through the course of two meetings with him, he supported going ahead with the elections on time which helped further crystallize my own views and he too understood that despite our internal schisms, Quraishi and I were prepared to go ahead.

It was at this point that I came across an interview that former CEC T.S. Krishnamurthy gave wherein he observed[16] that 'Some of these happenings are political and election-oriented. Once the election is announced, all these people will fall in line. This may be some kind of tactic to say that elections cannot be conducted. But as far as the Election Commission is concerned, I am sure they will go by the dates as prescribed in the Constitution,' asserted Krishnamurthy. He added that unless there is 'a real fear that voters will not be able to come out to vote', the Commission would go ahead with the polls. Even

15 Since his retirement, he has authored *Kashmir: The Vajpayee Years*, Noida: HarperCollins, 2015, and co-authored with Asad Durrani and Aditya Sinha *The Spy Chronicles*, Noida: HarperCollins, 2018.

16 'Once elections are announced everyone will fall in line', in an interview to Shobha Warrior, Rediff.com, 6 October 2008.

during the 1996 Kashmir elections, the situation was pretty bad; still we conducted the elections.

The political parties were, of course, constantly reassessing the position from their own vantage points. The BJP perceived that the summer agitation had given it an edge especially in Jammu and pitched for elections to be held on time. The BJP general secretary and in-charge of party's J&K affairs, Arun Jaitley, strongly advocated timely assembly polls, adding for good measure that any delay in initiating the electoral process would prove dangerous for democracy in the state.[17]

Interacting with media persons, Jaitley raised doubts on the Congress-led UPA government's intentions about holding elections on time. He also questioned the intentions of the Commission in holding a second set of meetings with political parties, when it has already held a series of meetings earlier. He also alleged that the Union home ministry had adopted dilly-dallying tactics over the Commission's demand for adequate security in the state. He pooh-poohed the argument that the atmosphere in the Valley was not conducive. 'This argument holds true only for a few pockets in the Valley and the elections cannot be delayed in the entire state for them', he said.

When we returned to Delhi, there was still no unanimity amongst us. If anything, Gopalaswami was firmer than ever on not holding the election in J&K at this juncture, fearing a very low turnout. Both Quraishi and I, on the other hand, continued to be less concerned about the turnout, arguing that voter turnout in Srinagar in 2002 was even then as low as 4 per cent. On 10 October, which was a Saturday, Gopalaswami convened the meeting of the full Commission to finalize the schedule for the other five states that were also to go to polls. Ironically, the *Kashmir Times* would in its report dated 11 October, quote 'insiders' as saying that Election Commissioner Navin Chawla was opposed to the conduct of the Jammu and Kashmir elections in November and pressed for deferring them to May to hold them along

---

17 'Delay in J&K poll will send wrong signal: Jaitley', *The Hindu*, 15 October 2008.

with the Lok Sabha elections. I wondered who these 'insiders' might be, because the exact opposite was true.

The Commission held an emergent meeting this time on Sunday, 12 October 2008. In spite of several hours of discussion we were still not able to achieve unanimity. On 13 October 2008 the *Hindu* in its editorial urged that elections in J&K should be held on time. 'While it is likely that voter turnout in the Kashmir Valley will be low, as it was in 1996 and 2002, there is no real reason to believe a delay of some months will make things better. There is a political vacuum that needs to be filled in J&K; it is better it is filled by mainstream political parties than by the Hurriyat, especially its extremist elements. Any election in Kashmir is an exercise in risk-taking and the risk will not go away by delaying the exercise. The people of J&K have been through an awful lot. What they deserve is an elected Assembly and an accountable government – not the stasis of prolonged central rule.'

In spite of these and other editorial urgings Gopalaswami's stance remained unchanged and it prevailed. On Tuesday 14 October, we called in the press to announce poll dates, but only for the five states of Rajasthan, Madhya Pradesh, Delhi, Chhattisgarh and Mizoram. We deferred the decision in respect of J&K. This predictably led to an uproar in the press room. For by now it had become clear to everyone in the country that there were serious differences between us commissioners. The *Pioneer* reported, as it happened accurately, on 15 October 2008 that the 'Election Commissioners reportedly favoured early polls, the Chief Election Commissioner had reservations on the issue of voter turnout. The CEC is said to have even expressed his desire to put in a dissent note if the two Commissioners wished to submit a report for early polls in the strife-torn state.'

This decision of the Commission to separate the J&K election from the other states led to an immediate uproar amongst the political parties. The BJP expressed its unhappiness, while most of the other parties were restive over the suspense of not knowing whether to marshal their forces to prepare for the polls or to demobilize their workers. Gopalaswami continued to argue against polls in J&K

holding that a poor turnout would rob the exercise of the required legitimacy. Quraishi and I held on to our positions that there was no guarantee that there would be a higher turnout even if the election were to be held at a later date. It was a most unenviable situation.

What further complicated the situation, if that was possible, was that the Hurriyat Conference issued another boycott threat, this time threatening a 'bandh' on the very first day of the poll. This meant that the local poll officials would keep away from their assigned duties—a repeat of the threats that the Hurriyat Conference had made in 1996 and 2002, when the local staff abandoned their duties. Our main problem was that if the Urdu-speaking staff stayed away, this would paralyse the election. In 2002, Lyngdoh had called their bluff when he managed to mobilize nearly 4,000 Urdu-knowing officials from Punjab, Haryana, Uttarakhand, Himachal Pradesh, UP and Bihar.[18] He had almost four months to make necessary arrangements which included requisitioning special planes to fly them into Jammu and Srinagar. But then the Commission stood united. This was not the case then.

Two days after the first announcement, a final meeting to decide whether the elections should be held or postponed was convened in the Commission. All our principal officers were present, as were B.R. Sharma and Kuldeep Khoda, who had come from Srinagar for this purpose. When the latest Urdu 'bombshell' exploded, the CEC announced that the J&K poll would not be held. This came at a particularly difficult juncture. The Hurriyat Conference had declared a complete boycott of the polls and had also ordered the people to boycott the polls en masse. I was clear that if we postponed the elections, it would be tantamount to a Hurriyat 'victory', which they would certainly have claimed. At this point I asked the DGP that if we were successful in enlisting, even at this late stage, the Urdu-knowing staff as had been done in 2002, was he confident, as the senior-most police officer in the state, that he could provide the election machinery sufficient security to conduct a free, fair and transparent poll? A thoroughly professional officer, he answered

---

18 These officials had to be conversant with the Nastalik script of Urdu.

without a flicker of doubt that this was a question of the prestige, not just for the state, but for the nation, and that he was up to the challenge. His confidence was remarkable.

With tension crackling in the air, Quraishi and I decided to go ahead with the poll. *This became a two to one majority decision.* We asked our DEOs to immediately contact all the concerned state governments to provide the Commission their Urdu-knowing personnel so as to call the Hurriyat's bluff. By now, it had become clear to those in the room that in accordance with the Supreme Court order in the Seshan case, the majority decision of two commissioners vs the CEC would prevail (just as it had prevailed in the case of two earlier elections when I had put up dissenting notes). Gopalaswami was on the verge of storming out of the room. However, faced with the inevitable, he soon gave in. All this was played out quite transparently before over a dozen officials.

By 17 October, it became evident that by majority vote the J&K election would now be held simultaneously with other five states. On 19 October, five days after the first announcement, the Jammu and Kashmir election was announced,[19] without offering any reason for the delay. Nor was there any need to, because the press had spent five days reporting our internal difficulties. At the press conference, Gopalaswami announced that the Commission was taking a risk. However, it must be said that thereafter all three of us worked single-mindedly as one team just as we had done for the two elections when I had submitted dissenting notes.

Many in the country breathed a sigh of relief. B.G. Verghese, the respected columnist, wrote in the *Tribune* as follows:[20]

> The window of opportunity opened by the bold decision to go ahead with general elections in Jammu and Kashmir as scheduled must not be wasted. The government [sic] has wisely called the separatists'

19 Interestingly most of the mainstream groups welcomed the Commission's decision on J&K polls. See *The Hindu*, 20 October 2008,

20 'Election in J&K: Time for reconciliation', *The Tribune*, 3 November 2008.

> bluff. The electorate will do the rest. The staggering of the polls over seven days spread over a month may not be tidy but is nonetheless a prudent arrangement, as underlying the threat of a poll boycott is the menace of the gun.
>
> The invited presence of independent election observers will put these saboteurs and their pious front men on notice that they will be held accountable for sabotaging the democratic process of popular self-determination. A low turnout at some polling stations or constituencies will not invalidate exercise or the resultant mandate. It will render the obstructionists even more irrelevant than they are today. ... The Hurriyat and other separatist groups are an unrepresentative and confused lot who seek a post-facto electoral endorsement of a predetermined result about an aazadi that means different things to different men. ... The first thing to remember is that Article 1 and schedule 1 of the Constitution bind J&K to India. Article 370 is only a mechanism to regulate the federal relationship between Delhi and J&K. Anything beyond the three original heads of accession—foreign affairs, defence and communications—is prima facie negotiable.

Whilst our 'boardroom battles' were on in public display in New Delhi, there were newspaper reports that the army in J&K was apprehensive that militants (and elements across the border) who had been lying low, were actually getting ready to strike during the coming elections in order to disrupt them. Coming as it did from the General Officer Commanding (GOC), Maj. Gen. Kishan Singh himself, this was not a report that the Commission could afford to take lightly. On 10 November, the police detained four JKLF leaders including its chairman Yasin Malik and placed them in custody. Sajjad Ghani Lone, chairman of the Jammu and Kashmir People's Conference was already under house arrest.

Having taken the decision to hold the elections, the Commission visited both Srinagar and Jammu on 10 and 11 November, in order to make a fresh review of poll preparations. We once again met political parties and the senior-most officials of the state. This time, we announced the dates and the duration of the poll—elections would be held in seven phases which would begin on 17 November and end on 24 December. The counting of votes would take place on 28 December. It was also important to let the country know that we had called the Hurriyat's bluff by successfully mobilizing 3,500 Urdu-speaking persons from across several states so that any last-minute call for bandh or boycott would not affect us. To obviate any risk, these officials would be covered by Rs 10 lakh special ex-gratia in case of death on duty, Rs 5 lakh for serious injury and Rs 1 lakh for partial disability. The CEO, B.R. Sharma informed all political parties in our presence that they would receive equal treatment and provided requisite security. This was vital because without adequate security cover to all candidates, they would not be able to stand up to separatist threats or face agitators and others sent out to disrupt their meetings.

On 14 November, temperatures in Kashmir suddenly nosedived by 6 degrees Celsius. Six inches of snow fell in Gulmarg and the weather report predicted continuous snow in Kupwara as well. The Chang La and other passes, critical for connecting Leh with Nubara, and Zanskar with Kargil were closing. In the face of snowfall, the leaders of the principal local parties (both NC and PDP) had become pessimistic and felt that the atmosphere was not conducive for polls.[21] As if on cue, all the four important passes of Khardung La, Chang La, Sadhna Pass and Razdan Pass were rendered impassable by heavy snowfall. By Friday, 14 November, the National Conference formally demanded the postponement of elections in view of heavy snowfall. In the Commission we took the decision that come rain or snow, there would not be a change in the poll schedule.

With the onset of snow, choppers were pressed into service in both districts of Ladakh, i.e., Leh and Kargil, which would go to polls in the first phase on 17 November. This meant the airlift of election staff and security personnel to far-flung polling stations. Although some polling stations such as Ralakung and Phema had only a handful of voters (twenty-four and fourteen respectively), nonetheless the full complement of polling staff with one EVM and one security personnel were airlifted to these polling stations. In a later phase, one polling station would be set up just for two voters

21 *The Hindu*, 15 November 2008.

in Kathua. This spoke volumes for our belief that each vote mattered and that we were making every effort to obviate the need for voters to travel long distances to cast their vote. By 15 November, despite the snowfall of the previous day, polling staff, security personnel and polling materials successfully reached 103 polling stations located in ten remote constituencies.

The actual turnout of voters was astonishing. In spite of the separatists' call for boycott, the first phase of polling for ten constituencies was unusually high at 69.02 per cent. I was very pleasantly surprised because the 2002 poll had averaged only 45 per cent in its first phase and I had not expected much more. Meanwhile, three leading national dailies had the following succinct comments to make. The *Tribune* of 19 November 2008 observed, 'With an average polling percentage of 64, they have set a record other states going to the polls would find difficult to improve upon. Unlike voters elsewhere, those in J&K went to the polling booths under threat to their lives and limbs. The separatists had given a call to boycott the polls they described as sham. Even in constituencies like Gurez, Bandipora and Sonawari where the militants called the shots at one time, the voter response was very good.'

The *Times of India* of the same date reported, 'Given J&K's recent inter-regional conflict, divisive issues should have dominated the electoral agenda. Yet, reportedly, day-to-day concerns—the proverbial bijli, sadak, pani—drove the Valley's voters to the polling booths. They seemed to see political engagement as the way to get results on improving basic amenities.'

The *Hindustan Times* said', 'The gold standard for "free and fair elections" in J&K has been the 2002 Assembly polls. Both domestically as well as internationally, it was the first major assurance that Kashmir is not a "strange" place, only a battleground for those seeking to break away from India and those forcing the state to remain part of the country. If the morning shows the day, Monday's turnout and the general sense of enthusiasm show that the people of Jammu and Kashmir want things to change in their backyard. It will be up to the new government to focus on these "real" things and provide them.'

The second phase of the election, which involved six constituencies recorded 68.29 per cent of polling, which continued to surprise me let alone the sceptics. After the third phase where polling took place for five constituencies, when almost 68.22 per cent of voting was recorded, one of the Kashmir papers reported as follows: 'In arguably the fairest ever exercise of the Indian democracy conducted by Election Commission of India in Jammu & Kashmir, 67 per cent of the electorate today exercised franchise in phase-three of the polling in five segments of Kupwara district in Kashmir Valley. Even as the district remained sealed off for every unauthorized entry and the Valley outside reeled under undeclared curfew, voters in large numbers turned up at the polling stations while treating the separatist Hurriyat Conference's call for "total boycott" to Assembly elections with contempt.'[22] This would echo my exhortations to the CEO and DGP that while district borders may be sealed to prevent trouble-makers from entering the constituency, the candidates, people and voters in the constituency going to poll must feel free and safe to go about their business.

The *Tribune* would report again on 6 December 2008 as follows: 'Their turnout was impressive, strengthening their faith in the democratic system. The people of Jammu and Kashmir have particularly broken the previous records in all the phases of elections held so far. The people, especially women, have given a befitting reply to the separatists who had given a call for the boycott of elections. They turned out at the polling booths in large numbers without the fear of the gun. The turnout in J&K has been increasing in phase after phase.'

Not everyone was optimistic. Sajjad Lone, chairman of the People's Conference wrote a signed piece:[23] 'The participation rates in the first two phases of the Jammu and Kashmir election seem to have propelled New Delhi into a state of excitement. Barring

22 Ahmed Ali Fayyaz, 'Hurriyat's boycott calls spurned with 67% turnout in Kupwara', *Daily Excelsior*, 30 November 2008.

23 Sajjad Lone, 'Turnout rates means nothing', *The Pioneer*, 5 December 2008.

the two constituencies of Bandipore and Ganderbal, all the others that went to the polls are traditionally high-turnout zones. Still, the rate of polling is surprising. But the sanctity and relevance of these figures start to erode rapidly once we scratch the surface.' However, he conceded: 'In November 2008, for the first time in the past two decades, there was no violence during an election.' He added that 'Regrettably, the Indian state refused to withdraw its gun from the democratic battle and continues to insist on a version of selective democracy—an order that is tuned to their system. It is at best a stage-managed democracy that New Delhi wants.'

Later, it was estimated that as many as 3,023 election meetings, both large and small, had been organized. Of these, 1,641 were in the Valley and 1,382 in Jammu. This reflected, in no small measure, the climate of security that have been created by the district authorities. Indeed, there was hardly a day that I was not on the phone to both our CEO B.R. Sharma and the DGP. I always emphasized that it was not in anyone's interest, least of all the Commission's that a high polling rate would demonstrate the success of the elections. I reminded them of the fiasco of 1987, where a rigged election continued to evoke revulsion.

While we did not expect the security forces to 'pull out people to vote', they had to find the right balance to ensure that those who wished to canvas, support and vote must not be impeded by those who wished to disrupt the election process through violence. They had to be cognizant of this balance, not just over the period of five weeks but every single day and single hour, because one mishap would be enough to play into the separatist's hands and disturb the whole election.

After the fourth phase for eighteen constituencies, recording 59.24 per cent turn out, former Union minister Karan Singh gave a statement to the Press Trust of India, which was widely reported. Interestingly too, a Kashmir local paper, *The Rising Kashmir*, known for its hot-and-cold approach, quoted Karan Singh as saying, 'The turnout in Jammu and Kashmir was really very impressive. It belies the boycott called by the separatists.' Describing polling in Jammu and Kashmir as a 'practical vote', Singh said the people of the state, like elsewhere in the country, are 'interested in development, job opportunity and getting over their problems. It [the vote] could be a turning point in Jammu and Kashmir.'[24]

The polling percentages continued to surprise us in the Commission. In the fifth phase, for twenty constituencies, it was as high as 58.5 per cent while the percentage for the sixth phase was 65.93 per cent. The voter turnout for the seventh and final phase involving twenty-one constituencies fell to 52 per cent. After the seventh and last phase was over, the *Hindu* in its editorial on Monday, 29 December 2008 wrote: 'The Election Commission of India has been brilliantly vindicated in its judgment of how people would respond to challenging circumstances. For the PDP, the returns from the incendiary communal campaign it ran this summer, and from its efforts to reach out to secessionists, have been quite disappointing.'

The *Asian Age* writing on 2 January 2009 stated: 'The electorate of Jammu and Kashmir in its wisdom did not hand over the reins of power to either a regional party or to a national one. A coalition government between a regional and a national force thus became inevitable. This carried its own message. It is fairly clear that the 60 per cent electorate that turned out to vote, even in the Valley, did not fully place its trust in a regional political entity. There was no question, of course, that it will back a national party all way. With the National Conference once again emerging as the first party in the state, the role of the balancer fell to the Congress.'

M.V. Kamath in his column, 'Odd Man In' summarized the election pithily with his five indisputable points:[25]

> One, the elections were the freest and fairest and most credible ever held in the state in the last six decades. Two, the voters' enthusiasm is a slap on the face of separatists who had tried their best to encourage

---

24 'JK polling practical vote: Karan Singh', *Rising Kashmir*, 8 December 2008.

25 'Favourable tide in Kashmir: Elections herald a new era', *Free Press Journal*, November 2008.

people to boycott the elections. Instead of boycotting the elections, the people with the overwhelming majority of 61 per cent went to the polls all on their own without anybody's persuasion or outside pressure. Three, the poll results are an indication that the people of Jammu & Kashmir are in step with the integration of the state with India and there could not have been a better referendum. Four, it is a warning to the greatest terrorist organization in the world, the Pakistan Armed Force-funded Inter-Services Intelligence (ISI) that henceforth its interference with the political life of the state will not be tolerated by the people themselves. Five, the democratic message is conveyed to Pakistan that there is no more a 'Kashmir issue' and any effort to raise it will be anti-people.

But not everyone agreed with this assessment. In his recent book, *The Kashmir Dispute 1947-2012*, A.G. Noorani wrote: 'The results of the recent elections to the Legislative Assembly of Jammu & Kashmir call for a calm, realistic appraisal. To begin with, the long queues in all the seven phases of the elections reflect a clear snub to the Hurriyat for its call for boycott of the polls. The voting was manifestly free. Yet, two caveats are in order. By all recognized tests of free and fair elections, the right to call for a boycott is as vital as the right to vote. This right was systematically denied. The Hurriyat's leaders were put either in prison or under house arrest. For seven consecutive weeks Mirwaiz Umar Farooq could not lead the Friday prayers at the Jamia Masjid in Srinagar. Uniquely, undeclared curfews were the norm. They are a form of repression whose other features need no mention.'[26]

Perhaps, the Oped article in the *Tribune* of 4 January 2009 puts the 2008 assembly polls in J&K in perspective:[27]

---

26 A.G. Noorani, *The Kashmir Dispute 1947-2012*, 2 Vols, New Delhi: Tulika Books, 2013.

27 O.P. Sabherwal, 'Verdict in Kashmir: Democracy, good governance can tackle separatism', Oped article, *The Tribune*, 4 January 2009.

The 'silent' majority has spoken. The spectacular events in Jammu and Kashmir during the seven-phase elections to the State Assembly have unleashed the soft but vastly underestimated people's power as never before. It is democracy at play. Prime Minister Manmohan Singh has rightly described the event in pithy words: 'Democracy has won whichever party may have won or lost.' But beyond this commonality, the Kashmir scenario has its distinct features and a jittery history, the lessons of which have to be re-learnt.

One should recall, in particular, the botched events of 1987 and after. The most widely participated election of 1987 led to traumatic events if the nineties. Why? Because the elections were horribly rigged. Even a minority of dissidents—possibly 14 or 15 winning contestants—were suppressed. When the ballot box is lost, the gun culture flourishes, and that is what happened in the nineties. Not only did the dissident Muslim minority parties turn to the gun, but the rebellion gained credence because of excesses all around—giving the Islamic jihadis based in Pakistan an outlet. It is a costly experience, but imbibing this experience has brought about the turn in the Kashmir scene. The free and fair elections of 2002 were a dress-rehearsal to the present 2008 elections.

It would, however, be foolhardy to think that the Kashmir groundswell is now well set. Much more needs to be done to ensure that there is no retrogression in Kashmir. The lessons of recent history point to the need for a many-sided effort to ensure that the achievements of the 2008 elections are not undone.

Prophetic words indeed.[28]

28 The results of the recently held municipal polls in Jammu and Kashmir stand testimony to the wisdom of these comments. While 35.1 per cent of the people exercised their franchise in the state, the turnout in the Kashmir Valley was only 4.2 per cent, *The Economic Times*, quoting PTI, 16 October 2018.

10

Electoral Reforms

GIVEN some of the distortions that have been spelled out in Chapter 4, electoral reform in India is long overdue. Yet, no government or political party has chosen to seriously address the proposals made by the Election Commission of India. It is true that over the years many committees and commissions have been set up by various governments to study the problems. For the most part, their recommendations gather dust. This is a pity because these reports were thoughtful, incisive and the result of painstaking work, where a large number of stakeholders were consulted and their views taken on board. Some of these reports are now too dated to have any resonance, but the spirit of their advice remains valid, which is to move the country towards cleaner politics by offering recommendations to reduce, if not altogether eliminate, the ills beginning to affect the body politic. With that end in view, the Indrajit Gupta[1] Committee was set up to explore

1 Indrajit Gupta (1919–2001), long-standing politician of impeccable integrity belonging to the CPI. Union home minister (1996–98). This was a dramatic reversal of roles as the home ministry had banned the CPI on three occasions, with many of its members, including Gupta, being sent to prison for long intervals. Drawn from one of the Bengal's most distinguished families, Gupta studied at St Stephen's College, Delhi, and Cambridge University. He was first elected to parliament in 1960. He was one of India's longest serving parliamentarians. He

public funding of elections as a solution to cut the Gordian knot with one powerful stroke.

The Commission too has, over several decades, continued to press the government of the day to initiate legislative reform. It was as early as in 1997 that the then CEC, M.S. Gill, addressed Prime Minister Vajpayee on the anxiety that the Commission felt regarding growing criminalization within political parties. In 2004, T.S. Krishnamurthy compiled a list of fifteen reform proposals to which he added another seven that were pending. Six years later, in 2010, I wrote to Prime Minister Manmohan Singh drawing his attention to the need to equalize the removal procedure for the election commissioners, and bring this on par with that followed in the case of the chief election commissioner. The most recent compendium of reform proposals was compiled in 2016 by the then CEC Nasim Zaidi. These have been uploaded on the Election Commission website and are in the public domain.[2]

Some of the inquiry commissions and committees set up by various governments over the last three decades included the Goswami Committee on Electoral Reforms (1990); the Indrajit Gupta Committee on State Funding of Elections (1998); the National Commission to Review the Working of the Constitution (2001); the Second Administrative Reforms Commission (2008) and the Justice J.S. Verma Committee on Amendments to Criminal Laws (2013). The Law Commission produced an important report on Reforms of the Electoral Laws (1999), followed by another Law Commission Report (2014) spelling out equally valuable recommendations. One could argue that a substantial field had been covered. The recommendations in their essence sought to free the body politic of many of its ills, principally the scourge of money and muscle power. They offered remedies to the ills from within,

---

served three times as pro tem speaker, and served on many parliamentary committees. In 1998, he headed the Committee on State Funding of elections.

2 https://eci.nic.in/eci_main/ElectoralLaws/HandBooks/PROPOSED_ELECTORAL_REFORMS_01052017.pdf

while also proposing far-reaching reforms that included replacing private funding with state funding.

The principal reason for the failure of the implementation of reform proposals lies in their being regarded by different stakeholders through differing prisms. The Commission views them from the prism of reform—seeking amendment to the electoral process in terms of constitutional and statutory changes. The intelligentsia, think tanks, political and social scientists and the various 'election watch' groups view this from more of less the same prism. The Supreme Court, by its various important judgments in some vital election-related cases, appears to share the same vision and has by and large endorsed the views of Election Commission. However, the most important stakeholders—the players on the field—view these proposals from an altogether different prism. Over the last three decades and more, important recommendations made so far by the Commission have therefore not seen the light of day.

From the point of view of those who have served in the Commission, what is more disappointing is that there had been some announcements that meaningful reforms would soon be ushered in. In 2010, during the course of speeches made at the diamond jubilee celebration of the Election Commission, the then prime minister, Manmohan Singh, the then leader of the Opposition, Sushma Swaraj, and the leader of the UPA, Sonia Gandhi, all spoke in favour of initiating urgent reforms. In 2014, Prime Minister Modi also gave similar assurances. The manifestos of the principal political parties also committed them to electoral reform. But no substantial action followed.

~

For purposes of this chapter, I have chosen to confine myself to five reform proposals. It is not that the others are not important. They are and need to be acted on just as urgently.[3] For paucity of space and equally for emphasis, I have sought to examine closely one proposal

3 EC proposals for electoral reforms in 2004. See Annexe 1 at the end of this chapter.

that I believe is vital to the inherent structure of the Commission. Five others seek to administer a kind of chemotherapy to the state of our democratic (ill)health. These should be seriously considered by the government and parliament, not in partisan terms, but for the well-being of the country, if we are not to slide into a plutocratic or oligarchic state—far removed from the ideals of our freedom struggle during which our forefathers were killed, lathi-charged, jailed for long years without trial or remedy.

Reform One: Purge Criminality and Tackle Breaches of Spending Limits

The Commission has been all too aware that in order to eliminate or lessen 'money and muscle power', there has to be a concerted attack directed at those candidates who have serious criminal records, compromised the statutory spreading limits, or have attempted to bribe voters to win elections. This multi-pronged attack is also directed at those political parties who do not disclose fully the source of the funds they collect. Greater light too needs to be shed on the accounts and on auditing procedures of political parties. There are a growing number of political parties that register themselves with the Commission (after fulfilling the basic criteria) but have no intention of fighting elections, creating instead a kind of 'benami bazaar' for collecting funds, taking advantage of the loopholes in the law, which permit those contributing to their coffers to enjoy the benefit of tax exemptions.

Amendment of Section 8 of the Representation of People Act, 1951

Towards addressing the issue of criminality head on, the Commission has written repeatedly to successive governments that Section 8 of the Representation of the People Act (RoPA), 1951 should be amended to disqualify those persons from contesting elections who are accused of such serious offences as are punishable by five years' imprisonment or more. The Commission believes that as soon as charges are framed by a court, *even* when trial is pending thereafter, there exists sufficient grounds to debar such candidates from contesting elections. The Commission has held that this is a 'reasonable restriction'.

Section 8 of the RoPA stipulates a two-year sentence as a prerequisite for disqualification from contesting an election. The underlying principle behind Section 8 is the presumption of innocence until proven guilty. But since the right to contest elections is not a fundamental right, an amendment to Section 8 can take away the right to contest on the loftier principle of the purity of elections.

This proposal to amend Section 8, not surprisingly, hit a wall of resistance: it was first referred to a parliamentary committee chaired by E.M.S. Natchiappan, MP, which, after deliberation and consulting several stakeholders (including the Commission, which supported the amendment), concluded that such an amendment would result in the misuse of the criminal justice system. The committee held that those in power could foist false cases upon political rivals, thereby seeking to eliminate them from forthcoming elections. The committee also observed that a person was presumed to be innocent until convicted. This committee, instead, recommended that a satisfactory answer lay in the setting up of special courts with day-to-day hearings that would result in speedy justice, ensuring the guilty politicians met their just deserts at the earliest.

An ordinary citizen might be forgiven for believing that the political establishment had closed ranks to thwart the Commission's proposals. Not surprisingly, in election after election to parliament or state assemblies, civil rights bodies and election watch NGOs continue to document the high percentages of contesting candidates with criminal antecedents, leading inescapably to the conclusion that most political parties *prefer* to nominate such persons if they have a strong 'winnability factor' in their favour.

In 2009, K.K. Venugopal, senior Supreme Court advocate, who is presently the Attorney General, wrote in support of amending Section 8.[4]

---

4 K.K. Venugopal, 'Re-democratising the electoral system', *The Hindu*, 9 April 2009.

> Under criminal law, there are at least three stages at which an accused can be relieved of charges. A magistrate trying an offence has first to take cognizance of the charge sheet and then satisfy himself that prima facie an offence has been made out, after applying his mind to the statements and the documents annexed to the Police Report. The case could be closed at this stage. Thereafter, the accused has an opportunity at the time of framing of charges to show that no prima facie case is made out or that no reasonable grounds exist to suspect him of the commission of the offence. He would then be discharged. Lastly, an accused could seek quashing of charges under Section 482 of the Criminal Procedure Code.
>
> It would, therefore, be incorrect to apply presumption of innocence, in a wooden fashion, to the issue of disqualification of a candidate contesting elections without taking note of the damage that otherwise would be caused to the democratic process. Section 8 of the RP Act will have to be amended so that a person against whom charges have been framed by a court for an offence mentioned in Section 8(1), or a person who is charged with an offence which carries a sentence of imprisonment of more than two years, would stand disqualified.

Venugopal, however, argued in favour of a charge sheet being filed *a full year prior* (emphasis added) to the notification of elections, instead of six months as has been sought by the Commission. He argued that 'otherwise a rival could easily file a false case and have a charge sheet framed, leaving no time for the accused to get a discharge or have the charge sheet set aside'.

This matter of debarring candidates with a criminal past was recently heard by a five-judge constitution bench of the Supreme Court. The Commission in its affidavit reiterated its stand and asked the Supreme Court to direct the Centre to amend the law to bar charged politicians facing trial for serious offences with the caveat that these cases should have been registered six months prior to polls.

'Don't get into areas forbidden by the Constitution', is what the Central government said to the Court in answer to the question, 'Can we give power to the Election Commission to deny symbols to political parties who field criminals as candidates?' On behalf of the Centre, K.K. Venugopal, this time in his capacity as Attorney General, argued according to his brief (although this was the exact opposite of his earlier 2009 averment). 'It was for elected representatives to decide, not the court,' adding that 'the court is touching an area forbidden by the Constitution'. The Attorney General made the first formal admission by any government to date when he added: 'The Court must realize the reality in the country. The cap on election expenses is one of the biggest jokes in the country. Candidates spend around 30 crores in a constituency.' One of the judges, however, disagreed with the Centre when he said, 'Until parliament decides, we can direct the Election Commission to add one condition to the Symbol Order saying if a person has criminal charges he will not get a symbol. We are not stepping into a parliament arena.'[5] The court has, however, thrown the ball into the parliament's court.[6]

Reform Two: Transparency of Funding and Spending

A big lacuna exists that enables donations to political parties to be made with relative anonymity. There is no constitutional or statutory prohibition that bars anonymous donations to political parties. There is, however, an indirect partial ban of anonymous donations through the requirement of declaration of donations under section 29C of the RoPA, 1951. While this clause requires political parties to declare their donations, such a declaration is statutorily mandated only for contributions above Rs 20,000 only. The result has been that the bulk of donations have deliberately been made for amounts below this ceiling. As a case in point, a sum

5 '"Don't Get into Area Forbidden by Constitution": Centre To Supreme Court', NDTV, New Delhi, 21 August 2018, https://www.ndtv.com/india-news/a-supreme-court-suggestion-has-centre-warning-of-serious-consequences-1903963.

6 'Supreme court leaves decision on criminal netas on parliament', *The Economic Times*, 25 September 2018. See also Chapter 4, pp. 134–43.

of 19,999 need not be disclosed. This loophole enables donors to make, if they wish, several tranches of donations, all under the bar of Rs 20,000. These amounts can also be given in multiples, thereby escaping the net of disclosure.

The Law Commission, in its Report No. 255 (March 2015), had recommended that all parties should submit the names and addresses of donors, regardless of the amount or source of funding, for contributions over Rs 2,000 through a new section 29D of the RoPA. The Commission also recommended that a maximum of Rs 20 crore or 20 per cent of the party's entire collection, whichever was lower, could be anonymous. The Commission recently suggested that the cut-off figure should be brought down from Rs 20,000 to Rs 2,000. This also formed part of the budget speech in 2018 wherein the finance minister proposed that all amounts above Rs 2,000 must be declared with the donor's PAN card details. However, these reform proposals have not as yet been acted upon. They will necessitate amendments to the Representation of the People Act, 1951.

There are three manifestations of the malaise that exist. The first is the vast overspending by candidates. It is well known that this far exceeds statutory limits. In 2009, the statutory limit of spending by a candidate for a Lok Sabha election was Rs 40 lakh, while the ceiling for the assembly polls varied from Rs 8 lakh to Rs 28 lakh depending on the size of the state.[7] Yet, unbelievably, election expenses filed by the candidates to the Commission were startlingly below their limits. A study prepared by the Association for Democratic Reforms (ADR) has shown that the number

7 The limit was raised to Rs 70 lakh in time for GE 2014, after the government accepted a proposal made by the Commission to raise the expenditure limit from Rs 40 to 70 lakh for Lok Sabha constituencies, on a sliding scale of Rs 22 to 54 lakh for smaller constituencies. Simultaneously, limits were also enhanced to between Rs 20 and Rs 28 lakh, depending on the size and population of the state, for assembly constituencies. Legislation was passed in time for GE 2014. The enhanced ceiling is still a fraction of real costs.

of MLAs declaring *no* (emphasis added) expenses for public meetings and processions was as high as 58 per cent. The number of MLAs declaring zero expense on campaigns through the print and electronic media was also as high as 58 per cent. 56 per cent of MLAs declared nothing for campaign workers. Five per cent of the MLAs revealed that they had spent *no* (emphasis added) money on the use of vehicles. With these unbelievable declarations at hand, it has become difficult for the Commission to press the government to increase the limits of statutory spending. What is widely accepted is that in fact the spending by candidates far exceeds the statutory limits, but often with the help of clever accountants they are able to declare unrealistic figures to the Commission and get away with it. The principal reason for such low declarations is to leave themselves sufficient leeway to add to their items of expenditure, should the election observers come up with proof of such spending.

The second malaise lies in the lack of transparency regarding the funds that political parties collect. It can be no one's case that elections can be conducted without adequate spending power. But what is adequate? Unlike the United Kingdom (on which country our parliamentary model is based) where the constituencies are relatively small, the size of the average Indian constituency (and its population) inevitably requires much larger amounts. Let us examine the average government spending per candidate since the first election of 1951–52. According to one estimate, the first general election saw government spending (not candidate spending) at 60 paise per voter. By 2004, the government spending rose to Rs 17 per elector but fell to Rs 12 in 2009.

This might help us understand candidate-wise spending. Each candidate needs to travel in his or her constituency, for which vehicles and fuel are needed. Their supporters also need to fan out. This requires infrastructure such as campaign managers, a basic staff, money for 'chai-pani', etc. Funds are needed to erect stages, prepare campaign material such as buntings, posters, flags and all the other paraphernalia that is needed to reach out to constituents, often spread over a large area with a sparse population, or sometimes a smaller area with high density.

The Commission's case is that the source of funding, as well as the full amount of funds collected, should be disclosed and be open to scrutiny. There was a time when most political parties, especially those that were cadre-based, could collect small donations of a rupee or two to finance their elections. That phase of fund collection is long since over. 'Bucket collections' are now rarely the norm; the occasional photograph showing people garlanding candidates with currency notes is more for publicity. Funds are now collected by a wide variety of means, one of which is through corporate donations. While corporates are permitted to donate up to 7 per cent of their annual profits, most of them prefer to donate funds anonymously. For in this anonymity lies their protection. Even when they distribute their largesse amongst rival parties, they try to keep these donations secret so that no party would know how much they may have given to their rival parties. The convenient loophole which still exists is that donations under sums of Rs 20,000 provide complete anonymity. A donor may choose to contribute a sum of Rs 5 crore, but as long as this amount is paid in multiples of less than Rs 20,000, no disclosure is necessary. Political parties are aware of this loophole, and accept it even though they may be bitter rivals in the field.

It needs to be added that it is mandatory for political parties to submit their funding details if they wish to avail of income tax benefits. If they decide not to, no mandatory declaration is required. This too is a loophole that the Commission seeks to plug.

There is no dearth of recommendations about political funding reform. In 2001, the National Commission to Review the Working of the Constitution suggested that 'political party accounts must be audited like the accounts of any public limited company and should be published yearly with full disclosures under predetermined account heads.' No action has been taken in these intervening years.

Political parties are, perhaps, dependent on corporate funding in so far as declared income is concerned. It is also widely acknowledged that the bulk of political finance makes its way clandestinely and illegally, usually on the eve of elections, from disparate sources.[8] It is believed that there is a large reservoir of undeclared money that is brought into the country by some candidates or some political parties, through multifarious channels before major elections take place in the country. This source of funding is extremely difficult to trace. (One of the most welcome developments, in this context, was the way the Aam Aadmi Party raised funds, and won so overwhelmingly the elections to the Delhi assembly in 2013.)

The third aspect lies with respect to spending by political parties in pursuance of their political manifestos. As long as these funds are not spent on any particular candidate, there is no ceiling on spending. Political parties may spend any amount on their declared 'star campaigners'. These can be up to forty in number for recognized central parties and up to twenty for recognized state parties. There is no ceiling on spending for transportation (which includes planes, helicopters and vehicles) as well as on the infrastructure cost for elections campaigns including the cost of meetings, stage, mikes, tents, etc. These add up to a huge chunk of electoral expenses. Thus the political party machine can make up for the statutory limits placed on individual candidates.

The bulk of electoral expenses are spent on publicity, both print and electronic, which has emerged as the largest share of the spending pie. During my time in the Election Commission we tried to separate 'star campaigners' from candidates. We passed an order that if the 'star campaigner' visited a constituency, the candidate in question could not share the stage or rostrum with the star campaigners, who could only speak in general terms about their party's programme. It was a thin line and probably did not make too much of a difference.

---

8 E. Sridharan, 'Overview of Political Finance in South Asia, with a Focus on India', University of Pennsylvania Institute for the Advanced Study of India, 15 December 2015; see also 'Reforming political finance', *Seminar*, October 2001, www. India-seminar.com/2001/506.

Having said this, the Commission and its observers have made it increasingly difficult for the candidates in question to throw their money around with impunity. At the end of the day, the candidate is afraid that the Commission could produce proof of overspending, which would then be used by rival candidates to file an election petition challenging the validity of his win.

Is there a way out and what might that be? An answer to the problem of less-than-transparent fund collection and excess spending, may well lie in state funding of elections. This could mean either state funding of political parties or state funding of candidates themselves, or both. This has been the subject of various committees including the Indrajit Gupta Committee set up for this very purpose. I do believe that herein lies a solution, in whole or in part.

Reform Three: Making Bribery in Elections a Cognizable Offence

Some of the most disquieting trends that have emerged in recent years have arisen in some of the southern states where 'deep pockets' have chosen to invest in elections, confident that the returns would enrich them manifold, in terms of prestige if not the accrual of wealth. This was exemplified in a bye-election held in Chennai on 21 December 2017 to fill in the vacancy caused by the death of Jayalalithaa. I was invited to participate in a TV show where I was asked to comment on the 'sting operations' the channel's investigative reporters had just conducted. What the visuals revealed were doubly disquieting. Not only were some political parties and candidates out to bribe voters, but voters, too, were vociferous in demanding their share of money and 'freebies'. The modus operandi used by election managers was nothing if not ingenious: political parties were handing out only a token twenty-rupee note to voters. But this was actually a promissory note that offered much more. They could be encashed (after the election) for sums ranging from five to ten thousand rupees. This manifest bribery was telecast for the whole country to watch. The Commission was all too aware of this growing cancer but each time the candidates managed to devise newer methods to hoodwink our observers.

In 2012, the Commission recommended to the government to amend the existing law to make bribery during elections a *cognizable* offence, thereby enabling the police to arrest a violator without a warrant. The Commission's proposal to amend Section 171(b) of the Indian Penal Code to make this a cognizable offence under the Criminal Procedure Code (CrPC) still awaits the government's nod.

Reform Four: Power to Deregister Political Parties That Do Not Contest Elections

Section 29A of the RoPA, 1951 empowers the Election Commission to register associations and bodies as political parties. However, there is no constitutional or statutory provision that enables the Commission to *deregister* those political parties who simply do not bother to contest elections at all, or contest them very irregularly. Before Section 29A was introduced in 1989 (vide Act 1 of 1989), the registration of political parties was regulated by the Commission under its own powerful order (Election Symbols [Reservation and Allotment] Order, 1968) which was far more effective. The introduction of Section 29A, far from helping to control the flood has had the effect of opening the floodgates: the number of associations seeking registration as political parties climbed sharply, at the rate of almost eight or ten every month.

What soon became clear was that most of these outfits, after getting registered, began to collect funds, without any intention to contest elections either to parliament or state legislatures. Since the government took no steps to curb this tendency, the Commission set some preconditions, such as demanding copies of electoral rolls that listed the names of at least 100 members of that party, and also increasing the processing fee. But these were at best minor obstacles. When I was CEC, the number of registered unrecognized parties grew to over 1,099; of these only 363 or 31.24 per cent contested the 2009 elections. By 2014 the number of registered parties rose to 1,703. Of these parties only 464 or 27.5 per cent contested the 2014 elections. By December 2017, the number climbed to 1866. Of this number only fifty-six are *recognized* by the Commission as registered national or state parties. In April 2018, there were seven recognized national parties; twenty-four recognized state parties, while the number of unrecognized parties had shot up to 2,044.

How many of these 'parties' submit donation reports to the Commission? In a study conducted in 2013 it was found that only 5 per cent of these unrecognized parties submitted their donation reports for the financial year 2013–14. Having done so, they could claim an income tax exemption. 95 per cent did not bother. Clearly, the rest were money laundering machines that successfully evaded tax scrutiny. These unregistered, unrecognized parties were nothing but a means to collect 'black money'.

Contrast this with the figures of political parties in other countries. In 2018, the total number of political parties in six countries put together was 388 (the UK 140, the USA 54, Brazil 33, Japan 42, Australia 12 and South Africa 47). Unlike in India, the UK's Electoral Commission can conduct an audit of accounts of parties, a power consistently denied to the Election Commission of India. In addition, the UK Electoral Commission has the authority to seek information from each party as to which constituencies they wish to contest from. Should they fail to do so, the Commission can proceed to deregister that party.

Reform Five: Constitutional Protection Regarding the Removal of Election Commissioners

For several years, the Commission has sought equal constitutional protection for its members by seeking amendment to Article 324(5), to make the procedure for the removal of election commissioners the same as that for the chief election commissioner. Under the Constitution, the CEC can be removed only by impeachment, by following a procedure similar to that for removal of judges of the Supreme Court. This entails that the impeachment process must be initiated by at least 100 members of the Lok Sabha or fifty members of the Rajya Sabha. It must be supported by two-thirds of MPs of that House present and voting. This, in reality, makes the procedure for removal of a Supreme Court judge or the CEC distinctly more difficult than the procedure to remove an election commissioner.

However, the Supreme Court in the Seshan judgment[9] confirmed the complete equality of all the three commissioners in terms of decision making. Indeed, the apex court went so far as to chide T.N. Seshan for his behaviour towards M.S. Gill and G.V.G Krishnamurthy. The court spelt out in so many words that the two commissioners could overrule the CEC, by a two-to-one majority decision. However, *perhaps inadvertently*, the court did not travel the last mile to equalize the removal procedure for the election commissioner bringing it on par with that of the CEC. To overcome this lacuna, several CECs have written over the years to the government of the day, seeking to insulate the election commissioners from executive interference by making the removal of the commissioners as difficult as that of the CEC.

In view of the imbroglio that arose in my own case (see Chapter 12), the CEC held that he had the authority under the Constitution to recommend the removal of an election commissioner. When he set this process into motion, a major crisis erupted in the country, with the government (and several legal luminaries) opposing his unilateral action as being bad in law. Therefore, in order to guard against such an eventuality ever arising in the future, I chose to write to Prime Minister Manmohan Singh on 22 January 2010 on the need for the government to initiate reform. I was already the chief election commissioner and therefore was constitutionally protected. Lest the two election commissioners at the time—S.Y. Quraishi and V.S. Sampath—be misunderstood in some quarters, I decided that I alone would sign the letter, although the full Commission had seen and approved it. The text of this letter is placed at the end of this chapter (Annexe 2).

9 *T.N. Seshan vs Union of India and others* (1995) 4 SCC 611.

This was not the first time that the issue had been raised by the Commission with the government. In 1997, M.S. Gill first wrote to Prime Minister Vajpayee on the subject. In 2004, T.S. Krishnamurthy had once again addressed Prime Minister Vajpayee as follows:[10]

> To ensure the independence of the Election Commission and to keep it insulated from external pulls and pressures, Clause (5) of Article 324 of the Constitution, *inter alia*, provides that the Chief Election Commissioner shall not be removed from his office except in like manner and on like grounds as a Judge of the Supreme Court. However, that Clause of Article 324 does not provide similar protection to the Election Commissioners and it merely says that they cannot be removed from office except on the recommendation of the Chief Election Commissioner. The provision, in the opinion of the Election Commission, is *inadequate* [emphasis added] and requires an amendment to provide the very same protection and safeguard in the matter of removability of Election Commissioners from office as is available to the Chief Election Commissioner.

In December 2015, the then CEC, Nasim Zaidi, would once again write to the government as follows:[11]

> Initially, the Commission had only a Chief Election Commissioner. On October 16, 1989 two additional Commissioners were appointed but they had a very short tenure of barely a few weeks till January 1, 1990. It was not until October 1, 1993 that two additional Election Commissioners were appointed and the concept of a multi-member Commission came into being. The Commission has since remained a three-member body but there is no bar if the government chooses to increase the number of Commissioners. Clause (2) of Article 324, makes clear that the Election Commission shall consist of a Chief Election Commissioner and 'such number of other Election Commissioners, as the President may from time to time fix'. However,

10 See Annexe 1 at the end of this chapter.

11 Letter of Nazim Zaidi, chief election commissioner to Law Minister Sadananda Gowda, D.O. No. 3/ER/2015/755, Enclosure.

> the tenure of the CEC was ensured for the full term largely because Article 324(5) of the Constitution stipulated that the removal of the Chief Election Commissioner from office shall be on 'like manner and on the like grounds as a Judge of the Supreme Court'. This was spelled out to mean that the CEC could only be removed by impeachment by Parliament, with 2/3rd of the members present and voting. In other words, the removal of the CEC was made very difficult in practical terms. The Election Commissioners did not enjoy this protection. Article 324(5) specifies that any other Election Commissioner (or a Regional Commissioner) shall not be removed from office except on the 'recommendation of the Chief Election Commissioner'.

The Goswami Committee noted this discrepancy in its report on electoral reforms in 1990. It had recommended that the 'protection of salary and other allied matters relating to the Chief Election Commissioner and the Election Commissioners should be provided for in the Constitution itself on the analogy of the provisions in respect of the Chief Justice and Judges of the Supreme Court. Pending such measures being taken, a parliamentary law should be enacted for achieving the object.'[12]

The Commission has, time and again, in its various recommendations and reports, reminded the government of the day that the current wording of Article 324(5) is 'inadequate' and requires an amendment, to bring the removal procedures of election commissioners on par with the CEC and to provide them with the 'same protection and safeguards(s)' as the chief election commissioner.

The Supreme Court in 1995 in the case of T.N. Seshan, held that the CEC is not superior to the election commissioners [ECs], rather is at the same position as the other election commissioners by stating: 'As pointed out earlier, the scheme of Article 324 clearly envisages a multi-member body comprising the CEC and the ECs. The RCs may

12 'Report of the Committee on Electoral Reforms, May 1990, Government of India, Ministry of Law and Justice, p. 10.

be appointed to assist the Commission. If that be so the ECs cannot be put on par with the RCs. As already pointed out, ECs form part of the Election Commission unlike the RCs. Their role is, therefore, higher than that of RCs. If they form part of the Commission it stands to reason to hold that they must have a say in decision-making. If the CEC is considered to be a superior in the sense that his word is final, he would render the ECs non-functional or ornamental. Such an intention is difficult to cull out from Article 324 nor can we attribute it to the Constitution-makers. We must reject the argument that the EC's "function is only to tender advise to the CEC".'

In a matter that is presently before the Supreme Court, the court sought the AG's help on a PIL seeking parity in removal of election commissioners, thereby insulating the Commission from executive influence. The petitioner, advocate Ashwani Kumar Upadhyay averred that though the political spectrum favoured more autonomy for the Commission, no party in government had taken the legislative steps to grant parity in the procedure for the removal of the commissioners. The government has, however, turned down this plea.

Reason for the Proposed Amendment

Clause (5) of Article 324 of the Constitution provides that the chief election commissioner shall not be removed from office except in the same manner and on the same grounds as a judge of the Supreme Court. The chief election commissioner and the two election commissioners enjoy the same decision-making powers, which is suggestive of the fact that their powers are at par with each other. However, Clause (5) of Article 324 of the Constitution does not provide similar protection to the election commissioners and it merely says that they cannot be removed from office except on the recommendation of the chief election commissioner.

The reason for affording protection as enjoyed by a Supreme Court judge in matters of removability from office to the chief election commissioner was to ensure the independence of the Commission from external pulls and pressures. Therefore, the rationale behind not affording similar protection to other election commissioners is not explicable. The element of 'independence' sought to be achieved under the Constitution is not exclusively for an individual alone but for the whole institution. Thus, the independence of the Commission can only be strengthened if the election commissioners are also provided with the same protection as that of the chief election commissioner.

The present constitutional guarantee is inadequate and requires an amendment to provide the same protection and safeguard in the matter of removability of election commissioners as is available to the chief election commissioner.[13]

ANNEXE 1

D. O. No. 3/ER/2004
Dated: July 5, 2004

Dear Mr. Prime Minister,

Electoral reforms have been engaging the attention of the Parliament, the Government, the Press and also the Commission for a long time. Some measures were implemented in the past to remove glaring lacunae in the law. Our recent experience in the just concluded general elections to the 14th Lok Sabha, however, reaffirms our belief that further steps need to be taken in this regard quickly.

My predecessors have been very regularly addressing the Government in the last six years on different subjects requiring reform. Certain new issues obviously have come up based on the experiences gathered by us in the recent past.

I enclose two sets of notes on areas of immediate concern to us in the Commission requiring your urgent attention. In the first part,

13 The Law Commission in its 255th Report (2015) endorsed the view of the Commission and suggested the following changes to be brought in Article 324:
In sub-section (5), delete the words 'the Election Commissioners and' appearing after the words 'tenure of office of'; in the first provision to sub-section (5), after the words 'Chief Election Commissioner'

we have set out certain urgent proposals for electoral reforms in areas that have not been taken up in the past by the Commission and which have arisen due to implementation of certain laws enacted or based on certain directions given by the Supreme Court and the High Courts. In the second part, we reiterate some of the pending proposals that remain unresolved and which in no way are less important than the proposals in the first part.

I, on behalf of the Commission, would urge the Government to give immediate consideration to these issues and if possible, undertake necessary legislation so that the same can be made effective well before the next tranche of legislative assembly elections due in some states. The Commission will be happy to explain and discuss these ideas whenever necessary and also react to proposals, if any, which the Government may have.

Yours sincerely
(T. S. Krishnamurthy)

Dr Manmohan Singh
Prime Minister of India
South Block
New Delhi

Proposals for Electoral Reforms[14]

1. Affidavits to be Filed by Candidates on Criminal Antecedents, Assets, etc.
2. Need to Increase the Security Deposit of Candidates
3. Criminalisation of Politics
4. Restriction on the Number of Seats from which One May Contest
5. Exit Polls and Opinion Polls
6. Prohibition of Surrogate Advertisements in Print Media

14 https://eci.nic.in/eci_main/PROPOSED_ELECTORAL_REFORMS.pdf

7. Negative / Neutral Voting
8. Appointment of Appellate Authority in Districts against Orders of Electoral Registration Officers
9. Compulsory Maintenance of Accounts by Political Parties and Audit Thereof
10. Government Sponsored Advertisements
11. Political Advertisements on Television and Cable Network
12. Composition of Election Commission and Constitutional Protection of all Members of the Commission and Independent Secretariat for the Commission
13. Expenses of Election Commission to be Treated as Charged
14. Ban on Transfers of Election Officers on the Eve of Elections
15. All Officials Appointed in Connection with Conduct of Elections to be included in Clause (7) of Section 123

Pending Proposals

1. Anti-Defection Law
2. Use of Common Electoral Rolls at Elections Conducted by the Election Commission and the State Election Commissions
3. Simplification of Procedure for Disqualification of a Person Found Guilty of Corrupt Practice
4. Same Number of Proposers for all Contesting Candidates - Amendment of Section 33 of the Representation of the People Act, 1951
5. Making of False Declaration in Connection with Election to be an Offence
6. Rule Making Authority to be Vested in Election Commission
7. Registration and De-registration of Political Parties – Strengthening of Existing Provisions

ANNEXE 2

Recommendation to Prime Minister Manmohan Singh made by CEC Navin B. Chawla on 22 January 2010.

As far back as in 1998, the Commission had mooted a proposal that Article 324 of the Constitution may be amended to provide, *inter alia*, that the constitutional protection should be the same for the Chief Election Commissioner and other Election Commissioners. This proposal was reiterated by Dr M.S. Gill, the then Chief Election Commissioner in his D.O. Letter No. 3/ER/1999 – J.S. II/240, dated 22nd November 1999 to the then Prime Minister. A copy of his said letter and relevant extract relating to the above proposal of the Commission is enclosed for ready reference.

Subsequently, the above proposal to provide the same protective umbrella to Election Commissioners has been reiterated by the Commission from time to time. An extract of item No. 12 from the Proposals on Electoral Reforms sent by the Election Commission to the Govt. in July 2004 is enclosed for ease of reference.

It will be appreciated that in the original scheme of the Constitution, as envisaged at the time of its adoption in 1949, the Election Commission was mainly contemplated to be a Single Member Body consisting of the Chief Election Commissioner, and Election Commissioners were proposed to be added from time to time as and when there were general elections to the Lok Sabha or the State Legislative Assemblies. This is evident from the following statement of Dr B.R. Ambedkar, chief architect of the Constitution of India, while introducing draft Article 289 (present Article 324) in the Constituent Assembly on 15 June 1949:

> Sub-clause (2) says that there shall be a Chief Election Commissioner and such other Election Commissioners as the President may from time to time appoint. There were two alternatives before the Drafting Committee, namely, either to have a permanent body consisting of four or five members of the Election Commission who would continue in office without any break, or to permit the President to have an ad

> hoc body appointed at the time when there is an election on the anvil. The Committee has steered a middle course. What the Drafting Committee proposes by sub-clause (2) is to have permanently in office one man called the Chief Election Commissioner, so that skeleton machinery would always be available. Elections no doubt will generally take place at the end of five years, but there is the question, namely, that a bye-election may take place at any time. The Assembly may be dissolved before its period of five years has expired. Consequently, the electoral roll will have to be kept up-to-date all the time so that the new election may take place without any difficulty. It was, therefore, felt that having regard to these exigencies, it would be sufficient if there was permanently in session one officer to be called the Chief Election Commissioner, while when the elections are coming up, the President may further add to the machinery by appointing other members to the Election Commission.

Therefore, in order to ensure the independence of the Election Commission and keep it insulated from external pulls and pressures, it was, *inter alia,* provided in clause (5) of Article 324 of the Constitution that the Chief Election Commissioner shall not be removed from his office except in like manner and on like grounds as Judge of the Supreme Court and that his conditions of service shall not be varied to his disadvantage after his appointment. However, similar protection was **not** extended to the other Election Commissioners and it was merely provided in the said Article 324 (5) that they cannot be removed from office except on the recommendation of the Chief Election Commissioner.

With the passage of time, and in view of the fact that the Election Commission has now become a three-member body on a regular basis, fully occupied with one election or the other throughout each year because of the totally changed political scenario from the one that prevailed in early 1950s, the above mentioned limited protection to the Election Commissioners in the matter of their removal from office and conditions of service is considered inadequate, if the independence of the Election Commission is to be ensured in the true spirit of the Constitution.

You may kindly recall that the Supreme Court had observed in *S.S. Dhanoa Vs. Union of India* [(1991) 3 SCC 567] that:

> there is no doubt that two heads are better than one, and particularly when an institution like the Election Commission is entrusted with vital functions, and is armed with exclusive uncontrolled power to execute them, it is both necessary and desirable that the powers are not exercised by one individual, however, all-wise he may be. It ill conforms the tenets of the democratic rule.

I am sure that the above observation of the Supreme Court must have been one of the important considerations which weighed with Government while converting the Election Commission from a Single-Member Commission to a Multi-Member body in October 1993.

I may further submit that the Constitution has made special provisions in Article 324 to provide for the autonomy to the Election Commission in its allotted domain of conducting elections and to insulate it from executive interference to the whole Commission as a constitutional entity and not to the Chief Election Commissioner alone as an individual. Election Commissioners are now an integral part of the Election Commission. Parliament has already recognized this fact while enacting amendments to the Election Commission (Conditions of Service of Election Commissioners and Transaction of Business) Act 1991, in 1993, by providing the same term of Office to the Chief Election Commissioner and the two Election Commissioners, establishing parity in terms of their salaries, allowances and other conditions of service and, more importantly, giving them equal say in respect of decision making in all matters falling within the jurisdiction of the Commission. Thus, they are now equal in all respects with the Chief Election Commissioner. The following observation of the Supreme Court in the case of *T.N. Seshan vs Union of India and others [(1995) 4 SCC 611]* aptly brings out the above position of election commissioners vis-à-vis the chief election commissioner:

> There can be no doubt that the Election Commission discharges a public function. As pointed out earlier, the scheme of Article 324 clearly envisages a multi-member body comprising the CEC and the ECs [election commissioners]. The RCs [regional commissioners] may be appointed to assist the Commission. If that be so the ECs cannot be put on par with the RCs. As already pointed out, ECs form part of the Election Commission unlike the RCs. Their role is, therefore, higher than that of RCs. If they from part of the Commission it stands to reason to hold that they must have a say in decision-making. If the CEC is considered to be a superior in the sense that his word is final, he would render the ECs non-functional or ornamental. Such an intention is difficult to cull out from Article 324 nor can be attributed to the Constitution-makers. We must reject the argument that the EC's function is only to tender advice to the CEC.

In the context of the above illuminating observation of the Hon'ble Supreme Court, kindly permit me to bring to your kind notice two unwarranted episodes which not only eroded the image of the Election Commission in public estimation but also created unpleasantness between the Chief Election Commissioners and Election Commissioners, adversely affecting the harmonious functioning of the Commission. In 1993, when the Election Commission was converted into a multi-member body, the then Chief Election Commissioner, Shri T.N. Seshan, did not take kindly to the appointment of the two Election Commissioners, Dr M.S. Gill and Shri G.V.G. Krishnamurthy. Not only did he challenge their appointments before the Supreme Court alleging mala fides against the Government, but also refused to associate them with any work in the Commission for more than one and half years, until his Writ Petition was dismissed by the Apex Court. He did not consider them to be at par with him because he was of the view that Article 24(5) placed him on a higher pedestal and that the Election Commissioners could even be removed from office on his recommendation. Again, a similarly unwarranted situation was created recently, when my predecessor Shri N. Gopalaswami first took a stand unilaterally before the Supreme Court that he could suo motu recommend the removal of an Election Commissioner under Article 324(5) of the Constitution and, then, in fact, proceeded to recommend to the Hon'ble President that I may be removed from my office as Election Commissioner. It goes to the credit of the Government under your sagacious leadership that the Government refused to accept Shri Gopalaswami's recommendation and the Hon'ble President was advised, and she chose, not to accept his said recommendation. The Commission strongly feels that so long as the provisions of Article 324(5) stand as they are, recurrence of episodes of the nature described above cannot be ruled out in future, again bringing the Election Commission into serious disrepute and shaking the confidence of millions of citizens in the integrity and neutrality of the Commission.

11
Emerging Trends

THERE are five main challenges that emerged from the sixteenth general election in 2014, indisputably the most mammoth election the world had ever seen. The first is the sheer numbers: 815 million voters on our electoral rolls, an addition of almost 100 million over the last general election. A 100 million is almost equal to the entire population of the Philippines and almost four times that of Nepal.

Second, with an increase of that size in five years, several states witnessed record turnouts, leading one to foretell that the overall voting figures in 2019, when the number of voters is likely to be 900 million, would break the record of 2014. Several factors could contribute to this: the presence of a 'wave', or the sheer energies of political parties enlisting younger voters or even the Election Commission's drive towards higher voter participation, or all the three.

The third challenge is that almost twenty million young voters between the ages of eighteen and twenty-two years would step out to vote for the first time. From my own frequent campus visits over the last decade, it is clear the earlier apathy has given way to a new burst of enthusiasm. Apart from those directly involved in campus elections, the mass of students on campus, while largely unaffected by divisive political voices, clearly seek a more promising future for themselves. They have realized (as evidenced by millions of voices on social media), that elections and representative governance are a means to that end. Make no mistake, there is a huge force out there. Our politicians should be cognizant too of their aspirations.

The fourth challenge, unfortunately, lies in the divisive voices aimed at creating communal or caste divide for electoral gain. The onset of the election season almost invariably sees a sharp increase in the frequency of inflammatory and vitriolic speeches, more often by fringe leaders rather than mainstream voices. As election fever catches on, the more extreme and dangerously divisive utterances, often in the heat and passion of electioneering, tend to receive disproportionate attention in our media. Worse still, communal and caste stereotypes are sought to be ignited to polarize voters, breaching in the process the Constitution, statutes and the model code of conduct.

The fifth challenge is one that I have discussed in chapters on paid news and post-truth, where fake news masquerade as the truth. Dangerous forces outside the country's borders can easily infiltrate election campaigns from afar, as we have witnessed in the November 2016 US presidential election, where Russia is alleged to have destabilized Hillary Clinton's campaign by hacking into email servers of the Clinton campaign and sending the files to Wikileaks. No one could have possibly visualized just a few years earlier that such events could be conceived, let alone come to pass. Today this is the subject of a Congressional inquiry.

These are some of the many challenges that the Election Commission of India and the political establishment at large must contend with. However well and fairly the Commission goes about its task, at the end of the day, it is an umpire acting for a limited period. Nevertheless, both the Commission and the political class have now to be cognizant of this new era of a proliferating social media and electoral interference. Against this new and alarming backdrop, our political establishment must be alive to these new dangers and try to uplift the discourse to a level that we—a mature democracy that has always conducted our elections on time and invariably witnessed an orderly transfer of power—have grown to expect.

Simultaneous Elections

Holding simultaneous elections in theory is certainly a feasible proposition. It may under certain circumstances even be a desirable one. However, there are important prerequisites before it can seriously be considered. Important constitutional changes as well as changes to statutes will need to be made. These require to be preceded by the widest political consultation before they can be taken up by parliament. It must be remembered that the Constitution's outcomes were determined by debates and deliberations of the Constituent Assembly that sat for almost three years.

It is true that the Commission at present is kept busy with elections throughout the year, almost without respite. It is either conducting elections or preparing for the next round. For instance, GE 2014 was spread over nine phases from 7 April to 12 May 2014, making it the longest election in the country's history. The general elections were clubbed with polls to four state assemblies. Four other assembly elections followed in as many months from September to December 2014. The MCC was, therefore, in force from practically mid-February to December 2014 in the whole country or in large parts thereof. As a result of this inordinately long period, it is not surprising that many governments chafed at the lengthy imposition of the MCC, which they believed did not permit them to fully govern.

In terms of election management, there are many valid reasons for the length of time involved. For the conduct of elections has become increasingly complex. One of its prerequisites is the Commission's need for large numbers of Central police forces to be placed at its disposal. With our continental size and now almost 900 million voters, this can exceed over 1,000 companies (almost 100,000 uniformed men) belonging to such Central government police forces as the CRPF, CISF, BSF, etc. Why should this be, particularly when law and order is a state subject? Are the states concerned not equipped with their own forces? The reason is that the political players themselves now repose less faith in state police forces during election time. They tend to view them, I believe unfairly, as pro-government in power. The requisitioning of such sizeable Central police forces from the home ministry is not easy. It is dependent on the home ministry's own security needs at a particular juncture. It is for them to take the final call on the quantum of force that they can spare from their current engagements.

In 2009, the Commission had sought 1,000 companies, but to my disappointment we got considerably less, a little more than half. As a result, we had no option but to stagger the election period from perhaps three or four phases into five phases, spread over almost four weeks. The Central forces were required for myriad duties: from law and order duties to safeguarding polling stations prior to and on the election day, to guard the EVMs after the polls and to watch over the counting stations on the day of counting. Another vital requirement in 2009 was the Commission's need for almost 2,500 general and expenditure observers. We were criticized in some quarters for stretching the elections too long and with more phases than necessary. Yet, the phases in turn, were tailored to the quantum of police force made available, as well as the number of observers we received. In effect one fed upon the other.

Now, if simultaneous elections were to be considered, with all the concomitant needs for Central police forces and observers, the elections may well have to be stretched over a longer period of time. The political contestants would themselves demand the critical placement of security forces and observers. Having become integral parts of electoral management, it would be difficult for the Commission to scale back the numbers. Were the security forces to be too thinly stretched, for example, in some vulnerable states, there could be every possibility of election-related violence that would impact on the very conduct of peaceful elections, which the country has rightly come to expect. It would also put the reputation of the Commission on the line. It is not as if the Commission is unaware of the pressures put on the Central and state governments. For deploying a large number of observers does deplete the Central and state governments of much of its own administrative backbone.

Simultaneous elections would additionally demand a larger allocation for the hardware involved—EVMs and now the VVPAT machines. Of all these requirements, additional hardware is in one sense the less difficult component, because their procurement (while it involves lead time for manufacture), comes with a one-time cost and fulfils the Commission's needs for up to fifteen years. The Commission has calculated that the additional cost to the exchequer in the case of simultaneous elections would be to the tune of Rs 9,284.15 crore, but with some extra requirements factored in, it would tend to cost about Rs 10,000 crore.

Simultaneous elections are not new in India. It may be recalled that the first four general elections (in 1951–52, 1957, 1962 and 1967) were held simultaneously with state assemblies. The country was then under the domination of a single party. With the rise of regional parties, this pattern was disturbed for the first time in 1968–69. This was when the Congress party's hegemony was challenged for the first time, and many of the elected governments in several states fell due to defections. Thereafter, mid-term elections to Lok Sabha and state assemblies were conducted each time a government concerned lost the confidence of the House in question.

The Constitution prescribes five-year terms for the Lok Sabha and state assemblies (six in the case of Jammu and Kashmir). Any change in this cycle would now necessitate amendment of several related Articles of the Constitution. If a new pattern of simultaneous polls is sought to be introduced, the existing terms of some Houses will need to be extended or shortened, perhaps as a one-time measure. But there are important lacunae which need to be addressed. Detailed political consultations are needed to determine what would need to be done if thereafter any state government again loses a confidence vote. Would there be a spell of president's rule in the concerned state? More importantly, who will administer a Central government in the case of an early dissolution of the Lok Sabha? There is no provision in the Constitution for any interim measure at the Centre. If the government falls in, say, thirteen days, as happened to the late A.B. Vajpayee's government in April 1996, or after thirteen months as it happened in 1999 when the Vajpayee government was lost by a single vote, would that require an immediate re-election for the Lok Sabha and state assemblies in the whole country? In case a government falls midway through its term, what might be the apparatus that could ensure governance for the remainder of its term? These are important questions that need deliberation and constitutional changes.

The Commission has not been averse to the idea of simultaneous polls per se. It had itself suggested as early as in 1983 that a system should be evolved so that elections to the Lok Sabha and state legislative assemblies could be held simultaneously. So, too, had the Law Commission. The Law Commission headed by Justice B.P. Jeevan Reddy, in its 170th report tabled in parliament on 29 May 1999 averred that 'we must go back to the situation where the elections to Lok Sabha and all the Legislative Assemblies are held at once'. No serious debate immediately followed these proposals.

These and related questions were more squarely addressed in the report of the parliamentary standing committee under E.M.S. Natchiappan, MP, tabled on 17 December 2015. It offered a possible solution: the holding of elections in two distinct phases. In the first, a clutch of state assembly elections could coincide with elections to the Lok Sabha. The remaining could be held after a period of two-and-a-half years. It would be kind of halfway house. When this proposal was tabled in 2015, the committee recommended that in the current Lok Sabha itself, some assemblies could go to polls in November 2016 while the rest could go along with the GE 2019. It also suggested that elections to all state assemblies whose terms end prior to or after a time period of six months to one year from the appointed election date could be clubbed together.

The pros and cons are being debated. There have been some quite sharp arguments on both sides. Those in favour point to the need to curtail the length of the MCC and reduce election expenses, (although the cost of elections is quite difficult to calculate with any degree of accuracy). For instance, a Niti Aayog paper pegged the cost of GE 2009 at about Rs 1,115 crore.[1] In February 2009, the figure

---

1 Bibek Debroy and Kishore Desai, 'Niti Aayog for Simultaneous Lok Sabha, Assembly Polls from 2014 to minimize expenditure', a Niti Aayog paper, Firstpost, 30 April 2017.

budgeted by parliament was Rs 1,120 crore while the actual spending for the general elections plus the three assembly elections that went to polls simultaneously, was pegged at about Rs 1,483 crore. This figure jumped dramatically in GE 2014, which was estimated to have cost variously between about Rs 3,426[2] and Rs 3,870 crore—an increase of at least 150 per cent to the exchequer. But in both 2009 and 2014 these figures were only what the governments spent. The actual money spent by parties and candidates was considerably more. The Centre for Media Studies placed the estimate for GE 2014 in the region of Rs 30,000 crore.[3] Much more modestly, the Commission has ventured an estimate of Rs 4,500 crore as government spending for simultaneous elections.

The lengthy duration of the MCC has often been blamed for holding up all development programmes, and this has been cited to justify the demand for simultaneous polls. A Niti Aayog discussion paper lists this rationale. 'There are compelling reasons in favour of simultaneous elections: suspension of development programmes, welfare activities due to frequent imposition of Model Code of Conduct, massive expenditures by government and various stakeholders on frequent elections, black money, engagement of government personnel and security forces for a prolonged period of time, perpetuation of caste, religion and communal issues, etc.'[4]

However, fingers being pointed at the MCC are not based on facts. The Commission has time and again clarified that normal day-to-day activities of government must proceed apace. It emphasized that the announcement of elections *was not* an excuse for some bureaucrats to go on a pen-down strike as it were. The normal work of government

---

2 Report in *The Hindu*, 23 May 2016.

3 'India set challenge U.S. for election-spending record', Reuters, 9 March 2014.

4 Bibek Debroy and Kishore Desai, 'Analysis of Simultaneous Elections: the "What", "Why" and "How",' a discussion paper, Para 6.4, http://niti.gov.in/writereaddata/files/document_publication/Note per cent20on per cent20Simultaneous per cent20Elections.pdf

must go on. Only *new* schemes that could tilt the level playing field, or such schemes that are contractor-driven and can generate black money, should be kept in abeyance. No calamity-related work should be stopped even for a minute. In pursuance of this, I had set up a mechanism in 2009, to obviate delays. One of our DECs met a designated joint secretary from the cabinet secretariat on a *daily* basis, to consider any and every proposal on which some ministry had doubts about impinging the MCC. I believed it worked quite well.

What are the broad views of the political parties? The BJP was always keen on simultaneous elections. L.K. Advani was one of the first to moot the idea when he was the deputy prime minister (2002–04). The BJP manifesto for GE 2014 favoured it. In the July meeting, the AIADMK supported it. The Trinamool Congress termed it 'anti-democratic and unconstitutional'.[5] The NCP believed that it was 'not feasible'. The CPI-M pointed out 'practical problems'. The CPI held the proposal to be ideal but not practical. 'There will be mid-term polls in states due to political instability in the states. The terms of such legislative assemblies cannot be reduced, to have simultaneous elections to legislative assemblies and parliament. It will be undemocratic. There is a possibility of mid-term poll for parliament also, due to the ruling party losing majority, as it happened earlier. To conduct the elections simultaneously, all the legislative assemblies cannot be unilaterally abolished for no fault of them.'[6] In other words, it could alter the democratic and federal character of India. In August 2018, in an eight-page letter, the BJP chief has written to the Law Commission arguing that one election would help curtail expenditure and ensure that the nation is not in 'election mode' throughout the year. He

5 'Opposition flays idea of holding simultaneous polls, terms Law Commission proposal "a complete misadventure"', Press Trust of India, 8 July 2018.

6 *The Economic Times*, 30 September 2017.

dismissed the Congress party's stand that it would affect the federal nature of the country as baseless.[7]

Those averse to simultaneous elections argue that state and national elections are often fought on different sets of issues. In simultaneous elections, voters may end up being swayed by either national or regional or even local issues. Conversely, this could lead to national issues being ignored, local issues being swept away by a national 'wave'. Large national parties that have the capacity to launch expensive and well-organized campaigns could engineer their own 'waves'.

The president of India and the prime minister have urged simultaneous polls in 2019. Perhaps the dilemma was best exemplified by former president Pranab Mukherjee, a politician and statesman known for his erudition and who has been in public life for six decades, who initially favoured the idea but would soon thereafter term implementation to be 'very difficult'.

Former chief election commissioner, O.P. Rawat, has advised caution, holding that the legal framework first needs to be in place. 'It is possible only when you make all the necessary amendments to the Constitution, Representation of the People Act, and other relevant laws. Those amendments have not yet been made, because you will have to take all political parties on board,' Rawat said. As late as 23 August 2018, the Commission announced that it was not possible to carry out simultaneous elections in 2019,[8] citing also that it does not yet have enough VVPATs at its disposal.

Compulsory Voting

From time to time voices have been raised in support of compulsory voting. This has sometimes been mooted to face the challenge of urban apathy, as for instance during GE 2009, only 41 per cent of

7 *The Indian Express*, 15 August 2018.

8 'Chief Election Commissioner on holding simultaneous polls: No chance at all', *The Indian Express*, 23 August 2018.

Mumbaikars chose to vote, having instead taken advantage of a five-day stretch of holidays to leave the city. Another reason given in favour of compulsory voting is that in the first-past-the-post (FPTP) system, candidates can get elected with as little as 20 per cent of the vote share. This, in turn, raises the question whether a candidate getting elected by such a small percentage truly represents the constituency at all. If there were compulsory voting, it is argued, it will be likely that the winner is elected on a more representative vote share.

When this subject comes up in discussion, the case of Australia is almost always cited. At a conference in 2017, I asked a senior official of the Australian Election Commission how they managed to administer compulsory voting in their country. It should not be forgotten that the total voting population of India is now almost 900 million, while the entire population of Australia is under twenty-five million. Their voters number 16.07 million. Despite their comparatively small numbers, the official said that it was very difficult for them to collect the statutory fine of A$20 imposed on about half a million defaulters. According to the law they are required to issue a minimum of three show-cause notices to absentee voters by registered post. If the fine is still not paid, legal action must be initiated. In the end, said the official, the total administrative cost incurred far exceeded the amount of the fine! On an earlier occasion, when I had put this question to my then counterpart, the chief election commissioner of Australia, he admitted that this legislation had been passed at a particular juncture of the country's history. Today, he said, his government was unlikely to pass such a law.

In India, the electoral right of a voter is defined in section 171A(b) of the Indian Penal Code and in Section 79(d) of the RoPA, 1951, which ensures the right of a person to stand or not to stand for elections, to withdraw from being a candidate or refrain from voting at election. Therefore, 'not voting' had become a part of an individual's fundamental right of freedom of expression.

Enforcing compulsory voting in a country of our size is virtually impossible without causing enormous hardship, not to mention a plethora of administrative and judicial difficulties that would arise. Not only have I gone on record to say that compulsory voting is virtually impossible to implement, I have also questioned its very desirability. During GE 2009, when 58.2 per cent or 417 million voters chose to vote, 41.8 per cent or 299 million voters, chose not to.[9] Again in GE 2014, 33.62 per cent voters, or 274 million did not vote. It would be unfathomable for the Commission, or any other body, to follow up on these cases of default. A counter-argument may be that were voting compulsory, the figure of non-voters would come down sharply. But even if this came down, for instance, to ten million non-voters, the Commission would still not have the wherewithal or the funds for follow-up. Cases of final default would end up in our courts, which are already so clogged as to make our judicial system amongst the slowest in the world. And as elections are held at frequent intervals, the cases for default too would mount commensurately.

In my view, there is also a moral reason not to embark on this path. Millions of our people work in the unorganized sector. They have no fixed jobs; most of them are daily wagers; many live at subsistence level. Can we really expect the poorest of the poor to forego their daily wage to instead stand for a few hours in a voting queue awaiting their turn? As a former head of elections, I would rejoice to see high voting percentage levels, but not, for instance, at the cost of a mother who might need to take her sick child to the hospital. Or face the wrath of an employer who refuses to permit a worker her statutory right to vote and threatens to deduct a day's wage. Even in the organized sector, employers are usually reluctant to give their workers the day off, although they are obliged by law in most states to do so. (I had personally encountered employer resistance at some meetings I had addressed in Mumbai). There is

---

9 How would our comparatively small administrative structure issue millions of registered letters, await and sift replies, proceed afresh in cases on non-compliance and thereafter flood our overworked and understaffed judicial system with millions of possible defaulters?

a moral dilemma here and the voter must be allowed to decide his or her own priorities. At the Commission's end this would entail issuing notices to millions of non-voters, followed by providing adequate opportunities to defaulters to explain why they did not vote, and thereafter giving them a hearing in a quasi-judicial capacity. This would throw up more administrative work than the Commission could cope with. Finally, having defaulters obtain judicial verdicts through our judicial process, not to mention lawyers' fees involved, would make it all improbable. It would add millions of new court cases after every election to the already existing mountain of pending cases.

The Totalizer: A Method to Prevent Post-Poll Victimization

The introduction of the totalizer is a reform suggested a decade ago, in 2008. I have introduced it in this chapter because it is presently pending before the Supreme Court.

What exactly is a totalizer? It is a simple mechanism introduced into the EVM which enables it to jumble up and add the votes polled in a collective of fourteen polling booths, without revealing the voting pattern of any one booth. Because it allows votes cast in fourteen booths to be counted together, it is quite similar to the earlier system of mixing ballot papers from different booths in a drum. Because it seeks to mask booth-wise voting patterns, it would make it more difficult for retaliatory action by candidates/ parties who even now seek to 'punish' those voters and localities who may not have voted for them; this being achieved by blocking MP or MLA funds, or else diverting infrastructure projects, in order to teach recalcitrant voters 'a lesson'. In GE 2014, the then deputy CM of Maharashtra threatened to cut off water supply in Baramati; more recently a minister in Madhya Pradesh and a well-known scion of a political family, landed in a controversy after she was heard threatening voters in a bye-election held in February 2018, that people who vote for the opposition party would not receive the benefit of government schemes.

~

As new problems emerge, election processes are continuously updated or refined. In 2008, the Commission became aware that the totalizer would be a useful addition in its arsenal for GE 2009.[10] We approached the law ministry seeking an amendment to the Conduct of Election Rules to permit its introduction. However, our reference to the law ministry went to a parliamentary committee, where no action ensued. After GE 2014, the Commission once again addressed the law ministry. The law ministry asked the Commission to seek the views of political parties but when this was done, surprisingly no unanimity emerged amongst them. The BJP, Trinamool Congress and the PMK opposed the measure; their views were that details emerging from booth-wise performance of candidates were important for booth management. The INC, NCP and BSP supported the introduction of the totalizer. The CPI-M agreed in principle but favoured its introduction in a phased manner after carefully observing its efficacy.

In 2014, a PIL was filed in the Supreme Court requesting it to step in to prevent candidates from intimidating voters in areas that had rebuffed them. The Law Commission and the Election Commission have since filed affidavits in support of the proposal; the NDA government has stoutly opposed it. The Commission tested the totalizer method after the counting of votes in the Bhadohi assembly seat in UP. The counting had been conducted in the normal manner, but the totalizer machine was tested to recount votes after the declaration of results. There was no discrepancy.

Should the apex court rule in favour, it will enable the Election Commission to put into place a further level of secrecy to prevent the disclosure of patterns, possibly in time for the next general elections.

10 The Commission approached the law minister in 2008 with a proposal to amend the Conduct of Election Rules to permit its introduction.

12

The Chief Election Commissioner: First among Equals?

IN this chapter I propose to focus on the crucial issue of the wholesome functioning of the Election Commission that is in many ways critical to the future development. There are two main issues involved here. The first is to instill a sense of security in the election commissioners, which can only come through a constitutional amendment that makes the procedure for their removal the same as that for the chief election commissioner, thereby giving the same protection to the election commissioners as accorded to the judges of the Supreme Court. The second issue is to give legal sanctity to the tradition of the senior-most election commissioner taking over as CEC on the retirement of the incumbent, so as to eliminate the discretion of the executive.

I have referred to the unfortunate imbroglio within the Commission when the then CEC, N. Gopalaswami, suo motu recommended my dismissal from the Commission. The CEC had held that he had the authority under the Constitution to recommend the removal of an election commissioner. This was a case of constitutional overreach, leading the government to reject his recommendation.

The furore that ensued led to a number of significant commentaries on the subject by arguably the country's foremost legal and constitutional luminaries. Their voices should be regarded as objective expressions of concern on an issue that awaits urgent resolution.

N. Ram, the then editor-in-chief of the *Hindu*, wrote the most detailed and lucid reports on this subject from 31 January till 12 February 2009. The *Hindu* also editorially commented on the controversy. There were several other reports and commentaries in the press, some of which I have reproduced below.

In so far as the commentaries are concerned, it is necessary to include the opinion dated 12 April 2006, of Ashok Desai, former Attorney General of India and senior advocate, for it was his opinion that CEC B.B. Tandon officially sought and upon whose advice he acted. It was on this opinion that the affidavit he filed in the Supreme Court was based. (This was obtained by the *Hindu* newspaper through RTI and it has been reproduced here with the permission of the *Hindu*.) What I also consider of value was the opinion piece (also carried by the *Hindu*) which was the interpretation of Article 324(5) by Justice (Retd) S. Mohan, former judge of the Supreme Court, (dated 9 February 2009). A week later, on 16 February 2009, former CEC T.S. Krishnamurthy commented on the then raging issue at a function in Chennai with these words: 'The anomaly pertaining to appointment or removal of Election Commissioner should have been set right in 1991 itself, when two more officers were appointed by the Centre. But it was not so. The disparity among the officers can be removed if all of them are treated alike.'[1]

I have chosen to incorporate a few other indispensable views, including those of jurist Fali Nariman, the widely acclaimed constitutional authority; the late P.P. Rao, a doyen of constitutional law; Soli Sorabjee, former Attorney General; former law minister Shanti Bhushan; and columnist Harish Khare. In doing so, I have suppressed my own voice in order to provide objectivity to the larger

1 'Fine-tune Election Commissioners appointment procedures: former CEC', *The Hindu*, 16 February 2009.

question at hand. The purpose here is not to rekindle controversy but to present the facts in the hope that what I see as a glaring lacuna can be conclusively addressed in a manner that would strengthen the Commission and free its commissioners from the 'whims and caprices' not merely of the CEC of the day but also of the government.

~

After I became the chief election commissioner—and constitutionally secure—I wrote to Prime Minister Manmohan Singh on 22 January 2010[2] on the need for the government to initiate this reform to guard against such adventurism on the part of the CEC ever arising in the future. The sum and substance of my case to the PM was for his government to provide the election commissioners similar protection from removal as is presently accorded by the Constitution only to the chief election commissioner.

I pointed out to the PM that till 1989 there was only the chief election commissioner, who was constitutionally protected by Article 324. On 16 October 1989, the government of Rajiv Gandhi appointed two additional commissioners, namely Messrs S.S. Dhanoa and V.K. Seigell, for a term of five years or until they reached the age of sixty-five, as prescribed for the CEC. Because of a curious turn of events detailed elsewhere, their tenures would last barely ten weeks. The 1989 general election to elect the ninth Lok Sabha saw the defeat of the Rajiv Gandhi-led government to be replaced by that of V.P. Singh. The new government abolished the two posts by a simple notification on 1 January 1990, allegedly because the two commissioners had angered the Haryana politician Devi Lal, who later became deputy prime minister.[3] This led one of the two affected commissioners, S.S. Dhanoa to challenge this decision in

---

2 See Annexe 2 to Chapter 10.

3 This incident is recalled by J.M. Lyngdoh in his book *Chronicle of an Impossible Election: The Election Commission and the 2002 Jammu and Kashmir Assembly Elections*, chapter titled 'EC survives first packing', New Delhi: Penguin Books, 2004, p. 67.

the Supreme Court. Although the Supreme Court agreed that his removal was arbitrary, the court, nevertheless, upheld the decision of the government, ruling that because the president (meaning prime minister in cabinet) was the appointing authority, he held the power to rescind the posts as well. This would hold special significance in my own matter as it unfolded.

My own case played out somewhat differently. In the case of Dhanoa and Seigell, it was the government that chose to abolish the posts. In my case, while the government had no *stated* intention of abolishing the posts, Gopalaswami interpreted the Constitution to mean that as CEC he had the constitutional right, suo motu, to recommend to the government the removal of a fellow commissioner *without* awaiting a reference from the government. This play of events was precipitated at a critical phase of the fifteenth general election, practically on its eve, and just a few months before the CEC would himself demit office.

My letter to the prime minister sought to deter any further adventurism from *within* the Commission. It was in the same spirit that I had sought to introduce some equalizing reforms. One was that, henceforth, the CEC and both the commissioners *would jointly* write the confidential reports of all officials who served the Commission both at its headquarters and in the states. As any civil servant would recognize, this served to bring about parity between all three, because all officials would seek to serve the *Commission* as a whole and not be beholden only to its chief. This was a significant step towards the concept of primus inter pares spelt out in the Seshan judgment of the Supreme Court, that held that all three were equal, but the CEC would handle matters of administration so that there was no confusion in day-to-day work.

At the time of writing, the matter of providing constitutional protection from removal is being heard in the Supreme Court. The Commission in its affidavit before the court reaffirmed its two-decade-old stand that all the commissioners must be treated equally in the matter of their removal. Disappointingly, and in sharp contrast, the government's stand is that there can be no justification for bringing the conditions of removal of the election commissioners, who are statutorily appointed, on par with that of a permanent constitutional functionary such as the CEC. The government in its affidavit has further stated that the Commission was functioning 'smoothly', and since the petitioner had not placed any 'material backing' there is, therefore, no 'need for a change'.[4]

~

Since the larger issue continues to defy a solution, I am reproducing below—with permission—the detailed and lucid opinion pieces by N. Ram, then editor-in-chief of the *Hindu*, from 31 January to 12 February 2009, as well as related reports from the same newspaper.

'Shocking constitutional overreach'

> The 'recommendation' of Chief Election Commissioner N. Gopalaswami to the President that Election Commissioner Navin Chawla should be removed on the ground of bias is a gross constitutional overreach that is shocking to the democratic conscience. In the crucial weeks before the general election, it has provoked needless hostility and brought a political twist and divisions into the Election Commission. The Commission is a high constitutional body whose members are expected to rise above partisan sentiments and function with objectivity and distance from political players. It could certainly have done without a controversy of this sort. The recommendation itself was triggered by a petition filed by the Bharatiya Janata Party and stems from a misreading of the constitutional scheme of things. Under Article 324, the CEC is appointed by the President (that is, the political executive) and cannot be removed except by impeachment as in the case of a Supreme Court judge. The Election Commissioners too are appointed by the President and cannot be removed except on the recommendation of the CEC. Considering the scheme of Article 324 as a whole, Chief

4 'Can't have same removal norms for ECs and the CEC', *Hindustan Times*, 26 April 2018.

Election Commissioner B.B. Tandon and the Election Commission took the provisions to mean that since the appointing authority is the President, the CEC comes into the picture only when a proposal for the removal of an Election Commissioner comes before him from the President for his recommendation. This was, in fact, supported by the opinion former Attorney General Ashok Desai gave the Election Commission in which he was categorical that the CEC cannot initiate action against an Election Commissioner suo motu. The Law Ministry too was of the same view. Early signs that all was not well within the Election Commission came in mid-2007 when Mr Gopalaswami filed an affidavit in the Supreme Court claiming the power to recommend an Election Commissioner's removal even without any reference from the President. The court was hearing a petition filed by the BJP for Mr Chawla's removal. The claim of suo motu powers was a clear and unexplained departure from the position the Election Commission had taken all along, and the present recommendation rests on that shaky premise.

What makes the CEC's action particularly colourable is that it meets the demand raised in the BJP's petition—submitted first to the President, then filed in the Supreme Court, only to be withdrawn and submitted to the CEC himself in January 2008. Ostensibly, though, the CEC's 'report' rests the decision on different grounds. The BJP had asked for Mr Chawla's removal on the alleged ground that he was tainted by his past association with the Congress party and could not function in an unbiased manner. While ignoring his alleged past associations, the CEC has now read bias into Mr Chawla's specific opinions on the timing and manner of conducting elections in some states. The grounds alleged appear to be differences of opinion rather than any grave prejudice or misconduct. They have nothing to do with the standard laid down by the Supreme Court when it observed in T.N. Seshan, Chief Election Commissioner v Union of India (1995): 'Of course, the recommendation for removal must be based on intelligible and cogent considerations which would have a relation to the efficient functioning of the Election Commission.' The Court also pointed out that the power was conferred on the CEC to ensure that the Election Commissioners were not at the mercy of the political executive. It was a check on the executive's powers and a safeguard of the independence of the Election Commission as a whole. The Court went on to caution: 'If therefore the power were to be exercised by the CEC as per his whim and caprice, the CEC himself would become an instrument of oppression and would destroy the independence of the Election Commissioners and the Regional Commissioners if they are required to function under the threat of the CEC recommending their removal.' This fear of capricious action and of the protector turning tormentor has now come to pass with Mr Gopalaswami's recommendation.

It needs hardly be emphasized that the Election Commissioners cannot function effectively and independently if they are to live in fear of the CEC recommending their removal for one reason or another, including merely differing with him on some issue. They cannot perform their constitutional functions if the CEC continually entertains petitions against them from political parties and other groups. Even during the later period of T.N. Seshan as Chief Election Commissioner, when bitter and open conflict raged within the Election Commission, he did not think he could invoke the power to recommend the removal of an Election Commissioner. It is indeed inexplicable that an experienced administrator like Mr Gopalaswami should have chosen to act in a way that is neither constitutional nor fair. The saving grace is that the President is not bound to accept the recommendation, particularly as it is untenable on the face of it and unwarranted in the circumstances. Nevertheless, it is bound to leave deep scars on the Election Commission's institutional credibility and collective functioning.

(*The Hindu*, 1 February 2009)

'Chief Election Commissioner Gopalaswami "recommends" removal of Navin Chawla'

N. Ram

Suo motu act is constitutionally and democratically out of line, will damage institution

In a move guaranteed to stir up institutional and political controversy, Chief Election Commissioner N. Gopalaswami has suo motu sent a recommendation to the President that Election Commissioner Navin Chawla should be removed from office on the alleged ground of 'partisanship.' The President has forwarded the CEC's missive to the Prime Minister.

Mr Gopalaswami's action has raised eyebrows within the government on account of its timing as well as its departure from well-settled readings of the relevant constitutional provisions. The 15th general election, along with Assembly elections in some states, will be held in April–May 2009. Mr Gopalaswami himself will retire as CEC on April 20 and Mr Chawla will succeed him.

The sequence of events is as follows. On March 16, 2006, BJP Leader of the Opposition L.K. Advani and 204 MPs submitted a petition to President A.P.J. Abdul Kalam seeking the removal of Mr Chawla as Election Commissioner under Article 324(5) of the Constitution. A month later, BJP leader V.K. Malhotra sent a copy of this petition to the CEC. With the President forwarding the petition to the Prime Minister, the matter rested there with the political government evidently finding no merit in the BJP's allegations.

The BJP took the matter to the Supreme Court where its arguments seemed to make no headway. It withdrew the petition in August 2007. In January 2008, the BJP leaders took the matter up with the CEC who curiously received them in his chambers instead of scheduling a formal meeting of the three-member Election Commission to hear them out. Subsequently, Mr Gopalaswami served a notice on Mr Chawla and took a whole year to come up with his adverse recommendation. He is known to have rejected as irrelevant the BJP's allegations going back to the Emergency and so forth. He claimed that he based himself on his own experience and observations of Mr Chawla's work as Election Commissioner.

In his affidavit submitted to the Supreme Court, Mr Gopalaswami departed from precedent to claim that the CEC had suo motu power to recommend the removal of an Election Commissioner. He interpreted his predecessor B.B. Tandon's view as being the same as his. Actually, Mr Tandon's view was shaped by an opinion given by Ashok Desai, former Attorney General, in April 2006. That opinion clearly held that under Article 324(5), which was elaborately interpreted by the Supreme Court in its judgment in T.N. Seshan,

Chief Election Commissioner of India v. Union of India (1995), 'the CEC cannot act on his own and must await the reference through proper channels to be able to act on a complaint or petition seeking the removal of an EC'.

The Supreme Court in the Seshan case held that the Article 324(5) proviso for the removal from office of the CEC only through impeachment (as in the case of Supreme Court judges) as well as the proviso that the Election Commissioners shall not be removed except on the recommendation of the CEC ('based on intelligible, and cogent considerations') was designed to protect the independence of the Election Commission as a body from political or executive arbitrariness. The Court specifically held that 'if...the power [of recommending removal of an Election Commissioner] were to be exercisable by the CEC as per his whim and caprice, the CEC himself would become an instrument of oppression and would destroy the independence of the ECs...if they are required to function under the threat of the CEC recommending their removal.'

The well-accepted legal position is that the three-member Election Commission is a constitutional body of co-equals, with equal voting power, and the CEC is the first among equals with certain leadership and administrative responsibilities. Crucially, Election Commissioners, being appointed by the President, that is, the political government, without consultation with the CEC, can be removed only by the President, that is, the political government. (The CEC as well as ECs apply to the President for leave and forward their tour programmes to her.) A necessary constraint on the executive's power is that ECs cannot be removed without the recommendation of the CEC —after a formal reference is made by the executive.

Mr Gopalaswami is an able man with a great deal of administrative experience. He is well regarded in the services. But his suo motu act of adventurism, coming towards the end of his tenure as CEC, is constitutionally and democratically out of line. The Manmohan Singh government will no doubt give the CEC's unasked opinion the quietus it deserves. But its effect will be to stir up political controversy over an institution that has done its job of conducting free, fair, and peaceful elections creditably during Mr

Gopalaswami's tenure. The impact on the internal workings of the Election Commission of India can well be imagined.

(*The Hindu*, 31 January 2009)

'Gopalaswami's claims on timing of missive are seriously misleading'

N. Ram

Documentary record shows he hounded Navin Chawla and made light of constitutional considerations

Chief Election Commissioner N. Gopalaswami has been widely criticised, among others by top constitutional lawyers Fali Nariman, Shanti Bhushan and K.K. Venugopal, for the timing of his missive to the President just three months ahead of the 15th general elections and three months ahead of his own retirement as CEC. In response Mr Gopalaswami has gone on record essentially blaming Election Commissioner Navin Chawla for the timing, claiming that he sent his 'final reply' to the allegations made in the BJP's petition only on December 10.

A careful, item-by-item verification by the *Hindu* of the CEC's claims on what happened within the Election Commission between January 30, 2008 and January 12, 2009 reveals that they are seriously misleading.

On January 30, 2008, Mr Gopalaswami received in his chambers a Bharatiya Janata Party delegation led by Arun Jaitley. It submitted a petition making various allegations against Navin Chawla and demanding his removal as Election Commissioner. On January 12, 2009, the CEC sent his report to the President 'recommending' that Mr Chawla be removed from office under Article 324(5) of the Constitution.

First of all, more than half the delay is explained by Mr Gopalaswami's keeping the BJP's petition to himself between January 30 and July 20, 2008. He is now quoted in the press as attributing the delay on his part to a highly subjective factor, the differences he had developed with Mr Chawla over the timing of the Karnataka election. ('I put the petition on hold till the Karnataka election was over, lest it be misunderstood.')

Secondly, the timing is to be explained by the CEC's overbearing insistence, in tandem with the BJP's strident stance, that he had the power under Article 324 (5) of the Constitution to conduct an inquiry against an Election Commissioner, and make a suo motu recommendation on his removal. This usurpation of authority flew in the face of the Supreme Court's judgment in T.N. Seshan, Chief Election Commissioner v. Union of India (1995). It was a complete reversal of the stand taken in June 2006 by Mr Gopalaswami's predecessor, B.B. Tandon, and by the Election Commission itself in the Supreme Court. It also went against the legal opinion given to the Election Commission, on April 16, 2006, by Ashok H. Desai, senior advocate and former Attorney General of India. What constitutional or legal sanction other than the BJP's averments Mr Gopalaswami had for his dogmatic claim of suo motu authority over a fellow member of the Election Commission remains to be inquired into and explained.

The documentary record shows that he relentlessly hounded an Election Commissioner, who was supposed to be his equal, after demanding his 'comments on the issues raised' in the BJP's petition so that he could 'consider the matter for further appropriate action'. He peremptorily ruled out challenges to his locus standi and jurisdiction. He insisted, in his written communication with Mr Chawla, that the matter was solely 'between the Chief Election Commissioner and the Election Commissioner' and had 'nothing to do with the Central Government,' the appointing authority for the CEC as well as ECs.

The CEC rejected the constitutional contentions in Mr Chawla's elaborate reply of September 12 and demanded a response on 'the merits of the petition' as early as possible. Even Law Secretary T.K. Viswanathan's vitally important letter of clarification, dated November 7, 2008, which Mr Chawla forwarded to Mr Gopalaswami, was dismissed as irrelevant in the cat-and-mouse game the CEC seemed to be playing.

Mr Chawla's 'final reply' of December 10 was only a reiteration of the important constitutional points he made in his reply of September 12, plus a rejection of the BJP's allegations as 'motivated and entirely baseless.'

(*The Hindu*, 3 February 2009)

'How Chief Election Commissioner pursued BJP allegations'

N. Ram

The factual record shows that on July 21, 2008—six months after he received a petition from a BJP delegation in his chambers—Chief Election Commissioner N. Gopalaswami forwarded the allegations to Election Commissioner Navin Chawla in an officious letter. He asked him to offer his comments on 'the issues raised in the said petition at your earlier convenience to enable me to consider the matter for further appropriate action'. Ten days later, Mr Chawla courteously acknowledged the CEC's July 21, 2008 missive, saying that he would revert to him.

The CEC did not have to wait for long because on September 12, 2008 the EC sent his detailed and constitutionally substantive reply. In this, he questioned the locus standi of the CEC in this matter and called attention to 'the variance in the extant constitutional position qua Article 324(5) and your interpretation of the same'. He said that by way of abundant caution he had written to the Union Law Secretary, T.K. Viswanathan, to seek information on whether the President or the government had been apprised of the representation in the first place and also to ascertain the stand of the Central government. Pointing out that he had set out his response to the allegations in a detailed June 2006 affidavit in the Supreme Court, the Election Commissioner backed up his stand by enclosing along with his affidavit the affidavits of former CEC B.B. Tandon and the Election Commission's Secretary, K.F. Wilfred, and also Ashok Desai's legal opinion. Mr Chawla added that his response was without prejudice and should not be considered to be his reply on 'the merits' of the petition signed by Mr Advani and others.

In a letter dated September 17, the CEC peremptorily rejected the constitutional contentions in Mr Chawla's elaborate reply and demanded a response on 'the merits of the petition' as early as possible.

Even Law Secretary T.K. Viswanathan's letter of clarification, dated November 7, 2008, which Mr Chawla forwarded to Mr

Gopalaswami was given short shrift. In his letter to Mr Chawla, the Law Secretary confirmed that a copy of the petition signed by Mr Advani and other MPs had not been forwarded either by the petitioners or by the CEC to the President or the Ministry of Law and Justice. Neither had the Central government been consulted by the CEC before seeking Mr Chawla's reply to the allegations. Most importantly, the letter put on record the government's considered view that 'the removal of an Election Commissioner under the second proviso to Article 324(5) of the Constitution cannot be initiated by the Chief Election Commissioner except upon a reference or with the concurrence of the Central Government'.

Treating all this as irrelevant, the CEC sent two more reminders to Mr Chawla asking for a reply on 'the merits of the petition' and even prescribing deadlines. Finally, on December 10, Mr Chawla gave his reply, questioning the CEC's locus standi in detail and rejecting the allegations as baseless, devoid of evidence or 'any material to even warrant a suggestion of impropriety on my part as an Election Commissioner,' and made for 'extraneous considerations'.

The wonder is that as this unseemly drama was progressing and the internal blood-letting getting worse, the three-member Election Commission managed to conduct Assembly elections in six states. For five states, election announcements were made on October 14 and the poll completed on December 5. For Jammu & Kashmir, the announcement was made on October 19 and the poll completed on December 28.

Soon after this, Mr Gopalaswami, who will retire on April 20, fired what he thought was his Brahmastra. It seems to have backfired.

(*The Hindu*, 3 February 2009)

'Does the CEC have suo motu power to recommend removal of an EC?'

We publish here a letter, dated 7 February 2009, from Chief Election Commissioner of India N. Gopalaswami addressed to N. Ram, Editor-in-Chief of the *Hindu*, and Mr Ram's response:

Letter from N. Gopalaswami:

I am writing this with reference to the first page news under your byline which appeared in *The Hindu* on January 31 on my recommendation to the Hon'ble President for the removal of EC Shri Navin Chawla. May I draw your attention to the conversation we had on the previous day when you asked for confirmation of my sending a report and the reason for one-year delay and I had clarified that 6 months out of that was attributable to Shri Chawla himself. Despite that you wrote 'took a whole year...' When I pointed out to that on Feb. 1, you told me that you had mentioned it but I regret to say it was not.

I had also taken exception to the remarks 'curiously received them in his chambers instead of scheduling a formal meeting of the three-member Election Commission to hear them out'. Your observation was surprising inasmuch as the petition was addressed to the CEC, it was against one Commissioner, the third Commissioner was not concerned with it and there was therefore no question of the CEC receiving it [in] any manner other than all by myself.

You also wrote: 'Mr Gopalaswami departed from precedent to claim that the CEC had suo motu powers.' Pray what precedent? As regards my departing from my predecessor's views on this issue, on August 11, 2007, I had answered your paper's report on this point by quoting Shri Chawla's own stand supporting my contention. Shri Chawla's affidavit in the case confirms that the CEC's recommendation was a condition precedent for the appointing authority to consider removal of an EC and I quote 'However... a clear recommendation from the Chief Election Commissioner (CEC) recommending the removal is also a condition precedent and must exist.' As regards suo motu powers of the CEC, Shri Chawla himself not only concedes that but in fact goes further to say that CEC's credentials will be suspect if he didn't. I quote from Shri Chawla's written argument in the Supreme Court case: 'A Chief Election Commissioner knowing from his personal knowledge that an Election Commissioner is unfit to hold that office must be thoroughly incompetent or corrupt himself, if he takes no action at all. The assertion of Respondent No. 3 that he would not have taken action unless his comments were called for by the President is wholly untenable'.

May I also mention here that during our telecon on January 30, I had recalled to you that I had shared with you over lunch information on the several instances of Shri Chawla's partisanship on December 27, 2007 and you had confirmed it.

I am writing this to correct the impression the readers of your esteemed daily may have after reading the series of stories that your esteemed daily ran starting from January 31, wherein an effort appears to have been made to project facts which support the 'no suo motu power' theory. That ignores Shri Chawla's own contention strongly supporting the existence of suo motu powers with the CEC in the case before the Supreme Court. Further, I draw your attention to what the Supreme Court said in its order of Aug. 7, 2007 in that case: 'That CEC has no power of suo motu recommendation whether binding on the President or not is already negatived by binding judgements.' The very fact that many eminent jurists have taken a similar view goes to show that the existence of suo motu power is equally plausible.

May I request you to kindly publish the contents of this letter with the same prominence as you have given to the contrary view so as to bring full facts for the information of your readers who can then judge things for themselves?

Response by N. Ram:

Since the issues raised by Chief Election Commissioner N. Gopalaswami in his letter relate mainly to facts, it is necessary to respond to them in some detail by laying out the relevant facts assembled in our investigation:

Timing and delay

Para 1: The CEC's explanation for the one-year delay in his *suo motu* processing of the petition he received from a Bharatiya Janata Party delegation is factually inaccurate and misleading. As I have shown in an article, 'Gopalaswami's claims on timing of missive are seriously misleading,' published on page 1 of *The Hindu* of

February 3, 2009 a careful, item-by-item verification of the CEC's claims on what happened between January 30, 2008, when the BJP delegation presented its allegations, and January 12, 2009, when the CEC sent his recommendation to the President, leads to the following conclusion: 'More than half the delay is explained by Mr Gopalaswami's keeping the BJP's petition to himself between January 30 and July 20, 2008. Secondly, the timing is to be explained by the CEC's overbearing insistence, in tandem with the BJP's strident stance, that he had the power under Article 324(5) of the Constitution to conduct an inquiry against an Election Commissioner, and make a *suo motu* recommendation on his removal.'

As the article pointed out, this 'usurpation of authority' flew in the face of the Supreme Court's judgment in the Seshan case (1995); completely reversed the stand taken in June 2006 by Mr Gopalaswami's predecessor, B.B. Tandon; and explicitly went against the legal opinion (also published in *The Hindu* of February 3, 2009) given to Mr Tandon by Ashok H. Desai, senior advocate and former Attorney-General of India.

The article also established that when the CEC—following his unexplained six-month delay—sent the BJP's allegations to Mr Chawla and asked for a response, he did not have to wait long. The Election Commissioner sent him a detailed and constitutionally substantive reply on September 12, 2008 and subsequently forwarded Law Secretary T.K. Viswanathan's letter that affirmed that the CEC did not have *suo motu* powers of recommendation under Article 324(5). As my second article, 'How Chief Election Commissioner pursued BJP allegations,' published in the Op-Ed page on February 3, 2009 pointed out, Mr Chawla's letter of December 10, 2008 was only a reiteration of the constitutional points he made in his reply of September 12 plus a rejection of the BJP's allegations as 'motivated and entirely baseless.'

Mr Gopalaswami refers to telephonic conversations we had on January 30, 2009 and February 1, 2009 that I understood to be off-the-record (which is why I did not quote him). I do not want to comment on what he claims was said except to point out that after our Delhi bureau got in touch with the CEC to verify the information I had, he telephoned me and gave me background and details that I appreciated because they made the story we published on January 31, 2009 more informative and meaningful.

Meeting in chambers

Para 2: Meeting the BJP delegation in his chambers was clearly an action that flowed from this CEC's stand that he had, under Article 324(5), *suo motu* power to conduct an inquiry against an EC and make a recommendation for removal. But that the CEC has no such *suo motu* power under Article 324(5) is the widely accepted view of constitutional experts. It also makes democratic sense, as Justice S. Mohan, retired Judge of the Supreme Court, shows in his article 'Chief Election Commissioner: equal or superior?' published in *The Hindu* of February 9, 2009: '... it is logical to conclude that if the Election Commission is to function as a body, such *suo motu* recommendation by the CEC would nullify the function of the Commission. The Election Commissioners will be more interested in dancing to the tune of Chief Election Commissioner and try to be in his good books. This cannot be the intent of the Constitution under Article 324(5).' Going by this view, meeting the BJP delegation in chambers instead of convening a full meeting of the three-member Election Commission was out of line.

What precedent?

Para 3: The departure from precedent is indisputable for the simple reason that no previous CEC, not even T.N. Seshan, took the position Mr Gopalaswami did in his affidavit filed in the Supreme Court in August 2007. As I pointed out in my story of January 31, 2009, while Mr Gopalaswami interpreted his predecessor's view as being the same as his, Mr Tandon's view was shaped by Mr Desai's opinion. That clearly held that under Article 324(5), 'the CEC cannot act on his own and must await the reference through proper channels to be able to act on a complaint or petition seeking the removal of an EC.'

Let me also quote from Mr Tandon's counter affidavit of June 2006 filed in the Supreme Court: 'Since the President is the appointing authority, the removal can only be by the President. But the condition precedent to the removal of an EC is that he can be removed only on the recommendation of the CEC. If a complaint or petition by any person or group of persons is addressed to the President, seeking removal of an EC, CEC comes into the picture only when such complaint or petition is referred by the President to CEC for his recommendation in the matter. It is submitted that CEC cannot act on his own on such complaint or petition and must await reference from the President to be able to act on the complaint or petition seeking the removal of an EC.' Mr Gopalaswami interprets his predecessor's stand to relate specifically to a petition addressed to the President and not received officially by the CEC. A reading of Mr Desai's opinion, on which Mr Tandon based his stand, makes it clear that it makes no such distinction. It holds absolutely that 'the condition precedent to the removal of an EC is that he can be removed only on the recommendation of the CEC on a petition addressed to the President' and that 'the CEC cannot act on his own and must await the reference through proper channels to be able to act on a complaint or petition seeking the removal of an EC.'

Mr Gopalaswami's version of Mr Chawla's stand in a 43-page counter affidavit filed in the Supreme Court in June 2006 is highly misleading. He quotes one sentence from the affidavit on the CEC's recommendation being a condition precedent for the removal of an EC but not this clear assertion in page 17 of the affidavit: 'I therefore submit that in terms of Art. 324(5) of the Constitution of India, the recommendation of the Chief Election Commissioner becomes relevant only in an instance where the appointing authority, i.e., the President (acting on the aid and advice of the Council of Ministers) takes a decision to remove an Election Commissioner. I submit, however, that the recommendation of the Chief Election Commissioner is neither binding nor mandatory, definitely is not contemplated while considering the appointment of an Election Commissioner.'

The quotation on the incompetence or corruption of a CEC not taking any action despite 'knowing from his personal knowledge' that an EC was unfit to hold that office is from a written submission made in the Supreme Court by senior advocate Ram Jethmalani on behalf of Mr Chawla. The context of this statement is Mr Jethmalani's point that Mr Tandon 'was in office for more than a year after the

Memorandum reached him and yet took no action of any kind. It only means that the conduct of the Respondent [Mr Chawla] was wholly proper and called for no adverse comments or report. It is no longer denied that all the actions of the Commission after this Respondent's appointment have been unanimous.' To conclude from this that Mr Chawla concedes *suo motu* powers to the CEC under Article 324(5) is to go against all the material available, including Mr Chawla's affidavit, his detailed reply of September 12, 2008, his forwarding to the CEC of the Law Secretary's clarification of November 7, 2008, and his final letter of December 10, 2008. In any case, what position Mr Chawla or even Mr Tandon took on the question of *suo motu* powers under Article 324(5) is far less important than the constitutional provision itself.

Off-the-record interactions

Para 4: There is no need for me to comment on claims about what was said or not said in off-the-record conversations. What I can say is that in my regular interactions with him over many months, this CEC was extremely forthcoming (a quality [that] journalists everywhere appreciate). For his own reasons, Mr Gopalaswami has chosen not to mention the repeated opinion I expressed to him that, especially given the creditable overall performance of the Election Commission and its good external or public image, he should take the initiative to unify the Commission and remove the bad blood that affected its internal functioning.

What the Supreme Court said

Para 5: The sentence quoted by Mr Gopalaswami is in the paragraph of the Supreme Court's order summing up Mr Jethmalani's arguments. It remains to be explained or corrected in view of the senior lawyer's contention reported in the previous sentence that 'the Chief Election Commissioner has no power to make any recommendations under Second Proviso to Article 324(5) except on a reference made to it by the President of India while considering the removal of an Election Commissioner.' To say that this is what 'the Supreme Court said in its order of Aug. 7, 2007 in that case' is contrary to facts and misleading.

It is absolutely clear that the two-member bench (Justices Ashok Bhan and V.S. Sirpurkar) of the Supreme Court, in its order of August 7, 2007 allowing the withdrawal of Jaswant Singh's petition, did not express any opinion on the constitutionality of the *suo motu* powers claimed under Article 324(5) by the BJP and Mr Gopalaswami. The August 7, 2007 order could not have been clearer than this: 'The permission to withdraw the writ petition shall not be taken as an expression of opinion on the part of this Court regarding the questions involved. All questions and contentions of the parties are left open.'

For background, let me quote from our Legal Correspondent's report, published in *The Hindu* of August 8, 2007: 'Appearing for the Centre, Additional Solicitor-General Gopal Subramaniam contended that the CEC could not act *suo motu* in the matter. He argued that the Centre alone could proceed to take action against [an] Election Commissioner. He said this was a peculiar case where the CEC had filed an affidavit. And the petitioners, after withdrawing their petitions, would file a fresh representation before the CEC ... the affidavit of the CEC was silent on the role of the government, he said. The Bench told the Additional Solicitor-General: "We are not deciding the issue whether CEC has the power or not. We cannot stop anybody from filing the representation before the CEC but you can challenge the decisions taken by CEC on the representation. If the CEC commits [a] mistake then you can come to the court. We would then decide the matter."'

What emerges from all this is that the issues figuring in l'affaire Gopalaswami vs Chawla go beyond individuals. They relate to the future of an institution, the Election Commission of India, created by the Constitution, mediated and strengthened by judicial interpretation as well as by executive decisions and legislative change, and vital to the functioning of elective democracy. What is also clear is that the institution needs reform.

(*The Hindu*, 12 February 2009)

'End to an unedifying chapter'

With President Pratibha Patil rejecting, on the advice of the United Progressive Alliance government, Chief Election Commissioner N.

Gopalaswami's recommendation to remove Election Commissioner Navin Chawla from office, an unedifying chapter in the working of the Constitution should soon come to an end. The CEC's move was wholly indefensible in terms of both its constitutional overreach and its timing. It invoked non-existent authority and threatened to destabilize the functioning of the Commission during the very critical phase of the 15th general election that is to be conducted in five phases from April 16 to May 13. The government's advice to the President is unexceptionable, even as it was expected, given its public stand that the CEC's recommendation was totally out of line. The President's announcement makes it clear that the decision was reached after considering 'the report of the CEC, the Government's recommendation, constitutional provisions, and the Supreme Court judgment.'

It is unfortunate that the CEC should have got himself and his office embroiled in what started out as a political battle. It was in March 2006 that Bharatiya Janata Party leader L.K. Advani submitted a petition to the President charging Mr Chawla with being too close to the Congress party and seeking his removal. Traditionally, it has been the government in office that appointed to the Election Commission persons whom it considered suitable. There is much to be said for broadening the process of appointment to the Commission by associating the leader of the Opposition as in the case of the appointment of the Chief Vigilance Commissioner, for instance. Yet the BJP-led National Democratic Alliance administration had shied away from such self-denying reforms during its six years in office. It had instead followed the usual practice and appointed the members of the Election Commission on its own, including the present CEC, initially as an Election Commissioner. By now seeing virtue in denying the government of the day the unrestrained power to appoint Election Commissioners and questioning the UPA government's choice on the ground of bias, the BJP was clearly playing partisan politics. The main opposition party also approached the Supreme Court and it was there that the present CEC interposed himself between the political combatants with his claim of suo motu power. Following this claim, the party withdrew its petition and presented it later to the CEC for action. The Supreme Court itself, while allowing the petition to be withdrawn, left open the contested question whether the CEC did have the suo motu power to recommend the removal of an Election Commissioner.

It is clear from the constitutional scheme of things that the CEC cannot initiate action and recommend the removal of any of his colleagues, but instead must wait for a reference from the President for his recommendation. Article 324(5) of the Constitution provides that the CEC cannot be removed except by impeachment as in the case of a Supreme Court judge, and that an Election Commissioner 'cannot be removed from office except on the recommendation of the Chief Election Commissioner'. With the security of his or her tenure guaranteed, the CEC is expected to protect the Election Commissioners from arbitrary removal by the executive. The Supreme Court in its detailed analysis of the Article in T.N. Seshan's case cautioned that if 'the power were to be exercisable by the CEC as per his whim and caprice, the CEC himself would become an instrument of oppression and would destroy the independence of the ECs ...' If differences of opinion on the timing of the Karnataka elections, for instance, were to be treated as proof of bias and as a ground for recommending removal, Election Commissioners would be deterred from voicing their independent opinion and forced to go by the dictates of the CEC. The whole scheme and the deliberative and collective decision-making value of a multi-member Election Commission, with the Election Commissioners enjoying equal powers with the Chief Election Commissioner, would then come to nought. From a practical standpoint, if the CEC were to claim such a power, his or her office would be inviting representations from parties dissatisfied with some order or the other of an Election Commissioner. Former Attorney-General Ashok H. Desai, in his opinion tendered to the Election Commission on Mr Advani's petition, was clearly of the view that 'the CEC cannot act on his own and must await the reference through proper channels to be able to act on a complaint or petition seeking the removal of an EC.' This was also the position that Mr Gopalaswami's predecessor as CEC, B.B. Tandon, took in the Supreme Court.

It is clear, in any case, that the President alone can remove an Election Commissioner, and the President and the government are not obliged to accept a recommendation for removal from the CEC even if that were to be within his competence. Now that the decision to reject the CEC's recommendation on Mr Chawla has been made, it is imperative that the government must announce the appointment of Mr Chawla as the next CEC-designate without delay. The murky controversy raised by the BJP and by the CEC's recommendation is absolutely no reason to depart from longstanding practice. The government would also do well simultaneously to name the person who will replace Mr Gopalaswami as the third member of the Election Commission when he retires on April 20; this would obviate an appointment when the election process is under way. Without the distraction of an internal war that will do no good to its functioning, and with uncertainty over its composition removed, the Election Commission will be well placed to conduct the elections.

(Opinion, *The Hindu*, 3 March 2009)

'Chief Election Commissioner cannot act on his own': Ashok Desai Opinion

During the tenure of Chief Election Commissioner B.B. Tandon, the Election Commission of India sought the legal opinion of Ashok H. Desai, barrister, senior advocate, and former Attorney-General of India, on Article 324(5) of the Constitution. The key question was whether the CEC can initiate suo motu action for the removal of an Election Commissioner without a reference being made by the appointing authority, the President. This is the text of Mr Desai's confidential Opinion:

1. On 16.3.2006 Shri L.K. Advani, Leader of the Opposition in Lok Sabha, along with 204 other Members of Parliament submitted a petition to the President of India Seeking the removal of Shri Navin Chawla, Election Commissioner (EC) under Article 324(5) of the Constitution of India. On 17.3.2006, Shri V.K. Malhotra, Member of Parliament sent a copy of the said petition to the Chief Election Commissioner (CEC) for necessary action.
2. Subsequent events disclose that the President has forwarded the petition to the Prime Minister. But the Prime Minister has not yet forwarded it to the CEC. The CEC has not received the petition through any official channel.

3. The short question for consideration is whether the CEC can initiate suo motu action merely on the copy of petition sent to him by Shri Malhotra. The petition makes various allegations against the concerned EC, which relate to his activities during the period of internal emergency (1975-1977), his activities as a bureaucrat, his proximity to the Congress party, to the Trusts run by his family and to his functioning as an EC. The petition itself is addressed to the President with an appeal that the concerned EC should be removed under Article 324. It concludes with the statement that a copy is being independently sent to the CEC so that he can begin to act in the matter immediately.
4. The provisions about the Election Commission are contained in Part XV of the Constitution Article 324(5) which provides for conditions of service and tenure of office is of special relevance. It reads as follows:

   '(5) Subject to the provisions of any law made by Parliament, the conditions of service and tenure of office of the Election Commissioners and the Regional Commissioners shall be such as the President may by rule determine:

   'Provided that the Chief Election Commissioner shall not be removed from his office except in like manner and on the like grounds as a Judge of the Supreme Court and the conditions of service of the Chief Election Commissioner shall not be varied to his disadvantage after his appointment:

   'Provided further that any other Election Commissioner or a Regional Commissioner shall not be removed from office except on the recommendation of the Chief Election Commissioner.'
5. Thus, an EC can be removed from office only on the recommendation of the CEC. In T.N. Seshan, Chief Election Commr. of India v. Union of India (1995) 4 SCC 611 the Supreme Court elaborated on the scheme intended by Article 324 as follows:

   'However, the proviso to clause (4) of Article 324 says (i) the CEC shall not be removed from his office except in like manner and on the like grounds as a Judge of the Supreme

Court and (ii) the conditions of service of the CEC shall not be varied to his disadvantage after his appointment. These two limitations on the power of Parliament are intended to protect the independence of the CEC from political and/or executive interference. In the case of ECs as well as RCs. The second proviso to clause (5) provides that they shall not be removed from office except on the recommendation of the CEC. It may also be noticed that while under clause (4), before the appointment of the RCs, consultation with the Election Commission (not CEC) is necessary, there is no such requirement in the case of appointments of ECs. The provision that the ECs and the RCs once appointed cannot be removed from office before the expiry of their tenure except on the recommendation of the CEC ensures their independence. The scheme of Article 324 in this behalf is that after insulating the CEC by the first proviso to clause (5), the ECs and the RCs have been assured independence of functioning by providing that they cannot be removed except on the recommendation of the CEC. Of course, the recommendation for removal must be based on intelligible, and cogent considerations which would have relation to efficient functioning of the Election Commission. That is so because this privilege has been conferred on the CEC to ensure that the ECs as well as the RCs are not at the mercy of political or executive bosses of the day. It is necessary to realize that this check on the executive's power to remove is built into the second proviso to clause (5) to safeguard the independence of not only these functionaries but the Election Commission as a body. If, therefore, the powers were to be exercisable by the CEC as per his whim and caprice, the CEC himself would become an instrument of oppression and would destroy the independence of the ECs and the RCs if they are required to function under the threat of the CEC recommending their removal. It is, therefore, needless to emphasise that the CEC must exercise this power only when there exist valid reasons which are conducive to efficient functioning of the Election Commission. This, briefly stated, indicates the status of the various functionaries constituting the Election Commission.'

6. The principle that appears from the above is that ECs can be appointed by the President without consultation with the CEC. However, once so appointed, they can be removed only on the recommendation of the CEC, thus ensuring their independence from the executive of the day. The Court has emphasised that the CEC himself is under the legal constraints indicated when he acts under the Article.
7. There is a distinction drawn between the process of removal of CEC and the process of removal of an EC. Since the President is the appointing authority, the removal itself can only be by the President. But the condition precedent to the removal of an EC is that he can be removed only on the recommendation of the CEC on a petition addressed to the President. This would suggest that the CEC cannot act on his own and must await the reference through proper channels to be able to act on a complaint or petition seeking the removal of an EC.
8. This conclusion is also borne out by a pragmatic approach. The present petition is signed by as many as 205 Members of Parliament. It cannot, however, be ruled out that, in future, there may be petitions signed or supported by smaller groups or even individuals. It is difficult to see how the CEC can suo motu act on such complaints or petitions without awaiting a formal reference.
9. I am therefore of the opinion that, before acting in the matter, the Chief Election Commissioner must await the petition submitted to the President by Shri L.K. Advani on March 16, 2006 to be forwarded to him and not initiate an inquiry suo motu.

Ashok H. Desai
Senior Advocate
Place: New Delhi
Dated: April 12, 2006

(*The Hindu*, 3 February 2009)

Other legal luminaries also weighed into this debate. Senior Supreme Court lawyer P.P. Rao wrote in the *Tribune*, Chandigarh, on 18 February 2009:

> As the power of removal is vested in the President of India, no part of the power can be wrested by the CEC for exercise by him. Initiation of disciplinary action for misbehaviour can be done only by the appointing authority, which is also the disciplinary authority or its delegate. It has not been delegated to the CEC so far.
>
> The CEC and the ECs together constitute the Election Commission and they collectively exercise the power of superintendence, direction and control of the preparation of the electoral rolls for, and the conduct of, all elections to Parliament and state legislatures and of elections to the offices of President and Vice-President of India.
>
> The Chief Election Commissioner and Other Election Commissioners (Conditions of Service) Act, 1991, as amended, provides inter alia that if the CEC and his colleagues differ in opinion on any matter, such matter shall be decided by the opinion of the majority. In T.N. Seshan vs the Union of India, the Supreme Court rejected Seshan's contention that the CEC alone has decisive powers.
>
> The question arises, whether in the scheme of the Constitution when the CEC is not removable from his office except in like manner and on the like grounds as a judge of the Supreme Court, i.e. only after a judicial enquiry into allegations of misbehaviour or incapacity followed by impeachment by Parliament, is it conceivable that an Election Commissioner who enjoys equal power as a member of the Election Commission can be summarily shown the door on the suo motu recommendation of a CEC? The answer is an emphatic No.

Eminent jurist and constitution expert Fali Nariman told the *Hindu*[5] that the CEC may have the power under Article 324 (5) of the Constitution to recommend the removal of an election commissioner but this power cannot be used mechanically due to

5 *The Hindu*, 1 February 2009.

some difference of opinion with the other commissioners simply because he is a superior authority. It can be used only if there is a gross violation or if a person has become bankrupt. He further stated that the CEC's recommendation is not binding on the government. The eminent lawyer was more upset at the timing of Gopalaswami's recommendation. 'When we need a united Commission for holding the general elections, it [CEC's action] has divided the Commission and has done damage to the institution', he said.

Former Attorney-General and senior advocate, Soli Sorabjee shared Nariman's views: 'The power of the CEC to recommend removal of an EC is implied given the structure of the Election Commission. But the timing is unfortunate. It is for the government to take a decision to accept or not accept the recommendation. If there are cogent reasons for the government to reject the recommendation, it can do so.'[6]

Former law minister Shanti Bhushan echoed this: 'Appointments and removals are in the government's domain and a view by the CEC is to be given only if his advice is asked for.' He too questioned the timing: 'The matter has been pending for many months. If the CEC wanted to give an opinion, why did he wait for weeks before his retirement, which is due on April 20?'

In an article published in the *Hindu* on 9 February 2009, Justice S. Mohan—retired judge of the Supreme Court of India—argued that:

> The CEC cannot exercise his power suo motu because the members of the Commission are of equal status. If suo motu power is conferred on the CEC, it will amount to an assumption of superiority, which is not warranted and will obliterate the equality. This aspect did not specifically arise in the case of T.N. Seshan. However, it is logical to conclude that if the Election Commission is to function as a body, such suo motu recommendation by the CEC would nullify the function of the Commission. The Election Commissioners will be more interested

6 Ibid.

> in dancing to the tune of Chief Election Commissioner and try to be in his good books. This cannot be the intent of the Constitution under Article 324(5). Such a situation will never be conducive to an effective functioning of the Commission. The conclusion, therefore, is inescapable that the power of recommendation cannot be exercised suo motu.

Senior journalist Harish Khare's article 'Restoring Order at Nirvachan Sadan Statecraft'[7] probably sums up the issues at stake:

> Almost all sober students of Indian politics and most constitutional experts are unanimous regretting that the controversy caused by Mr Gopalaswami has damaged the institutional prestige of the Election Commission. Since T.N. Seshan's days, it has reclaimed—with considerable help from the judiciary and the democratic civil society—its autonomy against a wayward political class; and it has indeed used that elbow room to introduce an energetic notion of fairness in the electoral process. No longer can a ruling party—at the Centre or in the states—have an unfair advantage over its rivals and challengers. The Election Commission has become a role model the world over for a vigorous, neutral and detached umpire in a poll process that otherwise tends to be defined by intimidation, violence and corruption.
>
> It is precisely because of this success that the timing of Mr Gopalaswami's action bewilders even those who may be inclined to see some merit or reason in his animosity towards Mr Chawla. Coming as it does so close to the next general election, the Gopalaswami activism has the potential of distracting from the authenticity of the forthcoming poll process. Neither Mr Gopalaswami's friends nor Mr Chawla's detractors would want any further erosion in the credibility of the institution that is at the heart of the Indian democracy.
>
> [...]
>
> In fact, both the Prime Minister and the Law Minister have a responsibility to reject Mr Gopalaswami's recommendation but in a

7 *The Hindu*, 26 February 2009.

manner and language that would assure the nation that there is no dilution of the canons of good governance. Indeed, the Gopalaswami activism needs to be defeated, otherwise it would set a disastrous precedent, encouraging political parties to try to manipulate and browbeat the Election Commission and its officials.

Appendix: Elections in Bhutan

"It was always the desire of His Majesty The Fourth King to bring democracy to Bhutan for he believed very early in his reign that the destiny of the nation must be entrusted to the Bhutanese people. His Majesty's vision for a democratic Bhutan is bearing fruit with the three parliamentary elections that have been held successfully since 2008."

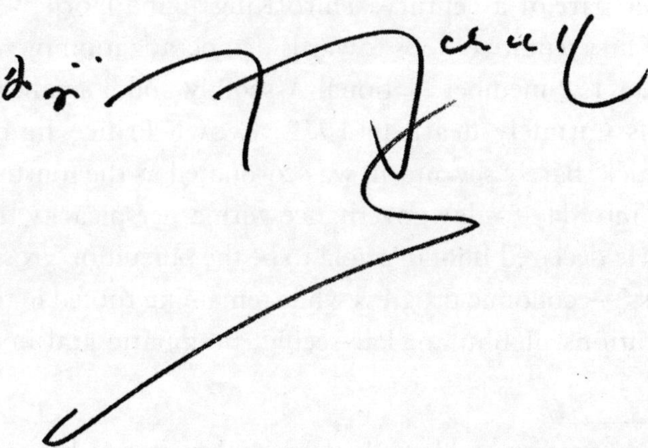

Queen Mother Ashi Dorji Wangmo Wangchuck

In May 2013, three years after my term ended as CEC of India, I was invited by the then CEC of Bhutan, Dasho Kunzang Wangdi, to observe the primary round of elections to the National Assembly.[1] At a polling station that I visited near Paro, I noticed an elderly, rather frail lady, perhaps in her eighties, enter the election booth supported by her granddaughter. As is Bhutan's custom on election day, both were formally dressed in their kiras. The presiding officer and the poll staff rushed to help her to complete the formalities. Then they led her to the voting compartment where lay the EVM. She had clearly never seen one before. She looked at it closely and asked some questions. Apparently satisfied and feeling she no longer needed their help, she waved them away. She waved away her granddaughter too. Her vote was secret and she intended it to be so. Later, I inquired of her why she had not voted in the first National Assembly election of 2008, as this seemed to be her first election. Her answer was crisp. She had always been content with the rule of the king, she said. Now that she had realized that he wanted democracy to take root, she decided to forget her aches and pains and had come to cast her vote.

Nestled in the great Himalayas, Bhutan remained in self-imposed isolation from the world. Tucked away between two huge neighbours, India and China, it remained an absolute monarchy for the better part of a century. Third King Jigme Dorji Wangchuck took the first tentative steps towards democratization by setting up, in 1953, a 150-member National Assembly and a smaller Council. Upon his untimely death in 1972, Crown Prince Jigme Singye Wangchuck, barely seventeen, was coronated as the fourth king. He plunged into day-to-day governance with a perspicacity that belied his age. He declared Bhutan's goal to be the pursuit of 'gross national happiness'—economic progress while remaining rooted in the culture and traditions of Bhutan. Far-seeing, pragmatic and importantly

1 I am no stranger to Bhutan's elections, having first been invited just after the Mock Polls in 2007, once again in 2009, when I was the Chief Election Commissioner and thereafter to observe the elections in 2013 and 2018.

someone who closely followed the history of the region, he realized that sooner or later there would be a democratic challenge to an absolute monarchy. Progressively, he began to liberalize the country's political system, moving rapidly towards a democratic constitutional monarchy. On his instructions a draft Constitution, mandating a parliamentary democracy, was drawn up and circulated to the people. Addressing the drafting committee which comprised eminent representatives of the government, the clergy and representative of the people, he said, 'It is important for all of us today to look into the future and to take the necessary steps to shape the destiny of our country. Bhutan must move with the times... (therefore) should not be deterred by the fact that democratic political systems did not work in some countries...'[2] He himself travelled tirelessly across the country, explaining to a bewildered populace that this is where their best interests lay.

The Constitution provided for a multiparty system with two parties in parliament (which was further elaborated in the Election Act). He encouraged the formation of political parties, created a National Assembly (parliament) of forty-seven members and the National Council (Upper House) of twenty-five members (five to be nominated by the king). This would be an apolitical body, candidates contesting as individuals and not representing any political party. The country would be run by a prime minister in cabinet, with a bicameral legislature that would hopefully ensure a real Opposition. The National Assembly would have a term of five years. Direct elections would be held under adult franchise. Bhutanese citizens above the age of eighteen could vote.

The Constitution which was adopted in July 2008, declared Bhutan to be a democratic constitutional monarchy, with clear separation of powers between the executive, legislature and the judiciary. The king would be the head of state while executive power would be exercised by the council of ministers. For the National Assembly there would be two rounds of voting, a primary round after

2 Speech reported in newspaper *Kuensel*, 31 December 2001.

which the two main political parties having the highest number of votes in the primary round would contest the general election. The prime minister would be a natural born citizen of Bhutan and could hold this office for two terms.

What could have been the reasons why a king, firmly ensconced on the throne, wish to move so dramatically towards creating a robust democracy, especially as his subjects sought no change? In the words of Her Majesty the Queen Mother Ashi Dorji Wangmo Wangchuck: 'It was always the desire of His Majesty the Fourth King to bring democracy to Bhutan for he believed very early in his reign that the destiny of the nation must be entrusted to the Bhutanese people. His Majesty's vision for a democratic Bhutan is bearing fruit with the three parliamentary elections that have been held successfully since 2008.'

By this process of self-abnegation, he set out to transform an absolute monarchy into a parliamentary democracy. In a world where democracies often enough spawn dictatorships (with rigged elections or warped constitutional amendments to remain in power), his decision attracted world attention, as did his voluntary abdication from the throne in 2006, at the age of fifty, in favour of his Oxford-educated son Jigme Khesar Namgyel Wangchuck. The abdication further catalysed the country's transition to a fully democratic government.

In 2006, Bhutan took another decisive step towards electoral democracy when it established the Election Commission. The basic structure of the Election Commission of Bhutan (ECB) would resemble India's. Although Bhutan had a tiny population in comparison, Bhutan too favoured a three-member Commission. Unlike India, the Constitution provided that the CEC and ECs would be selected by a broad-based panel comprising the prime minister, Chief Justice, Speaker of parliament, chairperson of the National Council and the leader of the Opposition. Dasho Kunzang Wangdi, Bhutan's distinguished auditor general, was selected to head the Election Commission. Dasho Chogyal Dago Rigdzin and significantly a lady, Aum Deki Pema were appointed commissioners.

The trio now faced a formidable task of setting up rules, regulations and electoral practice virtually from scratch. This was initially borne out in a somewhat amusing manner. In the absence of political parties or candidates, the ECB felt the need to create awareness by holding a 'mock election'. Candidates and voters alike needed to be made familiar with electoral procedures, not to mention an understanding of the functioning of EVMs that Bhutan had decided to use, eschewing the paper-devouring ballot papers. The problems seemed almost insurmountable. For a start there were neither political parties nor candidates. So four 'mock' political parties had to be set up. Each was assigned one of the four primary colours. Yellow stood for traditional values, red for industrial development, blue for fairness and accountability and green for the environment. Was it any surprise then that in the election conducted in April 2007 the Yellow Party won hands down, perhaps, because yellow is the colour associated with the king?

Dasho Kunzang Wangdi, was like me an alumnus of St Stephen's College in Delhi. Conscious of the enormous responsibility placed on his shoulders, he looked to India for support as he set about his work. He was acutely aware that he had rather less than two years (2006–07) to prepare for Bhutan's first national elections scheduled for 2008, with practice runs being held earlier. This entailed education of voters and stakeholders, encouraging the establishment of political parties, establishing a code of conduct to regulate their behaviour and creating various instruction manuals and much else that went into the voting process.

This included the training of officials and staff. Towards this end, he sought a long-term association of cooperation with the Election Commission of India by signing a memorandum of understanding (MoU) that covered all important areas of cooperation. I was a commissioner at the time. Thereafter, we helped in training their officials and arranged observation visits by Bhutanese officials to witness some of our elections to state assemblies. We shared information and expertise. We exchanged delegations.

However, it must be said that Bhutan's Election Commission, having wisely studied the world's leading democratic models, incorporated what suited their needs and traditions best. There were at least three very distinct differences between Indian electoral laws and practice. For instance, Bhutan favoured state funding of elections. It also decided that only graduates would be eligible to contest elections, which initially led to an outcry in a country of widespread illiteracy but this soon settled down. Another important (and may I add excellent decision) was to exclude anyone with a criminal record or accused of a felony in a pending case from contesting. Since the elections would be state-funded, the clergy, ordained or robed, which received its funds from the state exchequer, were astutely excluded from the electoral process. Hoping also to avoid multiplicity of parties, a two-party system was sought to be created. This they hoped would avoid the problems that arose from the compulsions of coalition politics that they saw elsewhere.

As a curious world watched, the ECB delivered elections on time. The elections for the National Council which were conducted in two phases (on 31 December 2007 and 29 January 2008), followed by elections to the National Assembly in March 2008, based on the first-past-the-post system, were acknowledged by observers to be an undiluted success. However, at this early juncture in Bhutan's history only two political parties (People's Democratic Party [PDP] and Druk Phuensum Tshogpa [DPT]) had registered with the Election Commission of Bhutan. Therefore, there could be no primary round of elections. The DPT was led by Lyonpo Jigme Y. Thinley and the PDP by Lyonpo Sangay Ngedup, both former ministers. The former won, and the leader was appointed the prime minister by the king.

By the time Bhutan was ready for the second parliamentary election in 2013, voter awareness had increased, in part through a number of voter education measures undertaken by ECB, and in part because of the burgeoning of social media.[3] Three more political

3 The ECB initiated a number of voter-education techniques including 'Democracy Clubs' in colleges and schools where mock elections were

parties had registered themselves the year before, which now enabled both a primary round (in May 2013) and a final one (in July 2013), with a voter turnout of just over 66 per cent. This time around the People's Democratic Party won the election, and its leader Tshering Tobgay became prime minister.

During Bhutan's third parliamentary election of 2018, I was once again invited as an observer to witness the polls on 20 April 2018 for the Upper House. This time the invitation came from the new chief election commissioner Dasho Chogyal Dago Rigdzin. That morning, in spite of a steady drizzle, I visited several polling stations. Once again, I was pleasantly surprised by the orderly queues of men, dressed in their formal 'khos' and the women in their beautiful 'kiras'. One could not be faulted for thinking that everyone was dressed for a formal occasion since this was quite unlike in any election queue that I had seen in any other country. I talked to many at random. A young first-time voter who had just turned eighteen said he was so excited that he could now vote that he had not slept a wink all night. Another first-time voter was a recent graduate from an American university. He had been unable to interrupt his studies to vote in the first election.

That night the results were declared. I noticed that a measure of growing voter awareness was that anti-incumbency was high, and many old faces found themselves voted out of power.

The elections to the third National Assembly demonstrated the steady progress that democracy has made. For the third time, Bhutan's voters have upset the applecart by changing their government. Democracy may have come late to the country but each election has revealed to me a steadily growing maturity that has accompanied an increasingly educated population.

Unlike the first election, but like the second, there were enough political parties to warrant a second round. This time too, the

---

held. Like India, ECB decided to celebrate National Voters Day (15 September), and an EVM Day to encourage familiarization with the machine.

primary round held on 15 September 2018 threw up a shock, when the ruling party, the People's Democratic Party (PDP) trailed to third place, not just disqualifying it from the final round but in the process wiping out its thirty-two seats in the same swoop. The final round on 18 October 2018 threw up yet another surprise, when a party that was born just five years earlier, the Druk Nyamrup Tshogpa (DNT), raced ahead to capture thirty out of the forty-seven seats, securing 31.85 per cent of the 70.73 per cent of the votes cast. The remaining seventeen seats were won by the Druk Phuensum Tshogpa (DPT) or the Bhutan Peace and Prosperity Party, the party that was in power for a term in 2008.

It was just a little over a decade ago in April 2007 that the country's newly set up Election Commission had to organize a mock poll to prepare the people for an imminent change to democracy. It was a difficult call for the first chief election commissioner, Dasho Kunzang Wangdi, since the people were not convinced. In fact, voter turnout was less than 30 per cent and those who did voted overwhelmingly for the Yellow party. With the voting almost double, and a third consecutive change, Bhutan has come a long way.

Having been to Bhutan seven times in the past decade, I have been able to witness for myself how democracy is beginning to take firm roots there. The Fifth King is, like his father, wise beyond his years. I have met him several times over the years and constantly been surprised by a maturity that belies his youth. There is in him the same sense of service that has marked his father's reign. He has been able to convert the veneration that still exists—rural Bhutan is still largely feudal in the way they look up to the royal house—into the strengthening of democracy. The Constitution of Bhutan no longer decrees an absolute monarchy; the king can technically be impeached and removed, and in any case must step down at the age of sixty-five.

Meanwhile, for reasons other than elections, I have interacted with ministers and bureaucrats in Bhutan and have encountered my share of red tape too. This is not always an unhealthy sign because at one level it demonstrates growing checks and balances in the system.

~

As Bhutan completed ten years as a democracy, representatives from political parties had gathered at a special forum held in the Royal University in March 2018 to discuss policies, issues and national priorities in an election year. There were voices that cautioned about the growing influence of money even in a state-funded electoral system. Others spoke for the need of a free media, yet cautioned about the negative role that social media was beginning to play. There was a healthy debate about what was going right and what was beginning to go wrong. The one steadfast refrain was both reverence and affection for the young king.

Appendix 2

GENERAL ELECTIONS IN INDIA		
General Elections	**Date**	**Chief Election Commissioner**
1st	23 October 1951–21 February 1952	Sukumar Sen
2nd	23 February–14 March 1957	Sukumar Sen
3rd	19–25 February 1962	Kalyan Sundaram
4th	17–21 February 1967	Kalyan Sundaram
5th	1–10 March 1971	S.P. Sen Verma
6th	16–20 March 1977	T. Swaminathan
7th	3 and 6 January 1980	S.L Shakdhar
8th	24, 27, 28 December 1984	R.K Trivedi
9th	22 and 26 November 1989	R.V.S. Peri Shastri
10th	20 May, 12 and 15 June 1991	T.N.Sheshan
11th	27 April, 2 and 7 May 1996	T.N.Sheshan
12th	6, 22 and 28 February 1998	M.S. Gill
13th	5, 11, 18, 25 September and 3 October 1999	M.S. Gill
14th	20, 26 April and 5, 10 May 2004	T.S. Krishnamurthy
15th	16, 23, 30 April and 7, 13 May 2009	N.Gopalaswami (First phase only), Navin Chawla
16th	7 April–12 May 2014	V.S. Sampath

LIST OF CHIEF ELECTION COMMISSIONERS			
No.	**Name**	**Took Office**	**Left Office**
1	Sukumar Sen	21 March 1950	19 December 1958
2	Kalyan Sundaram	20 December 1958	30 September 1967
3	S.P. Sen Verma	1 October 1967	30 September 1972
4	Nagendra Singh	1 October 1972	6 February 1973
5	T. Swaminathan	7 February 1973	17 June 1977
6	S.L. Shakdhar	18 June 1977	17 June 1982
7	R.K. Trivedi	18 June 1982	31 December 1985
8	R.V.S. Peri Sastri	1 January 1986	25 November 1990
9	V.S. Ramadevi	26 November 1990	11 December 1990
10	T.N. Seshan	12 December 1990	11 December 1996
11	M.S. Gill	12 December 1996	13 June 2001
12	J.M. Lyngdoh	14 June 2001	7 February 2004
13	T S. Krishnamurthy	8 February 2004	15 May 2005
14	B.B. Tandon	16 May 2005	29 June 2006
15	N. Gopalaswami	30 June 2006	20 April 2009
16	Navin Chawla	21 April 2009	29 July 2010
17	S.Y. Quraishi	30 July 2010	10 June 2012
18	V.S. Sampath	11 June 2012	15 January 2015
19	H.S. Brahma	16 January 2015	18 April 2015
20	Nasim Zaidi	19 April 2015	5 July 2017
21	Achal Kumar Jyoti	6 July 2017	22 January 2018
22	Om Prakash Rawat	23 January 2018	1 December 2018
23	Sunil Aurora	2 December 2018	Incumbent

NUMBER OF ELECTED REPRESENTATIVES			
States	**Lok Sabha**	**Rajya Sabha**	**MLAs**
Andhra Pradesh	20	11	175
Arunchal Pradesh	2	1	60
Assam	14	7	126
Bihar	39	16	243
Chhattisgarh	11	5	90
Goa	2	1	40
Gujarat	26	11	182
Haryana	10	5	90
Himachal Pradesh	4	3	68
Jammu and Kashmir	5	4	87
Jharkhand	14	6	81
Karnataka	27	12	224
Kerala	19	9	140
Madhya Pradesh	29	11	230
Maharashtra	48	19	288
Manipur	2	1	60
Meghalaya	1	1	60
Mizoram	1	1	40
Nagaland	1	1	60
Odisha	20	10	147
Punjab	13	7	117
Rajasthan	25	10	200
Sikkim	1	1	32
Tamil Nadu	39	18	234
Telangana	17	7	119
Tripura	2	1	60
Uttar Pradesh	80	31	403
Uttarakhand	5	3	70
West Bengal	42	16	294

NUMBER OF ELECTED REPRESENTATIVES			
Union Territories	**Lok Sabha**	**Rajya Sabha**	**MLAs**
Andaman and Nicobar Islands	1	Nil	Nil
Chandigarh	1	Nil	Nil
Dadra and Nagar Haveli	1	Nil	Nil
Daman and Diu	1	Nil	Nil
Lakshadweep	1	Nil	Nil
NCT of Delhi	7	3	70
Puducherry	1	1	40
TOTAL	532	245 including 12 Nominated members	4120

Largest Lok Sabha constituency by area: Ladakh in J&K, 173,266.37 sq. km

Largest Lok Sabha constituency by electorate: Malkajgiri in Telangana with 3,183,325 voters

Smallest Lok Sabha constituency by area: Chandini Chowk in NCT of Delhi, 10 sq. km

Smallest Lok Sabha constituency by electorate: Lakshadweep with 47,972 voters

Index

Acknowledgements

MY thanks begin at home. I have to thank my wife Rupika and my daughters, Rukmini and Mrinalini. They have been a fundamental part of my 'election' journey for many years—first supporting me through the exhilarating and exhausting years at the Election Commission, and then in their constant help with the writing of this book, including working on drafts through family holidays. Rupika, with four books to her credit, brought her experience as a writer and her profound intelligence to my aid. I was fortunate too in having Rukmini's editorial skills to assist me—that she works in publishing herself is something I took full advantage of, and saw first-hand how uncompromising and demanding she is as she wields her pen over an author's text! Mrinalini, the family designer, worked on cover options and read the text dispassionately to gauge its pulse. These are not perfunctory acknowledgements, for their skills have contributed much to the making of this book.

The only other person who went through the entire manuscript with a fine toothcomb was my publisher-friend, Dr Clive Wing. Familiar with India, having lived here years ago, he is removed enough from the Indian electoral scene to be able to raise many pertinent questions, the answers to which helped me to tie up several loose ends in the text.

N. Ram, presently chairman of The Hindu Group of publications, has been an influential presence in the writing of this book, discussing parts of the manuscript and helping me shape the book's contours. Both he and N. Ravi, editor-in-chief of *The Hindu* between 1991 and 2003, opened up the newspaper's archives for me. In Chennai, the former chief librarian of the *Hindu*, Mr V. Ganesan, provided me with all the copies I needed.

The late Madanjeet Singh, UNESCO's goodwill ambassador and prolific writer, and France Marquet continued to urge me ever since I retired to 'contribute to history' by writing an account of my years in the Commission. I am grateful to both of them for their gentle prodding.

Early discussions with V.K. Karthika, then publisher and editor-in-chief at HarperCollins, were invaluable as I sat down to write the book. Khozem Merchant's journalistic insights, honed over many years at the *Financial Times*, London, were very helpful too.

At the Election Commission of India, I sought clarifications from the then chief election commissioner O.P. Rawat on a few issues, and he was most forthcoming with his information. Senior Deputy Election Commissioner Umesh Sinha was considerate in helping me obtain documents and photographs from the Commission's archives. S.K. Mendiratta, former legal adviser, and K.F. Wilfred, senior principal secretary, obtained the information that I sought. I am in their debt. They are, of course, in no way responsible for my views.

It was during B.B. Tandon's stewardship of the Election Commission of India that I joined as commissioner and began to learn the ropes of how the ship at Nirvachan Sadan (the headquarters of the Commission) was steered. We had an able secretariat comprising in the main three indefatigable IAS officers, namely R. Balakrishnan, J.P. Prakash and, later, Vinod Zutshi. Our legal team and principal secretaries were integral to all the meetings of the Commission. The greatly experienced people whom I worked with at the Election Commission are the background of the knowledge that I bring to this book.

I also gained many insights into past workings of the Election Commission during informal meetings with the knowledgeable and amiable former chief election commissioner Dr M.S. Gill, as well as the erudite former election commissioner G.V.G. Krishnamurthy. Yet, it was the formidable former chief election commissioner T.N. Seshan who, in his inimitable style, gave me an hour's 'lecture' at his house in Chennai beginning with the encouraging words: 'Do you see my skin? Look at it carefully. It is the skin of a rhinoceros. If you have to do your job at the Election Commission, you had better develop it.' To which he added, 'Keep your head down and forge ahead.' This turned out to be rather useful advice which I followed.

For my chapter on Bhutan, I am greatly indebted to Her Majesty the Queen Mother, Ashi Dorji Wangmo Wangchuck, for her wide-ranging discussions as well as a note she sent me especially for this book.

At the Election Commission of Bhutan, I would like to acknowledge the help of the Chief Election Commissioner of Bhutan, Dasho Chogyal Dago Rigdzin, his predecessor Dasho Kunzang Wangdi, and present election commissioners Aum Deki Pema and Ugyen Tshewang for inviting me to observe successive elections and thereby witness the maturing of electoral democracy in their country.

For my understanding of the 1951–52 elections pertaining to the erstwhile princely state of Jodhpur, I am in the debt of Bapji Gaj Singh of Jodhpur. I would also like to express my gratitude to Mrs Jayanti Sen and Mrs Purabi Ward, daughters of the late Shri Sukumar Sen. Despite illness and distance, they shared valuable vignettes of their father's life and work.

The person who needs an award for deciphering my handwriting, and who painstakingly typed the drafts in her spare time, is Charu Pahuja (as did V. Seshu for the earlier part of the book). Sunil Binjola, with his deft computer skills, helped to verify facts, while Nidhi Binjola sorted out a large number of photographs and other materials. I am grateful to all four. Nearer home, my secretary Ramesh Miglani who has been with me for almost fifty years, had maintained my election notes meticulously, which were to be of immense help.

I am fortunate to have HarperCollins India as my publisher. From its decisive CEO Ananth Padmanabhan, I was privileged to receive the utmost consideration. Unless he was travelling, he always made time to have a cup of tea with me and, with a deft touch, would clear whatever queries I had. Warm thanks are due to Udayan Mitra, my publisher, for his constant guidance on various aspects of the book, without which I would have been quite lost. Senior editor Antony Thomas was meticulous in the final stages of the edit. We agreed and disagreed for over many an editorial issue, until we were both content. I'd also like to acknowledge Anish Cherian, who was offered to me by HarperCollins for a few months to assist me in my research. The India International Centre Library was my sanctuary, where the Chief Librarian Dr S. Majumdar and the entire staff were of considerable support throughout the two years that it took me to complete this book.